# A Compendium of Research in Home Management

# A Compendium of Research in Home Management

Maneesha Shukul

Veena Gandotra

Sarjoo Patel

AUTHORSPRESS

Publishers of Scholarly Books

Worldwide Circulation through Authorspress Global Network

**First Published 2011**
by
**Authorspress**

**Editorial**
Q-2A Hauz Khas Enclave,
New Delhi-110 016
e-mail: authorspress@yahoo.com

**Marketing**
E-35/103, Jawahar Park
Laxmi Nagar, Delhi-110 092
e-mail: authorspress@yahoo.com



**A Compendium of Research in Home Management**
**ISBN 978-81-7273-592-0**

Printed in **Shri Krishna offset Press Delhi-93**

# Preface

A need was felt since long by the researchers in Home Management/Family Resource Management regarding the availability of information about researches carried out in the field. The Home Management department, now known as "Family and Community Resource and Managemnt" Faculty of Home Science, (Family and Community Sciences). The Maharaja Sayajirao University of Baroda, is one of the prime institutions where a number of researches have been conducted. The present book is a compendium of abstracts of researches conducted at Masters and Doctoral levels during the period of 1964 to 2006. The areas considered for the abstract are the concepts of management, money management, time and energy management, participation in work at home, the perception regarding home management, housing and furnishing, consumer studies, environment, people with special needs, gender-based studies, energy management and gainful employment of women. Although an attempt is made to make the list exhaustive in these selected areas, any omission is non-intentional.

The book will prove to be a rich resource material for the researchers in colleges and universities. This would enable them to identify the thrust areas and the research gaps, and help them to plan out appropriate researches.

The authors are grateful to the researchers and their guides for their significant contribution to the field of Home Management/Family Resource Management/Family and Community Management.

*Veena Gandotra*
*Maneesha Shukul*
*Sarjoo Patel*

# Preface

# Contents


*Preface* — *v*

1. Management Concepts — 1
2. Money Management — 33
3. Time and Energy Management — 77
4. Participation in Work at Home — 99
5. Perception Regarding Home Management — 112
6. Housing and Furnishing — 117
7. Consumer Studies — 152
8. Environment — 211
9. People with Special Needs — 237
10. Gender-based Studies — 253
11. Energy Management — 267
12. Gainful Employment of Women — 286

# 1

# Management Concepts

Resources of the family are essential for achieving family goals. Without them, the process of decision making is ineffective. Each time you identify a goal to be achieved, you plan how to attain the desired outcome, identify the resources and plan how to use them. Although resources are used on a continual basis in our daily life, we need to decide the optimum allocation of resources in various combinations to achieve what we want. Everyone has many resources. Sometimes we is not aware of all the resources at our command. As a result, we are not able to use some of them at all. Even when we are aware of the resources, we may not be using them to the fullest extent.

Resources are defined as those material and human attributes that satisfy our wants. "They may be tangible or intangible. They vary for individuals, communities, states and nations. However all types of resources are used to achieve the family goals." They are the 'what' of management or the enablers one use to achieve the goal. Resources are the supply reservoir for use in the family's specific managerial functions.

Management is essential component of family living. It is a natural aspect of human association in the family. Since it plays a significant role in shaping our lives it is essential to understand the basic concepts of the home management process as applicable to all resources; and finally, the quality of life an individual achieves is dependent upon its use.

*Title: Factors Related to Decision-making Responsibilitie of Second Year Students, College of Home Science, S.N.D.T. University, Bombay.*

*Author:* Ila K. Master

*Guide:* Elizabeth Beveridge

*Year:* 1964

*Keywords:* Decisionmaking, responsibilities

## Introduction

Home science prepares for diversified roles that woman have inside and outside the home. The importance of home science is increasingly being realised by many in different parts of the country. Today home science education is given not only at the primary school level but also at the high school and college levels. Decision making is involved in every action, no matter whether it is conscious or habitual. Since adolescents of today are tomorrow's homemakers it becomes very important to know what decisions they are facing to make the learning meaningful.

## Methodology

A descriptive research design was used for the study. A questionnaire was used as a tool for collecting data. The sample of the study consisted of 95 students of second year college. Percentages and frequency were used for data analysis.

## Major Findings

Respondents belonging to families of five to seven members assumed somewhat more responsibilities than those from other sizes of families. The eldest and middle daughters showed little difference in the amount of responsibilities assumed by them. The amount of decision-making responsibilities increased as the income lowered. Respondents having hired help for more than three tasks assumed less responsibility at home than those having hired help for only three tasks. Respondents from families where the main homemaker was sick most of the time assumed more responsibilities than others. Respondents had maximum decision-making responsibilities in physical care and washing, starching and ironing of clothing, and minimum in clean-up and storage of food and purchase of food.

***Title: Decision-making Opportunities and Acceptance of New Ideas by Homemakers in One Village in India***
*Author:* Aji Parimala
*Guide:* Elizabeth Beveridge
*Year:* 1964
*Keywords:* Decisionmaking, acceptance of new ideas, homemakers

## INTRODUCTION

The community development programme initiated in the first five-year plan has provided an extension agency which serves and educates the farmer, the artisan, the woman, the youth in the village in India. Though many attempts have been made to sell new ideas to rural families through different programmes, new ideas are not accepted readily. In order to affect the life of the people, the approach must start with the home which is the basic unit of human society everywhere in the world. The extention worker who seeks to introduce change and guide decision making among Indian women must first understand the status, roles, patterns of power and social rank in the family. Unless she knows the extent to which women are free to make decisions her effort may be futile.

## METHODOLOGY

A descriptive research design was used for the study. The sample of the study consisted of 50 families selected through multi-stage stratified sampling technique from Mysore village. The interview schedule was used for collecting data which were analysed by using percentages.

## MAJOR FINDINGS

Wives had more opportunities in decision making in nuclear families. In decision making to try new ideas the influence of the other person was greater in joint families than in nuclear families. As to the acceptance of new ideas in joint families wives in the high income group said that they readily accepted new ideas to a greater extent than wives of middle and low income groups. In nuclear families wives in the low income group had more opportunities than in the middle income group to decide to try new ideas.

*Title: Some Management Practices of Selected Full-time Employed Homemakers of Baroda*

*Author:* Nisha. J. Dhawale

*Guide:* Jyoti Dangoria

*Year:* 1966

*Keywords:* Management practices, employed homemakers

## Introduction

Women of today are trying to combine two things together satisfactorily. They are management of home and outside employment. A number of women are accepting full-time jobs outside their homes due to some reasons, mainly economical ones. Management of home as such is a full-time job, so those women who take outside employment with it have to make satisfactory combination of management of home and outside employment. It is thought that as these married homemakers have to manage their jobs as well as their homes, management practices will be influenced, so the study of their management practices was conducted.

## Methodology

A descriptive research design was used for the study. The sample for the study comprised 60 married, full-time employed homemakers selected randomly. A questionnaire was used as a tool for gathering data. For data analysis average ranges and percentages were employed.

### Major Findings

A majority of the respondents ( 61%) received some help in their housework either by the family members or by servants. The overall management of food was done by the respondents themselves. In a majority of the cases purchasing, cleaning, storing, preparing and serving of the food was done by the respondents themselves. The help was received from the family members and servants. Practices followed by the homemakers due to limited time were using time- and energy-saving equipment, such as kerosene and gas stoves, pressure cooker, buying ready-made food, using preserved food. The reasons given for employment by most of the respondents were economical reasons such as to supplement family income and to meet increasing prices. Practices followed by the respondents were planning of expenditure ahead of time by 53 respondents, managing the income by pooling their incomes, planning jointly for the use of total income, and using the forms of saving such as bank accounts by 53, material goods like car, bicycle, house by 20, gold by 18 and piece of land by 18. With all these hardships majority of the respondents wished to continue their jobs.

***Title: Household Decision-making Patterns as Obtained from the Study of Homemakers***

*Author:* Jayshree Vamdagni

*Guide:* Nalini Ogale

*Year:* 1972

*Keywords:* Decision making, homemakers

### Introduction

Decision making is one of the important components of management. Every simple task involves decision making, a point which is overlooked by many. So homemakers should know when and what type of decisions are to be taken. Genuine decisions made by them contribute to the smooth running of a home and enable them to anticipate the problems rather than let them develop to a stage where it is not possible to control them. As decision making is an important component of management, it offers an intellectual challenge to homemakers. Even the simplest household task may involve decision making. Within the home, each activity presents more and more choice making, so decision making becomes a necessary task.

### METHODOLOGY

An interview schedule was used to collect the data. The sample comprised 100 families from Baroda city. The statistics used to analyse the data were simple percentages, mean, t-test and chi-square test.

### MAJOR FINDINGS

It was found that a larger percentage of independent decisions were made by the homemakers in nuclear families than those made in joint families. Husbands and wives consulted with each other more often in nuclear families than in joint families. It was found that the number of homemakers taking large number of independent decisions increased with the increase in their age. It was also found that there is a difference between the percentage of independent decisions taken by homemakers in joint and nuclear families.

*Title:* **A Study of Organisation Process used in Distribution of Household Tasks by Homemakers**

*Author:* Vijaya Kulkarni

*Guide:* Nalini Ogale

*Year:* 1975

*Keywords:* Organisation process, household tasks, homemakers

### INTRODUCTION

In the home the homemaker has to manage all kinds of resources available to her, and along with this she also has to manage various tasks of the household which are needed for survival, maintenance and welfare of the family. To carry out these tasks, she might use three processes of management, i.e., planning, controlling and evaluating.

The recent development in the theory of home management includes the organisation process as another important management process. No matter who plans and performs the tasks organising becomes a very important activity for the manager. Usually organising of the tasks would depend on the style of organising the tasks and the level at which it is to be performed. In all homes the homemaker is usually held responsible for the completion of the household tasks even though usually she gets some help from the family members or servants. So in getting this help proper organisation becomes an essential activity for the homemakers.

## Methodology

An interview schedule was used to elicit data. The total sample comprised 115 homemakers selected from Baroda city. The basis for sample selection was that the respondents should be married homemaker living with her family. On this basis a sample was drawn randomly. For data analysis percentages and means were calculated. t-tests and coefficients of correlation were computed to test the relationships.

## Major Findings

It was found that a majority had servants who helped in cleaning utensils and washing clothes. It was found that a majority of the homemakers planned and performed many of the tasks. The most used criteria for task distribution among the family members were past experience and age of the performer while it was the availability of persons in the case of servants.

The most used operation for the family members was authorising and the second most used was assigning tasks. It was found that the higher the socio-economic status the more the number of task distribution patterns were used. Assigning of the tasks for the family members was correlated with past experience, availability of person, nature of the task, sex, age and skills and abilities of the performer.

*Title: An Exploratory Study of Communication in the Management of Servants*

*Author:* Anita Vaish

*Guide:* Nalini Ogale

*Year:* 1976

*Keywords:* Communication, management, servant

## INTRODUCTION

In a home, the homemaker has to manage all kinds of resources available to her and also the various tasks of the household needed for the maintenance and well being of the family. To carry out these tasks she needs to use the process of communication basic to management. In carrying out any process of management, such as planning, controlling, evaluating, or organisation, the communication process is the foundation stone. Though the homemaker is chiefly responsible for managing the household work, it does not mean that she has to carry it out alone. In most of the families tasks are performed by the servants. For carrying out the household work, the homemaker has to communicate with the family members as well as the servants.

## METHODOLOGY

A questionnaire was used to collect the data. The total sample comprised 130 homemakers selected from some areas of Baroda. Data were analysed using simple frequency, means, percentages, and ranges.

## MAJOR FINDINGS

It was found that the most commonly used communication medium was verbal followed by audio-visual. Majority of the respondents used more than one media for communicating with the servants. Among the factors considered by the homemaker prior to the selection of the communication media the most important were reliability and honesty followed by past experience, age, skills, abilities, and training of the servants. For all the different household tasks a majority of the homemakers were satisfied by the use of verbal medium alone. The communication problems faced by most of the respondents included language problem, servants did not understand, servants were too young or old or illiterate to understand, difficult to guide, inattentiveness on the part of the servants, etc.

*Title: An Exploratory Study of Values Underlying the Family Decisions made by Homemakers*
*Author:* Bholi Pabha
*Guide:* Nalini Ogale
*Year:* 1977
*Keywords:* Values, family decisions, homemakers

## Introduction

Value is very precious as well as important to the person who holds it. An individual learns his values from varied sources which may include his closest associates, his religion, culture and his experience. Behaviour is intricately blended with the values held by the individual. In managing homes all families make decisions related to the different managerial activities taking place within or outside the home. From theory it is gathered that values underlie all decision making. An exploration of values underlying family decisions is essential to comprehend the vital role of values in management and their operation in decision making.

## Methodology

An exploratory study was planned. A questionnaire was used for data collection. The sample of the study comprised 60 homemakers selected purposively. Individual value profiles were made and values were analysed to examine which values underlined specific family decisions. For analysis, percentage, mean, median, kurtosis skewness and quartile deviation were used.

## Major Findings

Economic and social values are dominant normal characteristics of the group of the middle income homemakers. Though a majority of homemakers studied were graduate traditional values were still seen to be held significantly by them. This could be attributed to the fact that since customs and rituals were long established practices in our culture they still prevail dominantly even today. Values held by respondents do not change but their dominance changes with change in decision situations.

***Title: An Exploratory Study of the Styles of Motivation of Homemakers in Household Management for Self and Children***

*Author:* Kanchan Arora

*Guide:* Nalini Ogale

*Year:* 1977

*Keywords:* Styles of motivation, household management

## Introduction

There is some dissatisfaction among women about the performance of household chores which they perceive as duty. Therefore it is important to know what factors act as motivators for housewives. The study was planned with the purpose of ascertaining the motivators initiating household management by homemakers. It further attempted to find out the styles adopted by homemakers to motivate children for participation in household management. An attempt was also made to determine demographic and personal characteristics that motivate homemakers for household management and to determine styles used by homemakers to motivate children.

## Methodology

A sample of 125 homemakers were selected through various ladies' clubs. A questionnaire was administered at the meeting of the club. The data thus collected were coded, categorised and tabulated. Total scores, mean scores, frequencies and percentages were calculated.

## Major Findings

The conclusions drawn from the findings were that homemakers used affective motivators most of the time to motivate themselves. Within this category "Mental health" in terms of "happiness" and worries and "Nature of the job" were the most and the least motivating factors respectively. Physical and cognitive motivators were also used by a number of respondents. Temporal motivators were the least used. Type, size and income of family did not influence the use of motivators. Age, education and employment status of homemakers affect the use of cognitive and temporal motivators. However, cognitive motivators were used the most for children, while affective motivators were used less, and the least were physical motivators. As children grew older the use of affective and cognitive motivators increased and the use of physical factors decreased. The motivators used for younger age group were rewards of praise, encouragement, coaching, guiding and interest creation, while for older group they gave authority and independence.

***Title: A Study of Opinions of Adolescents towards Independent Decisionmaking***
*Author:* Mina Makhijani
*Guide:* Salma Nadvi
*Year:* 1977
*Keywords:* Opinions, adolescents, decision making

## Introduction

Adolescence, a period between childhood and adulthood, signifies the rapid changes taking place in the mental and physical conditions of an individual. The most significant of these changes are the ones in the decision-making process of a child. During this period he seeks an opportunity to try out his worth and tries to evade the restrictions imposed upon him as a child. In short, he seeks independence. And this is the time when an individual should be taught the fundamentals of the decision-making process. The role of parents here is, therefore, to provide the adolescent with enough opportunity and encouragement to make decisions independently so that it will help him in developing his skill of thinking.

## Methodology

A survey method was used for the study. A questionnaire was used to collect the data. The total sample comprised 150 adolescent boys and girls equally divided into two groups of 75 boys and 75 girls. They belonged to the age group of 17 to 22 years. The sampling technique was selective. For data analysis, frequency, percentage and mean scores were calculated.

## Major Findings

It was found that both male and female had similar opinions towards independent decision making. Respondents felt that an adolescent's friend circle creates a great impact on his behaviour and that the presence of an authoritarian figure also creates a barrier for him in making independent decisions. It was found that a majority of the male and female respondents made independent decisions in most of the areas. Male respondents felt that the most appropriate age for deciding mate selection was 24 to 27 years whereas females felt that 18 to 23 years was more appropriate. More than half of the respondents planned their expenditure so as to get an insight into money management.

***Title*: *A Study of Management Practices of Homemakers of Jorhat as Reflected in Use of Time and Money***

*Author:* Ruplekha Saikia

*Guide:* Asha Dass

*Year:* 1979

*Keywords:* Management practices, homemakers, time, energy

## Introduction

Management is a natural outgrowth of human association in the home environment. Gross and Crandall explain home management as a mental process consisting of three or more consecutive steps – planning, controlling and evaluating the use of family resources in order to achieve family goals. Time and money are the most frequently used resources. Time is the framework within which the day's activities are carried out and work is distributed. Money is a scarce resource and needs careful planning for optimum utilisation. The study focuses on finding out time and money management practices and their relationship with selected variables. It further attempts to the study utilisation pattern of time and money by homemakers of Jorhat.

## Methodology

A sample of 65 homemakers from two localities of Jorhat were randomly selected for the study. Only full-time homemakers were selected. The interview schedule was the tool used to collect data regarding use of management process, utilisation pattern of time and money in terms of expenditure pattern, credit and saving. A summated rating scale was used to study management practices. Data were coded, scored, tabulated and statistically analysed. Frequency, percentage, mean, chi-square and Pearson's Product Moment Correlation were used to test-hypotheses.

## Major Findings

The respondents were generally from the age group of 35 years and below. More than half had college level education; the income ranged from Rs. 750 to Rs. 1,800 per month and a majority belonged to the nuclear family. A majority of the homemakers sometimes followed steps of planning, controlling and evaluating, regarding the use of time. The reason given for planning was "to avoid last minute hurry and confusion". The reason for never planning was that "they could never work according to the plan". Nearly half of them had satisfactory management practices. There were significant differences in time management practices of home-makers according to this quality of management. Age was found to be significantly related to the quality of management, while education was not. Homemakers spent on an average 8.70 hr/day in rest and sleep, 6.63 hours in leisure and 8.65 hours in work. With regard to money it was found that a majority of the respondents planned use of money, and half of them had satisfactory money management practices. The quality of management did not affect their management practices. Age and education of homemakers did not affect their management practices. The expenditure pattern showed that percentage expenditure on food decreased with income, it remained the same for clothing, was more on housing in upper middle class and expenditure was more on education than on clothing.

Expenditure or recreation increased with income. Ninety per cent families saved and very few took credit. It was also found that homemakers' time management practices were significantly related to their money management practices.

***Title: An Exploratory Study of Long Range and Short Range Planning by Families***

*Author:* Manjari Agrawal

*Guide:* Nalini Ogale

*Year:* 1979

*Keywords:* Long-term planning, short-term planning

## INTRODUCTION

Successful management depends upon well thought out plans based on proper decision-making standards. Planning directs action towards goals. The study focused on finding the extent of planning used by families in the areas of financial security, standard of living, housing, education, personality development and retirement. Further it tried to scrutinise the nature of planning, the types of provision made and the use of the process of planning in setting goals. It also tried to find the opinion of respondents on planning out its utility.

## METHODOLOGY

A sample of 100 families were selected out of five colonies of Ahmedabad. Housewives and their husbands were also interviewed. The interview schedule was used and data were analysed through categorisation, coding, tabulation and statistical analysis. Summated scores, frequencies, percentage and median were calculated.

## Major Findings

The results showed that a majority of families, irrespective of income, made plans. Income level, education stage of family life-cycle influenced the kind of planning, difficulties experienced, implementation of plans and extent of certainty about attainment of goals. It was found that the middle income group did more long-term planning. Planning practices were not affected by goal preference. The highly educated had higher income, were in an expanding stage and made more detailed lifecycle plans. The certainty of goal achievement increased with the realisation of the importance of planning. Families in the expanding stage or in the contracting stage had high education, high income, were more certain about their goal attainment than those at the beginning stage of the life-cycle.

***Title: Managerial Process in Action: A Study among the Oraon Tribal Families***

*Author:* Mary Martha Thomas

*Guide:* Nalini Ogale

*Year:* 1979

*Keywords:* Managerial process, tribal families

## Introduction

Management is an indispensable part of family living. Some families do manage their affairs well while some manage them poorly. However, the success of a family living depends on how well its resources are managed. The use made of the family's resources and the extent to which the family goals are achieved in a large measure depend on how well they are managed and also on the managerial ability, interest and leadership of the homemakers and their ability to motivate all the members of the group. If the resources available to a family are to be directed towards improved family living, an intelligent and deliberate choice must be made. A good choice improves family living, a poor choice may result in wastage of resources or use in ways that fail to bring the desired outcomes.

## Methodology

A case study method was used for gathering data. An interview-cum-observation technique was used to get detailed information. Thirty families out of two hundred families were selected at random taking every sixth family from Phunduldinari village of Surgiya district in Madhya Pradesh. The data were analysed in case report and in a collective form using frequencies, percentages, means and median.

## Major Findings

Imparting higher education to their children and better economic and social status were the main goals expressed by the respondents. The resources of the families comprised those that were received by the effort of the members of the families and also those received through the community efforts. The families encouraged joint decision making on important financial matters. Most of the families had saved only under the compulsory schemes of the government. The families with higher income and educational status concentrated more on investing the same on land or agricultural work or house. The time managerial practices of the families indicated the busy life of a tribal housewife. The conditions of the kitchen were found to be very poor even though attempts were made by the housewives for maintaining it clean and tidy. Inadequacy of income, underemployment of the highly educated menfolk, attitudes towards women taking up gainful employment and lack of proper leadership for directing the younger population in the proper direction were some of the impeding factors that influenced the attainment of family goals with the available resources in spite of their strong will power for hard work and unity.

***Title: Decision-making Practices of Home Science Graduate Homemakers and Non-Home Science Graduate Homemakers in Relation to Selected Areas***

*Author:* Suvarnalata Gaekwad

*Guide:* Salma Nadvi

*Year:* 1981

*Keywords: Decisionmaking* practices, Graduate homemakers

## Introduction

In our day-to-day life we face a number of troubles or problems with choosing. The 'choice' part of the management process is extremely important while making a choice. Decision making is one of the important components of management. It is a blend of thinking and acting. It is important for everyone to know when, how and what type of decisions one should take. There should be deliberate thinking and a planned way to carry out the decision-making process for the smooth running of the home. To make decisions one should have practical and theoretical knowledge of the decision-making process, so education holds a pivotal position in the globe of decisions. Decision-making practices do not revolve only around the educational qualifications of an individual. There may be other contributory factors to similarities and differences in decision-making practices.

## Methodology

A survey method with a questionnaire was used as an instrument for collection of data. The total sample comprised 100 graduate homemakers, equally divided into two groups of 50 Home Science and 50 Non-Home Science graduate homemakers. The only basis was that they should have one teenage child. On this basis the selective sample was drawn. Simple frequency and percentages were calculated chi-square test was used to test the hypothesis.

## Major Findings

The practices followed by the home science graduates were more systematic and planned. Home science graduates took joint decisions in the areas of education, clothing, equipment and leisure time. The final decision was usually made by husband and wife keeping in mind the need and requirement of the family members. The purchasing of food was the area where the homemaker was the dominant decision maker. The practices followed by the non home science graduates were less planned and based more on experience rather than theoretical knowledge. Among both the groups of respondents values, goals and aspiration, standard, quality, need, interest, ability and budget were the factors considered. The way decisions were reached by the respondents in the study were more time-oriented. It was found that education is an instrument in the differences of decision-making practices.

***Title: An Exploratory Study of Commitment of Families to Energy Related Goals***
*Author:* Rachel George.
*Guide:* Nalini Ogale
*Year:* 1983
*Keywords:* commitment, energy, goals

## Introduction

Family goal commitment is the binding or pledging of family members to certain behaviour acts for the attainment of their family goals. Commitment reflects the willingness and determination of the family to allocate resources to attain their goals. It acts as a force which compels an individual to pursue certain lines of action consistently. Energy or power is one of the essentials required for the very existence and survival of man. The use and content of energy from the environment has been the key to man's ability to live, develop, socially control the environment and above all, to emerge into a mechanised era. In the process of socialisation, growth and development families assume the role of primary converters of energy from the environment. Families formulate goals that are associated with energy consumption in daily living, and they make innumerable decisions in relation to its behaviour which is concerned with energy consumption.

## Methodology

A descriptive research design was used, and an interview schedule was used to collect data. The sample of the study comprised 220 families selected purposively. Frequencies percentages and means were computed, and relational statistics like product moment correlations, F-test, t-test, regression were used to test the relationship between selected variables.

### Major Findings

The most popular mode of goal attainment was working toward a few goals at a time. The overall family commitment to type I goals was directly associated with ecoconciousness of husbands and homemakers. The educational level of homemakers was inversely related to an overall extent of commitment. As homemakers the education level increased sacrifices in abundant living and the level of living decreased. Family income ecoconciousness and the age of husbands, ecoconciousness of homemakers family size and the level of future goal attainment emerged as the major prediction of overall extent of commitment of family, while ecoconsciousness age, and the education level of homemakers and family income never seemed to be the major predictions of overall extent of commitment of families. Energy-related goals refer to objectives of the family in relation to energy consumption in family living. There are two major categories: type I energy goals include objectives pertaining to the acquisition of material goods in the quest for higher level of living which, when attained, lead to an increase in energy consumption, Type II energy-related goals cover objectives aimed at conservation of energy resource.

***Title: A Study of Resource- Management by Homemakers of 'Sewasi' Village***

*Author:* Sangeeta Joshi

*Guide:* Veena Gandotara

*Year:* 1985

*Keywords:* Resource management, homemakers

### Introduction

Management is an inseparable part of family living. As individuals and as a family everybody manages his personal affairs within a constantly changing world. Some families do manage their resources well while some manage them poorly. It is seen that rural areas, where over 76 per cent of the Indian population reside, are pronounced as areas of poverty, unemployment, illiteracy and low productivity. In today's situation where the government is taking steps for the rural upliftment it is best to know how the families of rural areas manage their resources and whether they are aware of the facilities provided for them by the government. The knowledge of their practices and awareness will be helpful for the social worker and other institutions in planning and carrying out strategies and programmes for rural upliftment.

## Methodology

A descriptive research design was used. An exploratory survey as well as a case study were used for the study. The sample of the study comprised 50 homemakers from low, middle as well as high income groups selected through stratified sampling technique from Sewasi village. Data were categorised, coded and tabulated, and expressed in frequencies, percentages and means. The coefficient of correlation was computed to test the relationship between selected variables.

## Major Findings

Food was found as the main head of expenditure, and the percentage decreased with an increase in the income. Credit was common mainly among low income group. Respondents were not having a satisfactory knowledge of many community resources. The management of resources was found to be poor among low income group and the best in middle income group. The respondents from nuclear families were better managers. There was an inverse relationship between the management of resources by the respondents and the size of the family to which they belonged. There was a direct relationship between the managerial behaviour and the level of education as well as between the managerial behaviour and the income of the respondents.

*Title: A Study of Family Managerial Behaviour in Energy Crisis Situation*

*Author:* Manju Goel

*Guide:* Nalini Ogale

*Year:* 1986

*Keywords:* Managerial behaviour, energy crisis

## Introduction

From the ecological perspective, a family is an energy-driven open ecosystem. Families are dependent on the natural environment for most of their energy requirements but a majority of them are unaware of this fact. The families do not make explicit decisions to consume a particular quantity of energy or to spend money on energy up to some fixed amount, rather families engage in activities of their choice to meet the family and individual goals, and in the process consume the amount of energy required but families need to change this attitude towards energy consumption. Further, the large share of family income would be consumed by the energy used. Thus, the present energy crisis situation calls upon families to demonstrate their ability of adaptability. Any change in the fuel availability and price would affect the families, especially the low and middle income families. The efforts to cope with such a situation would thus be the major concern of the family system as a whole.

## Methodology

A descriptive type of design was used for the study. An interview schedule was used to collect data. The sample comprised 260 households selected randomly. Data were analysed employing descriptive as well as relational statistics. The data were presented in frequencies, percentage, mean and standard deviation, and relational statistics such as chi-square Pearson product moment correlation, multiple correlation, coefficient, F-test and 't' test were used.

## Major Findings

The perception level of homemakers regarding energy crisis increases with the increase in the education level. The families are more affected during energy shortages than during their price increase. Conservation measures are generally adopted irrespective of any of the energy crisis situation. Homemakers shared concern for conservation of energy only to the extent of reducing expenditure on fuel by different ways without sacrificing their comforts and conveniences associated with energy use. Families have a flexible household standard which helps them to adjust to the crisis situation readily.

***Title: Woman's Lifestyle, Involvement in Decision-making, Performance Achievement and Role in Conflict Resolution: A Cross-sectional Study of Homemakers' Perceptions***

*Author:* Sangeeta Patel

*Guide:* Kamala Srinivasan

*Year:* 1989

*Keywords:* Women's lifestyle, decision making, performance achievement, conflict resolution, perceptions

## INTRODUCTION

The family is increasingly considered to be the managerial unit and hence the homemaker is a home manager. In a family situation and in other group living, decisions tend to be developed by all concerned. If satisfactorily made, they result in better decisions and more action. They may however be made at different levels of desirability based on the degree of resultant group harmony. If a conflict arises the most satisfactory solutions are those of integration and, in some cases, of acceptance of differences. Decisions focusing on roles are of special concern today since the social role of a wife and a mother are under reconsideration. Review of literature revealed that there is a need for the study on decision-making, especially on the lifestyles of homemakers and their involvement in various decision-making areas and their role in conflict revolution.

## METHODOLOGY

The research design of the study was predominantly descriptive-cum-exploratory. A interview-cum-questionnaire schedule was used to collect data. The sample of the study comprised 100 educated married homemakers. The study was conducted at Vallabh Vidhyanagar and Anand of Kheda district, Gujarat State. The statistics applied were frequency and percentage distribution, measures of central tendency, mean and standard deviation, and chi-square and t-test were used for testing the hypotheses postulated.

## Major Findings

It was found that irrespective of the education level, the type of family, the family income, the age of homemakers, the income of homemakers, their professions etc. barring a very few exceptions, the lifestyles of homemakers, their involvement in decision-making areas remain largely unaffected by the various demographic and socio-economic variables. It was found that lifestyles of homemakers among the selected sample were predominantly individualistic and influential. In terms of performance achievement, as perceived by the homemakers, a majority of the families were satisfied. A majority of the homemakers were found to be playing a positive role and very few a passive role, while none played a negative role in conflict resolution. A majority of the conflicts were mainly resolved through voluntary submission, compromise, integration, struggle and victory from homemakers' side and conversation.

*Title*: ***An Exploratory Study of Determinants of Optimum Utilization of Selected Community Facilities by Urban Poor families of Hyderabad.***

*Author*: Vijaya Nambiar

*Guide:* Nalini Ogale

*Year:* 1989

*Keywords:* Community facilities, Urban poor families

## Introduction

The movement of rural population to the urban areas have resulted in urban congestion, with the accompanying problems of provision of basic amenities to satisfy certain essential needs of all the inhabitants. The manner in which the basic needs of health, education and recreation of the urban dwellers, particularly the urban poor are met, has become institutionalized. The community facilities offer services of a free or low cost nature, which need to be optimally utilized by those who are in dire need, mainly the urban poor.

## Methodology

To explore constraints which act as catalysts or pose as impediments in the utilization of facilities and services, a study was conducted in the city of Hyderabad on 240 households belonging to low-low and low-middle-income class. An interview schedule containing standardized scale was used to find out the extent of awareness, utilization and satisfaction of families and the data were gathered.

## Major Findings

The findings reveal that the mean age of the homemaker was 36.5 and that of husband was 44 years. Most of the husbands from LLI category were either illiterate or were educated till primary school. A majority of the husbands were unskilled workers. A majority of the respondents had nuclear families. Their monthly income ranged from Rs. 501 to Rs. 1000. The health status of adults was good in a wide majority of the respondent's families. The space inside the house was used for play and study also. Regarding availability and awareness of respondents about community facilities and services, it was revealed that a majority pointed out to non-availability of a government hospital, balwadi and playground nearby the house.

A wide majority of the respondents were aware about free services of government hospitals, government high school, public libraries, museums and exhibitions. A majority were aware about the zoo and unaware of other recreational facilities such as swimming pool or fishing sport. One-third of the respondents had not utilized the community facilities but one-third had used the same for over 15 years. Only about one-fourth of the respondents utilized the government hospitals/health centre during an illness and a wide majority had never used the community health facilities.

About one-fifth of the children were sent to the government school. The use of health and educational community facilities increased with the decrease in income while the use of recreational facilities increased with the increase in income as revealed through the coefficient of correlation. There was a moderate satisfaction in the achievement of family and recreational goals by a majority of the families. Education and occupation of the head of the family negatively influenced the use of health facilities and services. The location of family or proximity from the house influenced the use of the community facilities. The study indicated a need to make offerings of the facilities better so that people were motivated to use them.

***Title: A Study of Determinants of Conflicts, between Youth and Parents in Decisionmaking***

*Author:* Chadha Inderjeet Kaur

*Guide:* Nalini Ogale

*Year:* 1991

*Keywords:* Conflicts, youth, parents, decision making

## INTRODUCTION

The need for independence becomes very important during adolescence, when the individual is called upon to make a decision. But while making decision adolescents face conflicts with their parents. The young rebel in their adolescence, because they feel that they are different from their parents, and want everything and have their own way. One major cause of conflict is the crisis of values in youth, and interference in youngsters' freedom by their parents in the choice of friendship between sex, dress, music, choice of life partner and social interaction.

## METHODOLOGY

The present research was a descriptive study. A purposive sampling procedure was used for sample selection. Fifty boys and 50 girls of M.S. University of Baroda who were graduates and doing postgraduation, and their parents, were considered for the sample. A questionnaire was used as a method of data collection. The statistics applied were percentage distribution, mean, standard deviation. Chi-square and t- test were used for testing the hypotheses.

## Major Findings

Regarding the extent of independent decision by students it was revealed that students had a lot of say regarding education, they do not participate independently in decision making as they have not been given enough experience at an early age in handling money. Regarding conflict it was found that fathers and boys have more conflict compared to fathers and girls. A large percentage of conflict between mothers and girls than between mothers and boys was evident. There was not much difference between values of parents and youth. Youth gave more importance to freedom, excellence, achievement and success while parents gave importance to economy, education and moral orientation. The gender bias among the parents in relation to son and daughter was evident. Thus the determinants of conflict were demographic characteristics of the youth, gender bias on the part of the parents, the extent of freedom given to children in decision making and value differences between parents and children.

***Title: Involvement of Women in Decision Process in the Management of Farm Households of the Hill Region of Uttar Pradesh***

*Author:* Promila Sharma

*Guide:* Nalini Ogale

*Year:* 1993

*Keywords:* Women involvement, decision making, management

## Introduction

Management is one of the important areas that requires careful decision making and planning on the part of individuals to bring about the change in the quality of life. Decision making is one of the important components of management that requires concrete planning on the part of the family members to perform the activities. Since women's contribution to economic development is vital, there is a need of proportionate increase of her involvement in the decisionmaking process. The role of women is vital, especially in the management of farms and houses. Rural women play a vital role in production activities, which increase their management responsibilities.

### Methodology

An interview schedule was used to collect the data. A multistage purposive-cum-random sampling design was adopted, treating purposive selection of Nainital district at the first stage; 23 families from large land-holding, 64 from medium and 113 from small land-holding groups were selected randomly.

### Major Findings

Rural women from hill areas were not much involved in buying decisions regarding food management. On the whole respondents' involvement in decisions related to maintenance of house and home decoration was low among all land-holding groups. Women had no power to participate in decisions like taking loans, savings and investments. Decisions related to education and occupation of the children were mostly taken by men. Marriage-related decisions were jointly taken. Involvement in financial decisions and decisions which required technical know-how related to farm decisions were low. Decisions related to storage of products and animal fodder were totally female-dominated. Respondents' involvement in decisions related to selling of products and deciding about selling price of the products was nil. A large number of respondents of all land-holding groups were wholly or partially performing tasks related to their farm. In spite of playing a significant role in productive work, women were not involved in the marketing of products of any type.

***Title: A Study of Decision-making Practices regarding Food Buying of the Middle Income Group Families Residing in Baroda City***

*Author:* Vrushali Vasant Datar

*Guide:* Asha V. Dass

*Year:* 1994

*Keywords:* Decision-making practices, food buying

## Introduction

Decision making is an integral part of the management of any organisation. It is not unique to management but crucial to it. When there is some problem to solve or some choice to be made or when an opportunity presents itself, some families are very authoritarian in which the husbands make most of the important decisions and others are made to follow his decision when implemented. But food is an area where the homemaker plays an important role of the decision maker and only at times may require the help of her husband or other family members. Food being the basic necessity of a family, today, due to the increasing population its management has become very important because the ratio at which the population is increasing is so high that even though the food production has improved and increased yet scarcity and limited income force the family to really manage its resources, making wise decisions in each and every aspect related to food.

## Methodology

The study was descriptive. A purposive sampling procedure was used for the selection of the sample population. Thirty housewives from Gujarat refinery township and 30 from I.P.C.L. Colony from middle income group were considered for the study. A questionnaire was used as a tool for collecting data. The statistics applied were percentage distribution, mean, and standard deviation. Chi-square was used for testing hypothesis.

## Major Findings

Decisions for the brand, quality, quantity, place and time of purchase of food were taken by housewives. Factors like nature of family members, preferences, prices, new products always influence the decisions taken. Intelligence, knowledge, judgement, taste, money always influenced the decisions, and resources like energy, confidence, attitude, faith, time, creativity influenced sometimes. A majority of the homemakers followed the steps of decision-making process. Age influenced the overall decision making practices regarding food purchases of cereals, grains, pulses and legumes because as the age increased the experience of the homemaker also increased.

*Title: A Study of Interpersonal Communication among three Generations in Selected families*
*Author:* Sarjoo Patel
*Guide:* Maneesha Shukul
*Year:* 2003
*Keywords:* Interpersonal Communication, three Generations, families.

## Introduction

Communication is continuously and intricately interwoven in the life of human beings. Communicating is a fundamental aspect of not only any individual but also of a family and a larger social organization. Today there is less common ground between the ideas and the ideals of older and younger generations. Communication thus becomes the crux to the relationship between grandparents, parents and youth. As such there is really no gap between generations, only a gap between talking and thinking, and thinking and doing that is indeed a communication gap. Today it becomes the need of the hour to evaluate the interpersonal communication amongst them. Once the assessment of the complexity and intensity of the problem have been made the solution thereof would become possible. Thus the study is of fact finding into the dynamics of inter-personal communication among the youth, parents and grandparents.

## Methodology

The research design of the study was descriptive in nature conducted on three generations of families living in Baroda City, selected through a purposive sampling technique. Fifty families were chosen and the case studies were undertaken of those families in which the extent of communication was found to be low. The Interview schedule was used as an instrument for gathering data. The data were analyzed employing the descriptive as well as the relational statistics. The data were presented in frequencies, percentage, mean and standard deviation t-test, and coefficients of correlation were used to test the hypothesis postulated for the study.

## Major Findings

A majority of the youths considered as a sample were females and a little more that one-third of them were male respondents. The mean age of the youth was 19.8 years, that of fathers was 49.1 years, mothers 46.4 years, grandfathers 73.8 years and that of grandmothers 71.4 years. It was found that all the fathers were employed whereas a majority of the mothers were not employed. A wide majority of the grandparents were not employed. The mean monthly income of the family was Rs. 21,980 and the mean number of family members was 6.3. It was observed that a majority of the parents and grandparents had a positive orientation towards liberation. A majority of the youths perceived their home environment as good.

It was found that 78 per cent of the youths had poor relationship with their fathers and 74 per cent of them had a poor relationship with their mother. A majority of the children and parents experienced a great extent of conflict whereas a majority of children and grandparents had a low extent of conflicts. The child-parent relationship experienced a high extent of barriers in communication.

The testing of hypotheses proved that extent of communication differed due to the occupation of the mother, was positively related with value orientation of three generations and with the extent of conflict, and negatively with the extent of barriers. The extent of barriers to communication were found to have a negative relationship with value orientation, home environment, parent-child relationship and the extent of communication but a positive relationship with the extent of conflict. The extent of conflict was positively related with age, extent of barriers and with the extent of communication, and negatively with value orientation and parent-child relationship.

*Title:* ***Attitude, problems and coping strategies of homemakers belonging to various forms of family***
*Author:* Sweta Patel
*Guide:* Maneesha Shukul and Sarjoo Patel
*Year:* 2006
***Keywords:*** Attitude, problems. Coping strategies, Homemakers, Family.

## INTRODUCTION

A family is a social unit. The concept of family is derived from the Latin word "famulus" which means servant. It is in fact an association which comprises a man, his wife, or wives, and the children, and in case of a joint family, it includes aunts, uncles, and grandparents too. The families have three major functions. First, marriage family serves to replenish society with socialized members. A second function of marriage and family for society is that they promote emotional stability of the adult partners and give children a place to belong to. Finally, by producing and socializing offsprings, marriage and family contribute to other institutions. In the past, people used to live in joint families.

A joint family is defined as two or three generations related by bonds of blood, live under the same roof and share the common purse and hearth. In the ancient times India was the home of joint families but gradually joint families started splitting into nuclear families because of disputes among the family members, which resulted in division of their property. Each member got small holdings which was not sufficient for the upkeep of their family, therefore the new family migrated to another place giving rise to a nuclear family. A nuclear family is defined as "a man and woman joined in marriage, with their children living under the same roof". Due to changing attitudes, lifestyles and thinking of people single-parent families are now emerging in society. A single-parent family refers to a private household including only one parent who may be widowed, separated, divorced or single, and has at least one child.

## METHODOLOGY

The study used the descriptive research design. Purposive sampling method was used for the selection of the sample. Only female homemakers were chosen for the study. For this, a questionnaire tool was selected for data collection. In total, 120 samples were taken for the present study. Description and relational statistics were applied for data analysis.

## MAJOR FINDINGS

The findings of the study revealed that most of the respondents were of middle age (36-45) group, were graduates and were not employed. Most of them had a monthly family income below Rs. 20,000 and had a medium-size family. An equal number of joint families, nuclear families and single-parent families were selected.

A majority of the respondents had a favourable attitude towards the joint family and a neutral attitude towards the nuclear and single-parent families. For testing of hypotheses ANOVA and co-efficient of correlation were computed. The findings show that there is a variation in the attitude of homemakers towards the joint family by family income, whereas there is a variation in the attitude of homemakers towards the nuclear family by form of family to which they belong; the attitude of homemakers towards the single-parent family varied with education, forms and size of family. Further problems experienced by homemakers varied with family forms only whereas coping strategies adopted by homemakers varied with the employment status and family forms. The computed correlation value revealed that there exists an interrelationship between attitude, problems and coping strategies adopted by homemakers to solve various problems. The findings would be beneficial for personnel in the field of home management, families and homemakers.

# 2

# Money Management

Of all the resources available to the family money is the most vital one. It constitutes a very important non-human resource. Money management is necessary for the fullest accomplishment of satisfaction in life. Proper financial management forces a person towards a careful selection of goals and alternatives which will help in satisfying his wants in order of their importance. It provides an opportunity to practise thrift and substantially increase savings through elimination of wasted expenditure. Many people recognise the importance of planning the expenditure but few people follow this practice in their personal life. In the Department of Home Management many studies have been conducted on financial management.

***Title: Money Management Practices of Third and Fourth-year Home Science Hostel Students in Baroda***

*Author:* Dass Asha

*Guide:* Jyoti Dangoria

*Year:* 1965

*Keywords:* Financial management, income, expenditure, savings

## Introduction

Financial management is necessary for the fullest accomplishment of satisfaction in life. All individuals and families have set goals for personal tastes, talents, ambitions and character which differ from individual to individual and family to family. Proper financial management forces a person towards a careful selection of goals and alternatives which will help in satisfying his wants in order of their importance. It provides an opportunity to practise thrift and substantially increase savings through elimination of wasted expenditure. Many people recognise the importance of planning the expenditure but few people follow this practice in their personal life. A student receives her income for her expenses from parents or others. She should weigh each proposed expenditure carefully in order to obtain the maximum benefit of her income. The study was conducted to find out how many students plan their expenditures, keep records of the expenditures and observe saving habits, their opinion towards the practices mentioned above, and to find out the average expenditures.

## METHODOLOGY

The sample chosen was third and fourth year Home Science students staying in the girls' hostels. The sample comprised 68 students. A questionnaire with a record sheet to record expenditure for a specific month was used to gather information.

## MAJOR FINDINGS

The average income of the third year group was Rs. 127.14 and that of the fourth year was Rs. 116.06 per month. The amount they received ranged between Rs. 50.00 and Rs. 200.00 per month. The average expenditure of the third year students was Rs. 79.20 and that of the fourth year was Rs. 69.69. Both the groups spent the highest on clothing and next on food. It was found that the third year students spent more on entertainment than on education while the fourth year students spent more on education and less on entertainment. Most of the students planned their expenditure because they thought that it was necessary for a proper use of income. Many students did not plan because they felt it did not work during an emergency. Most of the students kept a record to know how much they spend, while a few did not keep because it took a lot of their time. The average amount of savings was Rs. 17.76 in the third year and Rs. 11.06 in the fourth year, and they kept savings with themselves or in a bank. A majority of them learnt money management from their experience and from parents.

**_Title: Practices and Opinions of Families as to Saving Patterns_**

*Author* : Dhingra Sunita

*Guide* : Jyoti Dangoria

*Year* : 1966

*Keywords* : Income, savings

## INTRODUCTION

The problem of money is uppermost in the minds of most of us from the time we acquire an understanding of money matters. Acquisition of money is not the goal of life, but money is important in attaining the objectives of life. People are concerned with the problems of earning money but not of saving or investment. The immediate satisfaction that we get from savings is the knowledge that in future we can enjoy some goods and services. The motives for saving perhaps vary with the source and amount of family income. Saving is not an alternative to spending but only a device which enables an individual to spend in the future. The study aimed to find out the saving patterns which are prevalent among the families of two different income groups and their attitudes toward saving patterns. The findings of the study would be helpful for government and private agencies to know which are the common saving patterns utilised by the families, and they can encourage savings to accumulate more funds and use them for extending credits.

## METHODOLOGY

A survey method with an interview schedule was used to collect information. Stratified random sampling was used on the basis of income of the government employees with 100 samples in the Sangrur and Jind Districts of Punjab. The analysis was done by calculating percentages and averages.

## MAJOR FINDINGS

From the total number of 100 families, there were 31 families having an income ranging from Rs. 251 to Rs. 350, 20 families having income from Rs. 351 to Rs. 450, in families having an income from Rs. 451 to Rs. 550, 15 families having an income from Rs. 551 to Rs. 650, 12 having Rs. 651 to Rs. 750 and 8 in the last group, i.e., Rs. 751 and above. Nearly 5 per cent families were supporting their relatives and 20 per cent of the monthly income was spent for that. Just less than half of the families were found supplementing their income from other sources, such as property, part-time service and renting. A majority of them kept a certain portion of their income every month for saving. The percentage of income kept for saving was less among lower middle income group. The average amount of 14.86 per cent was kept per month for saving. Families saved for higher education of children, future emergencies, and marriage of children. Life insurance policies, bank saving accounts, provident fund and cash were common forms of savings. Most of the families did not prefer shares of companies and postal savings. Fifty per cent of them were not satisfied with the type and amount of saving they did.

***Title: Attitudes of Mothers Towards Learning Experiences for Children in the Management of Money***

*Author:* Shakti Chhaya

*Guide:* Jyoti Dangoria, Helen Wells

*Year:* 1967

*Keywords:* Attitude, money management

## INTRODUCTION

Money plays an important role not only in the economic sense but also in the psychological sense. It gives a feeling of security and confidence. If a healthy attitude toward money is developed in childhood the individual is more likely to assume his economic responsibilities towards himself, his family and society with less conflict. At home the parents play an important role in helping children learn, and their attitude will have some effect in the way they teach them. The attitudes often direct one's behaviour, and since a major source of developing attitude is in the home, it is important to know whether parents have a positive or a negative attitude towards money for children. This would help the teachers, extension workers and curriculum planners to plan their experiences for children and for parents.

## Methodology

A survey method was used with a questionnaire as a tool to collect the data. Systematic random sampling was used to draw 100 samples, i.e., students from selected schools of Baroda, whose mothers were the subjects of the study. But only 80 sets of the questionnaire were used to tabulate the data. The questionnaire also included a checklist of 70 statements to study the attitude. The data were tabulated with mean and median of the scores, and three categories were formulated.

## Major Findings

The family income ranged from Rs. 3,000 to Rs. 60,000 per annum. The educational level of the mothers was lower than that of fathers. Only six respondents were employed outside the home. The families were in the expanding stage of family life-cycle, with children of 11 to 20 years age. The amount of allowance ranged from no allowance to Rs. 30 per month. A majority of them did not give regular allowance. Snacks and pictures were the most common items of expenditure. Very few children saved money from the allowance in different ways, i.e., savings in the bank, buying defence certificates or using it in buying expensive items of personal requirement. The mothers belonging to nuclear families, with high income and higher level of husbands, education scored more on the attitude indicating a favourable attitude scale.

***Title: A Study of Expenditure Patterns and Attitudes of Selected Urban Families towards Money Management***

*Author:* Desai Chitra

*Guide:* Jyoti Dangoria, Helen Wells

*Year:* 1967

*Keywords:* Money as a medium of exchange, expenditure

## Introduction

Money as a medium of exchange facilitates the movement of goods and services from producer to consumer. The money which is spent for different items is known as expenditure. The pattern of expenditure varies from family to family, place to place and time to time. The income, home production of goods and services, size of the family, stages of family lifecycle, price level, location, availability of goods and climate conditions are the factors affecting the expenditure pattern of each family. In this study an attempt was made to determine the pattern of expenditure of urban families.

## METHODOLOGY

A survey method with an interview technique was employed to collect data. The of the study consisted of heads of households from three industries in Baroda city, whose income fell between Rs. 350 and Rs. 800 per month with a sample size 50. The analysis was made from income groups based on total family yearly income. The results were reported in percentages and means, and chi-square was calculated.

## MAJOR FINDINGS

The income of the families ranged from Rs. 4,100 to Rs. 25,000 per year. The mean family size was five and the families were in an expanding stage of family size cycle. The highest percentage of the income was spent on food and the percentage expenditure decreased as income increased. The next greatest percentage of income was spent on household expenses. A greater percentages of families lived in rented houses than in owned houses. Borrowing of money was practised at all income levels but not all families borrowed. Saving was done by 60 per cent of the families and the bank was the most preferable place for keeping savings; the post office was also preferred by them except the highest income group. Most of the respondents felt it necessary to have a budget to keep records and to save. Nearly half of the families felt that their income was adequate for their family needs. None of the respondents felt that their income was more than adequate for the work they did and the position they held. All respondents felt that it was necessary "to be more careful in buying" and "to earn more money". "To produce more at home" did not have a high rating by any of the families for balancing income with expenditure.

***Title: Dowry Practices of Patidar Patels and Maharashtrian Brahmins***

*Author:* Uma Sriramlu

*Guide:* Jyoti Dangoria

*Year:* 1968

*Keywords:* Dowry practices, Patel's, Brahmins

## Introduction

Dowry is in the form of money, goods and real estate which a woman brings to her husband at marriage. In the present times also this custom has been intensified and assumed scandalous proportions. It varies from family to family and caste to caste. The present study was planned to compare the expenditure incurred by two castes on dowry and to what extent they spent money on various item of dowry. An attempt was also made to find out the attitude, opinion and preference of parents towards their daughter's education, career before marriage and type of marriage. An analysis was also carried out to study the effect of dowry on the family finance.

## Methodology

The data were collected through interview technique with the help of a questionnaire. A sample of 100 families (50 from Patidar Patels and 50 for Maharashtrian Brahmins) were selected for 'C' ration card holding families. Systematic sampling design of selecting every third family from the list was selected. Data were analysed and reported in frequency and percentages. Pearson's Product Moment correlation was used to determine the relationship between income of the family and amount spent on dowry, and the income and the amount reduced per month after their daughter's marriage. An analysis of variance was used to find whether the allocation of expenditure on various categories was significantly different or not in both castes. To find the difference between families who had taken loan and who had not, the t-test was applied.

## Major Findings

The total income of families ranged from Rs. 450 to 5,650 per month. All families favoured education for their daughter; 75 per cent preferred the daughter to take up career before marriage. Arranged marriages were preferred. The custom of dowry was prevalent in all families. The items given in dowry were in the form of cash, jewellery, clothes, kitchen equipment of silver, brass and stainless steel. The amount spent ranged from Rs. 4,000 to 19,500 with a mean of Rs. 8,665. Patidar Patels spent more than Maharashtrian Brahmins. They spent more on cash, jewellery and clothes. The relationship between the income and the amount of dowry was not found significant. Families met expenditure from savings or took loans. Working daughters contributed towards their dowry. The total expenditure incurred by all families on their daughter's marriage ranged from Rs. 10,000 to Rs. 40,000 with a mean of Rs. 19,575. Patidar spent more than Maharashtrian Brahmins.

**Title: To Study the Attitudes and the Pattern Practised in Giving Pocket Money Allowance to Children by a Selected Group of Punjabi and Gujarat Families**

*Author:* Vasudev Indra

*Guide:* Vijay Taneja

*Year:* 1971

*Keywords:* Money as a resource, pocket allowance, attitude towards use of money

## Introduction

Money as a resource is valuable and is a matter of four functions: a medium, a measure, a standard and a store. Modern society today is characterised by rapid technological advancement and urbanisation. The changes have made the family more of a consuming unit than a producing unit. This change of family function has increased the importance of money in the lifespan of the family. For children, practical experience in handling small sums of money becomes vital; in this respect pocket money allowance becomes a purposeful tool in providing this training. But a proper attitude towards the use of money should be carefully and steadily built by parents. Hence, the study aimed to assess the attitudes of parents towards the giving of allowance to children, the pattern they follow and reasons for doing so.

## Methodology

A survey method with an interview schedule was used for data collection. The interview schedule included a summated rating scale to study the attitude, 180 male respondents from Gujarati families of Baroda and Ahmedabad and 180 male respondents from Punjabi families of Delhi and Ludhiana. These worked in government and private offices and institutions like medical, educational and engineering firms, and chosen to get a good representation of families. Data were analysed employing categorisation, coding, scoring and chi-square.

## Major Findings

A majority of the respondents gave an allowance to their children giving a fixed allowance once a month ranging from Rs. 5 to Rs. 20. The majority of the respondents felt that pocket money should be started for children between the ages of six and 15 years. There was an association between the amount of allowance and the income level of parents and the age of the children. The reasons in favour of giving allowance were that children can learn to handle money wisely, they develop the habit of saving early in life and parents do not have to worry with the day-to-day personal expenses of the child. Further, community, income and family size did not play an important role in the attitudes of fathers toward the giving of pocket money allowance to children.

*Title: Money Management Practices and Attitudes of Teenage Students in Baroda*
*Author:* Mary Jayashree
*Guide:* Nalini Ogale
*Year:* 1972
*Keywords:* Attitude towards money, money management practices

## Introduction

The ability to manage money can be acquired. Children should develop a proper attitude towards money in their childhood, so that, as adult individuals, they would be able to assume their financial responsibilities with confidence. The study was undertaken to know the students' requirement regarding money and their attitude towards money management practices. The finding of this study would be helpful in revealing the needed information to home scientists and curriculum planners in planning the experiences to be provided in money management courses in schools.

## Methodology

The data were collected using a survey method with a questionnaire. The data were collected from two schools in Baroda, and 90 students from ninth and tenth classes were randomly included for the study. The data were analysed using percentages, mean and chi-square.

## Major Findings

The monthly income of respondents' parents or guardians ranged from Rs. 201 to Rs. 1,000 per month. The respondents in the sample belonged to middle and upper socio-economic status. Out of 80 subjects, 80 received some allowance, so further analysis was limited to only 80 subjects. All the respondents received their pocket money either from their parents or / and their guardians. The range of the pocket money was Re. 1 to Rs. 35 per month. (Sixty-five per cent of the subjects received their pocket money by allowance method and 35 per cent of them received by dole method.) Few students borrowed extra money from their parents, relatives and friends as they were dissatisfied with the amount of pocket money they received. A majority of the respondents planned for saving and used various methods to keep their savings by depositing the amount in the bank or keeping their savings with their parents. Most of them spent a large amount of their allowance on entertainment and food, and a small share on postage, gifts and charity. More than half of the respondents showed a positive attitude on money management practices. The boys and girls had similar attitudes towards money management practices.

*Title: A Comparative Study of the Money Management Practices and Attitude Towards Money Management of a Selected Group of Female Hostel Students of M. S. University, Baroda*

*Author:* Kamala Srinivasan

*Guide:* Nalini Ogale

*Year:* 1973

*Keywords:* Financial management, attitudes and practices

## Introduction

Money plays an important role in the life of man as an instrument through which he can satisfy his physical, material and mental needs. The satisfaction of most needs demands the use of money. A family's financial management is influenced by a number of factors like socio-economic status, goals and values, the attitudes etc. As attitude plays an important role in shaping behaviour it is important that proper positive attitudes are developed in children right from a young age. Home economics courses have included subjects relating to financial management within the curriculum of home science. Hence, the study was planned with the objectives to measure the attitudes of students towards money management and to determine the factors affecting money management attitude and practices.

## Methodology

A survey method with interview schedule was used; and to measure the money management practices a descriptive rating scale was developed, and to measure the attitude towards money management a summated rating scale was developed. A total sample of 100 students for the study was randomly drawn from four year B.Sc. students from the science and other faculties. The data obtained were cateogirsed, coded, scored and tabulated. Statistics used to analyse the data were percentage, mean, median, standard deviation, chi-square and t-test.

## Major Findings

The findings were shown in two sections, i.e., fourth year home science students had undergone a course in personal and family finance, and were treated as trained students; the other group formed the untrained group. The average size of the family was large with 20 per cent of the respondents from joint family; 78 per cent of the respondents came from high income families and mean monthly allowance of the trained group was Rs. 184 and of untrained group was Rs. 197. Training has a positive attitude towards money management. Rural students showed a greater receptivity to training. The attitude towards money management and actual money management practices were not correlated.

***Title: A Study of Factors Related to the Food Consumption Expenditure of the Selected Families in Baroda City***

*Author:* Neera Bhatnagar

*Guide:* Nalini Ogale

*Year:* 1973

*Keywords:* Money management, consumption expenditure, food habits

## Introduction

Money is a scarce and limited resource. Effective money management becomes important to families in attaining maximum satisfaction through proper allocation of money resource for various heads of expenditure. Food is an important commodity which shows a large part of the consumption expenditure of families. Hence, homemakers have a tough job in maintaining well-fed families within their limited money income. It is essential to know what are the facts about expenditure for food to improve food management and to know the factors directly related to the food expenditure. The study aimed to know food consumption expenditure, food habits and factors related to them.

## Methodology

A descriptive survey method was used for the study. The interview method was chosen to collect information on demographic characteristics and food habits of the families, and the questionnaire method was chosen to collect information on the food consumption. The samples were collected from Alkapuri, Sardarnagar and Nava Yard from Sayajigunj area of Baroda city. A total of 105 samples were surveyed using the systematic random sampling, i.e., 35 from each area and three income groups. Categorisation, coding and tabulation with percentages, and mean were used to analyse the data.

## Major Findings

The mean income of the high, middle and low income group families were Rs. 3,258.67, Rs. 646.93 and Rs. 298.35 respectively. A majority of them were in the expanding stage of the family lifecycle. The mean family size was 7.6, 5.1 and 5.3 members in three income groups respectively. The average expenditure on different food items per family per day was Rs. 22.30, Rs. 11.14 and Rs. 8.75 in three income groups respectively. The percentage of expenditure on food was 26.16 per cent, 64.20 per cent and 96.82 per cent in three income groups respectively. In high and middle income groups families a majority were vegetarian and in low income group a large number of families were non-vegetarian. The total expenditure increased with the increase in the size of the family. Food habits also had an influence on food expenditures. In middle and low income group families the diet was not balanced. In general, the food consumption expenditure increased with the increase in the income for all families, but the percentage of the income spent decreased as the income increased.

***Title: Credit Practices of Middle and Low Income Group Families in Baroda, Gujarat***

*Author:* Rekha Saxena

*Guide:* Nalini Ogale

*Year:* 1973

*Keywords:* Credit

## Introduction

During early centuries, people resorted to their household expenditure by barter, to satisfy their needs or to meet emergency situations. When people borrowed money, they often found it difficult to repay loan on time, and many people defaulted. Credit permits consumers to use goods and services before having enough money to buy. Each consumer must be wise in using his credit, which depends on a number of variable factors. One of them is the size of the income, which affects the extent of using the credit. The purpose for which credit is used also has a bearing on how much debt is reasonable to assume. Therefore, it is very essential that consumers need adequate credit information for wise and proper use of this financial tool. The study was planned to know the type of credits used, types of credit, sources of borrowing money, purposes and factors influencing the credit practices of the families.

## Methodology

A survey method with interview schedule was used to collect data. A sample of 100 families was drawn from the area of Sardar Nagar and Kamatipura of Baroda. The criteria for the selection were that the respondents should be from a nuclear family and must be users of some kind of credit for household consumption. The data were analysed using frequencies, mean, median and percentages. Analysis was done on the basis of the family income to find out the types and purposes for which credit was used.

## Major Findings

All the families used an open account credit. Out of total sample, 70 per cent used cash credit and 46 per cent used instalment credit. Family income had more influence on the use of credit than family size. Instalment credit was commonly used by middle income group for housing, vehicles, furnishings. Cash credit was more frequently used for food, clothing and health purposes by low income group families, and for the purchase of vehicles and housing purposes by middle income group families. As the number of family members increased, the use of cash credit and instalment credit also increased. The uneducated group borrowed money from relatives, friends and neighbours, and respondents from high education group took loans from cooperative banks and societies. The main reasons for using credit in the low income group were to meet emergency situations and inadequate income, and in the middle income groups, because of their convenience and to meet expenditure.

***Title: A Survey of Life Insurance Practices and Opinions of the Selected Urban Families Residing in Baroda***

*Author:* Minaxi Baruah

*Guide:* Nalini Ogale

*Year:* 1974

*Keywords:* Life insurance, practices and opinions, financial plans, financial protection, savings

## INTRODUCTION

In day-to-day life man is confronted with many forms of risks and uncertainities, such as death, accident, injury leading to numerous difficulties. One of the problems is how to make provisions to take care of the family's financial loss, in case of the death of the main earner or during his inability to earn due to old age, illness, injury, loss of life in accident, fire, flood or loss of job. The severity resulting out of these conditions can be reduced to a certain extent by insuring oneself against these risks. The person who insures himself against risks is in a better position to cope with the unexpected emergencies and expected events in his life. Thus, life insurance is an integral part of a plan for financial security. The study was planned to assess how people are utilising this saving tool and what their opinions towards it are.

## METHODOLOGY

A survey method with questionnaire as tool for data collection was selected. The data were collected from 115 heads of the families from Alkapuri, Pratapgunj and Fatehgunj area keeping in mind that they belong to a nuclear family and have carried out life insurance after marriage. The data were coded and tabulated and analysed in terms of mean, median and percentages. Chi-square was computed to test the hypotheses.

## MAJOR FINDINGS

The mean size of the family was 5.95, the mean annual income was Rs. 13,050.5, and the respondents were college and school teachers, doctors and lawyers. The beginning stage of the married life was the most common period during which life insurance policies were purchased by a majority of the respondents. A small percentage of respondents discontinued the policy because of their inability to make premium payments regularly. The ownership of different types of life insurance policies and the amount insured were related to the income and the education of the respondents. The factors considered before the purchase of life insurance policies were income per month, size and premium, and future needs of the family. The most common reasons were "to provide financial protection to the family", 'to accumulate savings for old age', 'for education and marriage of the children and to meet unexpected emergencies in life". A majority of them had a favourable opinion towards life insurance as a form of savings and opinions were related to the family income and the age of the respondents.

***Title: A Comparative Study of the Money Management Practices and Attitude towards Money Management of a Selected Group of Female Hostel Students of M. S. University Baroda***

*Author:* Kamala Srinivasan

*Guide:* Nalini Ogale

*Year:* 1973

*Keywords:* Money management practices, attitude, students

## Introduction

Of all the resources available to a family, money is the most vital one. Home scientists have been pressing for inclusion of effective education in money management in the curriculum. This is in keeping with the national trend to give students training in the practical affairs of living. Proper training and guidance will help them to develop the type of value pattern that will enrich their entire lives.

The Faculty of Home Science offers personal family finance, consumer economics and family economics courses. The main purpose of these courses is to teach the principles of family finance management which will lead students to understand how a family can live in security by adopting suitable methods. Attitudes and values are an important indication of how one can expect people to behave in future situations.

## METHODOLOGY

A descriptive research study was undertaken. A questionnaire was used as a tool for collecting data. The random sampling technique was used to select the sample comprising 50 students from the girls hostel. The data were analysed statistically in terms of percentages and frequencies, and chi-square test and t-test were applied.

## MAJOR FINDINGS

The trained students reported a mean monthly allowance of Rs. 184, while the mean figure for the untrained group was Rs. 197. The mean monthly expenditure of the trained students for recreation was 18.47 per cent, for personal care 9.74 per cent and savings 3.48 per cent where as for untrained students for recreation it was 14.3 per cent personal care 8.10 per cent and savings 13.78 per cent.

The study showed that trained students did not apply the principles of money management in their practice of spending pocket money allowance.

***Title: A Comparative Study of Money Expenditure Incurred on Selected Ceremonies, Performed by Gujarati Anavil Brahmin and Baniya Families Residing in Baroda city***

*Author:* Maneesha Sinha

*Guide:* Veena Gandotra

*Year:* 1977

*Keywords:* Customs and ceremonies, expenditure

## Introduction

The individual or a family has limited resources to meet numerous wants, and there are a number of physical, social, economic, religious and cultural factors which affect the wants of people. Custom is one of the strongest. People in India perform various customs and ceremonies, especially those associated with marriage, birth, upanayanam and death, spending a considerable amount of money. How much expenditure was incurred on these ceremonies and how the families tried to finance them were the important objectives of the study and comparison was made for two selected castes.

## Methodology

A descriptive survey method with a questionnaire was used as an instrument for gathering data. Selective sampling of 100 families which belonged to the Anavil Brahmin and Baniya castes, and who had observed any one of the selected ceremonies within the last three years were selected. Categorisation, coding, and tabulation were done, and data were expressed in terms of frequency, range, mean and percentages. Chi-square and t-test were computed, and rank difference correlation was calculated to see the degree of relationship between the expenditure and income of the family.

## Major Findings

It was found that two castes, i.e., Anavil Brahmins and Baniyas, differed in the expenditure incurred on many of the items of expenditure on various ceremonies. Anavil Brahmins incurred more expenditure than Baniyas on the ceremonies. The families saved in advance to finance the ceremonies, yet still a few had to borrow money from others, sell their property, take loans from their provident fund. The reasons given for such expenditures were to gain recognition and acceptance in their group which in turn satisfied their wants of belongingness and gregariousness, and avoid helped to criticism from relatives and caste members. Families had the opinion that such expenditures should not be continued as it was difficult to finance such occasions due to the high cost of living, and they suggested performing the ceremonies in the simplest possible manner. As the income increased, the expenditure on the ceremony increased, but education did not help to change their deep-rooted ideas and customs. Hence there is a need to bring awareness and to change the values and attitudes of people. A cooperative effort should be made by the members of the caste to stop such practices.

***Title: A Study of Credit Practices and the Determinants of the Use of Credit by the Household of Udaipur City, Rajasthan State***

*Author:* Sushma Bhargava

*Guide:* Kamala Srinivasan

*Year:* 1979

*Keywords:* Credit practices, attitude towards credit

## Introduction

In this era of consumerism, we find that the role of credit has assumed a new dimension. It has now come to play an important role in the economic life of the families. Rapid advancement of technology has led to mass production of durable goods which in turn have increased the demand of families on their limited funds and consequently the notion regarding the use of credit for consumption purposes has also undergone a change. Being a relatively new phenomenon, there is an immediate need for educating the consumers regarding the proper and wise use of credit so that it serves not only as a tool that helps to tide over emergency expenditure but also as a tool that helps families to raise their standard of living. It was necessary to find out the extent to which credit is used, uses of credit, attitudes of homemakers towards credit, etc.

## Methodology

A survey method with an interview schedule was used for the study which contained the attitude scale to measure the homemakers' attitude towards credit use. A 100 samples were taken with stratified random sampling based on income. The data were coded, categorised, tabulated and analysed in terms of frequencies, mean, mode, median and standard deviation.

Chi-square, t-test and analysis of variance were employed for testing the hypotheses.

## MAJOR FINDINGS

A majority of the respondents belonged to the nuclear family with a mean size of 4.8 members and a mean monthly income of Rs. 780.50. Charge account credit was used by most of them mainly for buying milk, groceries, newspapers and magazines. Twenty-one per cent of the households used instalment credit for buying cycle. Sixty per cent of them used cash credit mainly for house construction and also for buying annual grains. A majority of the respondents had a negative attitude towards the use of credit. For the use and extent of the use of credit, income and socio-economic status emerged as significant determinants. Household size and the level of knowledge were not found to be affecting the use of credit. It was found that households with a positive attitude of homemakers used a greater amount of charge account credit. The socio-economic status and attitude formation gave partially significant results.

***Title: A Study of Investment Practices of the Families of Jammu City, Jammu and Kashmir State***

*Author:* Sudha Gupta

*Guide:* Shibani Mukerjee

*Year:* 1980

*Keywords:* Money as a resource, savings and investment, finance management

## INTRODUCTION

Money is an indispensable resource to mankind. In a predominant exchange economy it is being exchanged for commodities and services. No family spends the money it receives solely on consumer goods and services required for daily living; often a part is diverted into savings and investments. Although investment plays a significant role in the attainment of the long term goals of families and all-round welfare, studies related to this area are lacking. It is of great value to the home economists to know in detail how much and on what families invest their savings. The findings would benefit in teaching family finance management in institutions.

## Methodology

A survey method with an interview schedule was used to collect data. Purposive sampling was used to select 100 nuclear families headed by government servants working in selected offices of Jammu city with an income of Rs. 500 and above per month. The data collected were categorised, coded and tabulated using frequencies, percentages and means. Further F-test and chi-square were used to ascertain the level of association of the variables.

## Major Findings

The monthly income ranged from Rs. 500 to Rs. 3,000. More than half of the families had less than five family members. Half of the families were in the second stage of family lifecycle. A majority of the families were single earner families and the rest had a supplementary income from other sources. The mean age of the respondents was 36.6 years and the level of education ranged from high school level to professional degree level. The salaried urban families invested mainly on savings schemes, house, vehicle, equipment, furniture and education of their children. Livestock and stocks and shares were less popular items of investment. Every family has some motive behind its investment. In case of material possessions, the main motives are social status and prestige value. The income of the family affects the extent of investment more than the other variables, such as stage of family lifecycle, size of the family and age of the head of the family.

*Title: An Exploratory-cum-Descriptive Analysis of Banking Practices of Families and Customer's Evaluation of Working Efficiency of Banks of Baroda City*

*Author:* Sangita Kukreja

*Guide:* Kamala Srinivasan

*Year:* 1980

*Keywords:* Capital, savings, investments, banking system

## Introduction

In any economic development, capital occupies a position of strategic importance. The serious capital deficiency in underdeveloped countries is reflected in a small amount of capital equipment per worker, limited knowledge, training and scientific advances. These are serious handicaps in economic development and it is here that a bank can play a useful role. The role of banks in economic development is to remove the deficiency of capital by stimulating savings and investment. A sound banking system mobilises the small and scattered savings of the community for investment in productive enterprises. In this connection banks perform two important functions: they borrow in the form of deposits and lend in various forms of advances. The present study is justified with a view to determine banking practices of families, to ascertain homemakers' knowledge on banking and to assess the customers rating of working efficiency of their banks.

## Methodology

The study is both exploratory and descriptive with a survey method and an interview schedule for getting data. One hundred samples were randomly selected from three income groups on the basis of information received from the municipal corporation and income tax office of Baroda city. The data obtained were coded, tabulated and analysed in terms of simple frequencies, mean, mode, median and standard deviation. Chi-square test, t-test and analysis of variance were employed for testing hypotheses.

## Major Findings

A majority belonged to the nuclear family with a mean family size of 4.47 and a net disposable income of Rs. 1,766 per month. The mean age of male respondents was 42.9 years and of female respondents was 39 years. A majority of them were degree holders and belonged to category II of the socio-economic class. All the respondents had savings accounts as fixed deposit and recurring-cum-cumulative accounts with the reasons that they are for emergency purpose, making long term plans with more confidence and developing savings habits. Children's wedding and education were the purpose by the majority for holding a fixed deposit account. The knowledge of graduate and postgraduate respondents was found to be more then respondents who were below the graduate. The income and socio-economic status is at the increasing function of the extent of savings, and was partially accepted on the basis of F and t-tests. Family size and nature of occupation did not have any impact on the extent of savings. The educational level was an influential factor of banking knowledge.

***Title: Credit Practices of Rural Household and the Knowledge of the Head of Household Regarding Cash Credit***

*Author:* Toral Mehta

*Guide:* Rachel George

*Year:* 1981

*Keywords:* Credit, consumption, finance management

## Introduction

Credit is a term which in recent years has found a significant place in the finance management of many households. It is utilised in connection with the purchase of goods and services for personal and family consumption with a promise of future payments. Credit facility, if used judiciously, is a blessing while if misused, is a curse to the household. Learning to use credit in various ways to one's advantage is a part of the educative process in the society. The essential need of the day is, therefore, to educate the people in family finance and to reach consumers through teaching, research and counselling. To achieve this goal information about the credit practices of the rural households is needed which has been not explored fully.

## Methodology

The data were collected with a descriptive survey with the use of an interview schedule and knowledge test. One hundred and twenty households which used credit were selected through selective sampling from Kandari village from middle and low income groups. The data were analysed using categorisation, coding, tabulation and statistical analysis.

## Major Findings

The most popular kind of credit used was charge account credit for the purchase of daily required goods and services and consumption credit, that is, cash loan for meeting consumption expenditure / non-productive expenditures, mainly for marriage and housing expenses. Unlicensed lenders were the important sources of credit and then friends and relatives. Government and private licensed lending sources were not very popular sources. The reasons for using unlicensed lenders were easy availability, easy to approach, no interest charged. The households chose mainly monthly repayment plan to clear the debts. A majority of the households were able to pay off their debts as agreed up on. In general, the rural households did not make wise use of credits, such as phases like planning and record keeping. The respondents lacked knowledge about various aspects of cash credit, such as sources of cash credit, interest rate, etc. Income, education and employment status emerged out as factors influencing the sources of securing cash credit. Employment status, length of marriage and household income affected the extent of wise use of credit. Age of the head of the household, his educational level and experience were associated with knowledge and extent of wise use of credit by the households.

***Title: Worker's Awareness, Utilisation, and Evaluation of the Fringe Cum Social Security Benefits with Special Reference to the ESI Scheme in Two Private Organisations of Baroda City***

*Author:* Renu Kapoor

*Guide:* Kamala Srinivasan

*Year:* 1981

*Keywords:* Income insecurity, financial or social security

## Introduction

Man, being a social animal, faces a multitude of problems of varying nature, and economic problems are the most crucial ones.

Because of lack of adequate economic resources, solution for other problems also becomes difficult. The problem of income insecurity is faced by families all over the world. The rapid pace of industrialisation along with bringing a dynamic change in the economy has increased the economic hazards especially for the industrial workers who, on account of meagre economic resources, are incapable of affording the financial security for the family. Various financial / social security measures are provided from the workplace to help the families solve the problem of income insecurity to a large extent but its systematic implementation is a must. This study was undertaken to find out the worker's awareness, evaluation and utilisation of various personal and financial-cum-social security measures – the findings of which will help the authorities concerned for taking necessary measures.

## Methodology

A descriptive survey method with an interview schedule was taken for the study. Random sampling was done for selecting two organisations and for selecting 50 samples from each organisation. The data were coded, tabulated and analysed in terms of frequencies, mean, median, mode and standard deviation. Chi-square and t-test of variance were employed for testing the hypotheses.

## Major Findings

For the welfare of the employees, both the organisations had made provision for different kinds of fringe benefits. Ninety-five per cent of the employees were aware of it; 68 per cent of the respondents from chemical works and 56 per cent from textile mills had utilised it for various purposes, mainly for house construction and the least for business purpose. As the socio-economic status increased, the extent of use credit also increased. Large size families relatively utilised more amount of credit than the small size families. The opinion of the employees towards their union was neither too favourable nor too unfavourable. Maximum awareness of the employees was found with regard to sickness and medical benefits, and the least was regarding disablements, extended sickness, dependents and funeral benefits. Knowledge regarding terms and conditions and coverage of the scheme was influenced by the education and socio-economic status of the respondents. Evaluation of the workers regarding the nature and functioning of the ESI scheme from the point of view of convenience and human aspects showed that workers were not satisfied with the working of the scheme. They were not completely satisfied with whatever was being provided to them in terms of financial security. Respondents desired improvement in financial security measures in terms of increase in the existing pay scale, minimum wage, bonus rates and different allowances. Moreover, they reported that administrative procedures for obtaining various benefits under the scheme should be made more simple.

*Title: A Study of Money Management Practices of Retired People and Their Attitude Towards Money Management and Retirement*

*Author:* Kiran Ghai

*Guide:* Veena Gandotra

*Year:* 1982

*Keywords:* Retirement stage, financial security, attitude and practices towards money management

## Introduction

While financial security is of significance at any period, it is of particular importance at the retirement stage of the family. In India, after retirement, normally a person becomes a non-productive member of the family. So a proper financial plan becomes necessary to make provision for meeting the needs of today and tomorrow. Retirement seems to be an appropriate time to examine the management of family resources because of the changes in the established income and expenditure patterns, and the subsequent changes in the lifestyle due to reduced financial resources. Therefore, an attempt was made to study the money management practices of retired persons, their attitude towards money management and retirement.

## Methodology

The data were collected through a survey method using an interview schedule, money management practices scale and attitude scale. Samples were selected from two occupational groups, namely, Air Force and Post and Telegraph as public service organisations, and 60 samples were randomly selected from each occupational group. The data were coded, tabulated and analysed in terms of simple frequencies, percentages, mean and standard deviation, and chi-square and t-test were employed for testing the association between the variables.

## Major Findings

A majority of the retired persons were working after retirement because of economic stress on the family as the income decreased after retirement. The expenditure pattern differed among the income groups and occupational groups. The average amount of credit taken by retired people decreased after retirement and they used cash credit rather than instalment credit. A majority of the respondents were able to save before retirement but after retirement a few of them were able to save. They saved through provident fund as it was a compulsory deposit scheme. Different income group respondents reflected differences in their practices of handling money. Income and occupational differences, attitude of retired persons towards money management towards retirement showed decided influence on money management practices followed by the retired people.

***Title: Life Insurance Practices of Households and Customers' Evaluation of the Functioning of LIC - A Cross-Sectional Analysis***

*Author:* Rosetts Nazareth

*Guide:* Kamala Srinivasan

*Year:* 1984

*Keywords:* Life insurance practices, endowment assurance policy

## Introduction

Life is filled with risks of all kinds both in our homes and outside. Life insurance is a method that seeks to reduce the financial uncertainities arising from the natural contingencies of old age and death, and to bring about a comparable certainty in the case of possible misfortunes, injury and sickness. Life insurance made rapid progress in quantitative terms, but the quality has not kept pace. However, no empirical data was there to support the fact about how the quality of service had deteriorated. Hence, the study has been carried out in the area of life insurance practices of households along with their evaluation of the functioning of Life Insurance Corporation.

## Methodology

An exploratory-cum-descriptive design with a survey method of investigation was carried out with the interview schedule as the tool for data collection. A cross-section of a representative sample of hundred respondents of Baroda city were randomly chosen. The data were coded, tabulated, analysed in terms of frequencies, mean, mode, median and standard deviation, and t-test was employed.

## Major Findings

The mean family size was 3.4 persons and the mean income was Rs. 3,350 per month. Eighty-five per cent of the sample had a regular saving with approximately Rs. 292.19 per month. Only 27 per cent of the sample had life insurance purchased for them by their parents or near relatives. The most common life insurance policy taken for them was the Endowment Assurance Policy by 44 per cent of them and the mean face value was Rs. 20,370. Half of them had purchased their first life insurance policy in the beginning stage of the family lifecycle and rest had at other stages of the lifecycle. Only 16 out of 100 respondents took loan from LIC. Fifty-six per cent of the sample had a negative opinion towards the convenience aspect of LIC in Baroda. They were also dissatisfied, especially because of lack of proper guidance given to customers and the staff had not enough knowledge regarding life insurance schemes, terms and conditions. The income type of occupation had a positive relationship with the face value, premium rate and the number of life insurance policies taken that were partially accepted. Income and occupation showed significant results for the convenience aspect of LIC but not for the human aspect.

***Title: A Comparative Study of Attitude of Boys and Girls from Haryana and Gujarat towards Dowry***

*Author:* Leena Hooda

*Guide:* Veena Gandotra

*Year:* 1986

*Keywords:* Attitude, boys, girls, dowry

## Introduction

Dowry is the custom in Indian society. However, with changing time the attitude towards it are changing. The custom of dowry affects the financial management of the family also. The study focuses on the attitude of young boys and girls toward the practice of dowry. It further attempts to find out practices followed by families with regard to giving and taking dowry and their opinion towards it. An attempt is also made to study the effect of selected variables on the attitude of respondents towards dowry.

## Methodology

Data were collected through a questionnaire by contacting boys and girls at the place of their study. The sample comprised 200 respondents, 50 each of boys and girls from Haryana and Gujarat. Data were categorised, coded, tabulated and analysed in terms of frequencies and percentages. Coefficient of correlation and chi-square were used to test the relationship among variables.

## Major Findings

A majority of respondents belonged to class II of the socio-economic class in Haryana and in Gujarat. A majority of the respondents belonged to class I and class II. A majority of the families of boys in Haryana accepted dowry whereas in Gujarat, one-third accepted dowry. A major form of dowry was ornaments, clothing, furniture video and TV. Girls from Haryana felt they had received adequate amount of dowry while those from Gujarat did not feel so. Boys were looked upon as a necessity in the families of Haryana and Gujarat. Girls were also welcomed by both communities. Dowry was seen as a burden on the family and not as a girl's right. Opinion was not in favour of dowry. They were against dowry. Girls from Gujarat were more against than those from Haryana. All were aware of the Dowry Prohibition Act. A negative relation was seen between the socio-economic class and the attitude towards dowry. Attitudes differed among boys and girls and those from different education levels.

***Title: Impact of the Bank Credit Extended Under the Integrated Rural Development Programme on Status of Women and Family —A Comparative Analysis***

*Author:* Sunita Rana

*Guide:* Kamala Srinivasan

*Year:* 1987

*Keywords:* Credit – Family-oriented credit and women-oriented credit, status of women

## Introduction

Economic development requires the utilisation of a wide range of resources, both material and human resources. Women constitute almost half of the manpower resources of the country and is an important resource. The Indian Constitution gave great attention to the issue of improving the status of women. With this intention several programmes were formulated under the Sixth Five Year Plan, and the Integrated Rural Development Programme was one of the major programmes providing self-employment to women, especially the weaker section. Credit is given to women. The study was taken to assess the effectiveness of the programme intended for women and to study the awareness, knowledge and extent of utilisation of two types of credit, viz. family-oriented and women-oriented, and their relative impact on the status of women.

## Methodology

A survey method with an interview schedule was used to gather data which consisted of two descriptive rating scales: (i) to elicit information regarding extent of problems faced and (ii) to assess the perception of homemakers towards the impact of credit facility on her status in the family. A stratified random sampling was used to draw 100 sample, i.e., 50 from rural and 50 from semi-urban who had availed credit facility under IRDP. The procedures used to analyse the data were coding, tabulation and mean and standard deviation. Chi-square and t-test were also used to test hypotheses.

## Major Findings

The joint family system was existing predominantly in rural areas and the mean size of the rural family was 7.64 and 4.82 members in semi-urban area. The mean monthly income was Rs. 612 and in both areas 50 per cent of the respondents were illiterate. In semi-urban area 64 per cent of families reported to be saving as compared to 42 per cent of the families in the rural area. Most of the families borrowed money for consumption purpose. Most of them had a favourable opinion about bank credit facility. They showed low response to skill training classes. Community workers and neighbours were the sources of knowledge regarding 'bank credit' facility but they did not show a positive inclination towards learning of bank rules and regulation.

They took loan for sewing machine, business purpose, buffalo and other incidentals. The higher income families were getting a larger amount of loan as compared to the low income families. The larger amount was extended to male beneficiaries as compared to female beneficiaries. Male beneficiaries had more knowledge than female beneficiaries. The homemakers in women-oriented credit perceived more positively than family-oriented credit regarding the impact of credit on their status. Income and education were the determinants affecting the perception of women towards the status of women. Thus, women-oriented credit proved to be more effective in improving the status of women and family living as compared to family-oriented credit.

***Title: Educational Goals of Families and Cost of Education***

*Author:* Prathima Kosaraju

*Guide:* Nalini Ogale

*Year:* 1992

*Keywords:* Educational goals, families, cost

## Introduction

Education is the chief tool of social change and national development. It claims a considerable section of the national budget as well as family budget. As education is becoming more and more important, families spend a lot to educate their children. Expenditure on education is an investment expenditure and it begins to yield results after a generation in the form of jobs and earnings. So how much the families spend to educate children and whether educating the children gives some psychological satisfaction to the parents or not are to be found out.

## Methodology

A descriptive research design was used for the present study. The data were collected by a questionnaire. The study was conducted at Vijayawada of Andhra Pradesh State. The total sample consisted of 100 families. The study was limited to those families who had children who were still studying in school / college. The statistics applied to analyse data were frequency, percentage distribution, measures of central tendency, mean and standard deviation. Chi-square, ANOVA and coefficient of correlation were used for testing the hypotheses.

## Major Findings

Families spent a considerable part of their income on education of their children throughout the year and they even paid capitation fee to admit their children in good reputed schools / colleges. It was found that parents were satisfied regarding the education of their children. All the respondents had children whose achievement was average and above average. As the respondents were from middle income group they didn't find it difficult to spend on their children's education. It was found that the achievement of educational goals was not associated with income and education of parents. A significant relationship was found between the income of the family and the monetary cost of education of children.

***Title: Practices and Expenditure of Families Regarding Education of Their First-Born Child as a Means to Invest in Human Capital***

*Author:* Ami Majmudar

*Guide:* Maneesha Shukul

*Year:* 1995

*Keywords:* Human capital, investment, expenditure

### INTRODUCTION

Human beings, when treated as capital assets, are termed as human capital. Human beings are considered "capital" by investing in various aspects of human capital formation. The theory of human capital treats expenditure on education, health, on-the-job training etc. as investment expenditure. These expenditures form the human capital, i.e., it enhances the capabilities of individuals as workers and makes them more productive. Education comes at the highest order of importance because direct relationship exists between education and the earnings of a person. This fosters economic growth of the country. The importance of formal education has increased in the present age but the family provides an environment for a child's education to grow. Hence, an attempt is made to study the parents' practices for the education of their first-born child, the amount of expenditure and reasons for investment in human capital through education.

### METHODOLOGY

A descriptive survey with a questionnaire having a summated rating scale to score the practices was used to collect data. A sample of 112 families residing in Nizampura area of Baroda was purposively selected on the basis that the family should have their first child studied in standard 10th, 11th or 12th during the academic year 1993-94. The data were coded, tabulated and mean, standard deviation and percentage were applied. Canonical correlation and multiple regression analysis were applied to test the hypotheses.

## Major Findings

Almost an equal number of first-born boys and first-born girls were found in the same category with not much difference in distribution in each standard. The mean monthly income was Rs. 7,325. Respondents showed good practices related to provision of facilities. The total score on all types of practices, i.e., motivation, guidance, supervision, participation, authoritarian practice, etc. was high expression that their overall practices for education of the first-born child were good. The mean of total yearly expenditure on education and transportation was Rs. 7,901.4 with the highest yearly mean expenditure on private tuition fees. A majority of the respondents financed the education of the child from regular income and savings because they wanted their children to be independents; also they believed that it was their personal duty. More than half of them believed that education would enable them to earn enough in future. A majority of the respondents favoured a combination of degree and vocational courses for getting better jobs. They also agreed that expenditure on education of the child was an investment in human capital. This would be helpful to their family in future and they would be contributing to national development. There was a fairly good amount of relation between selected independent variables and practices for education, whereas no significant relationship was found between selected variables and total yearly expenditure on education of the first-child born in the family.

***Title: A Study of Extent of Utilisation and Satisfaction Experienced by the Families of Employees Regarding Selected Fringe Benefits Provided by Gujarat Refinery***

*Author:* Ramnani Sangeeta

*Guide:* Maneesha Shukul

*Year:* 1995

*Keywords:* Fringe benefits, utilisation of benefits, satisfaction from the use of benefits

## Introduction

Fringe benefits are those benefits which primarily are means in the direction of ensuring, maintaining and increasing the income of the employee. Gujarat Refinery has provided a number of fringe benefits to its employees and their families. The study was undertaken to know to what extent the employees utilise the selected fringe benefits and whether they satisfied with the benefits or not.

## Methodology

A descriptive survey with an interview schedule was used as a tool to collect data. The schedule contained summated rating scale to score the utilisation and satisfaction. A 100 samples were selected through systematic random technique. Categorisation, coding, tabulation, frequencies and percentages were used to analyse the data. Canonical correlation was applied to test the hypotheses.

## Major Findings

The mean monthly income was Rs. 6,555.45. A majority of the respondents possessed one or more than one vehicle, as the Gujarat Refinery paid the vehicle maintenance allowance to its employees. All the respondents used the medical facility at the Gujarat Refinery Hospital. The children's immunisation programme and visiting specialist doctors were not encouraged. A majority of the respondents were satisfied with the location of the hospital, physical conditions of the equipments in the hospital and cleanliness in the hospital. Respondents used transport facility when they or their husbands alone visited the city or by their children to go to schools at Baroda city, but when they went with the whole family then they used their own vehicles as the petrol allowance was paid by the Gujarat Refinery. A variety of recreational activities, such as cable TV connection, clubs, nights, parks etc. were provided and used by the respondents and most of them were satisfied by it. An indepth analysis shows that the respondents tapped the fringe benefits adequately. The result of the canonical correlation computed showed that there was a fairly good amount of relationship among selected variables and utilisation of selected fringe benefits but no relationship among selected variables and satisfaction experienced by utilisation selecting fringe benefits.

*Title: A Study of Financial Management Practices of Selected Families of Gujarat Refinery Employees at Jawaharnagar, Baroda*

*Author:* Nisha Pandey

*Guide:* Asha V. Dass

*Year:* 1997

*Keywords:* Financial management, management practices, process of management, credit

## Introduction

Families achieve financial peace of mind, not by wishing for more and more income, but by learning to manage their own income. As with all types of management, plans are unlikely to be carried out successfully unless some control is exercised. Control in financial management helps one keep in mind the decisions which were made in the planning stage, and gives one the assurance of knowing whether or not adjustments are needed. Evaluation in the light of family goals in financial management is important. By planning, controlling and evaluating, families can progress towards achievement of their economic goals. When they have less income and savings to meet their needs and wants they take credit. The study aimed to find out the financial management practices of selected low income families and the reasons for following the financial management practices.

## Methodology

A descriptive survey with an interview schedule was used. Purposive stratified random sampling was used to select 120 samples from Gujarat Refinery of Baroda. The data were coded and categorised, and relational statistics employed were frequency, percentage, mean, standard deviation, coefficient of correlation, and analysis of variance.

## MAJOR FINDINGS

The mean income was Rs. 3,581.10 per month; 58 per cent of the respondents followed fair planning practices and 40 per cent followed good practices. For controlling expenditure, an equal number of respondents followed fair and good practices. Regarding the evaluation step, 50 per cent had good and 43 per cent had fair practices; 72 per cent did not avail of credit. Thus, a majority of the respondents had fair practices regarding financial management. The financial management practices of the respondents were not influenced by their own age, education, their husband's age and education, family income and size of the family. The reason for the results not becoming significant may be due to that many financial benefits were provided from the company which reduced the disparity among the various income groups chosen for the study.

***Title: Expenditure Incurred and Practices Followed by Homemakers Regarding Health and Family Members***

*Author:* Trupti Arya

*Guide:* Maneesha Shukul

*Year:* 1997

*Keywords:* Good health, mental and physical well-being, sanitation practices, preventive and curative practices

## INTRODUCTION

Each individual wants good health, which is the condition of physical and mental well being that enables an individual to engage in the normal activities appropriate to his age. The health condition of a person and the socio-economic development go hand in hand. Health care is one of the most important of all human endeavours to improve the quality of the life of people. It implies the provision of condition for normal physical and mental development, and the functioning of the human beings. The homemakers, the main caretakers of the health of all family members, need to be aware of the right kind of practices which would keep the illness away from their family, thereby decreasing much of the expenditure on the treatment and even loss of life.

It was necessary to understand the practices followed and the expenditure incurred on health and also preventive measures taken by them so that the appropriate educational programme could be undertaken.

## METHODOLOGY

A survey method with an interview schedule having a summated rating scale to score the practices was used for the study. The sample consisted of 120 respondents selected through systematic random sampling from Pratapnagar slums of Baroda city. Data collected were coded and tabulated. Mean, standard deviation and percentage were used to describe the data. The hypotheses were tested through the Analysis of Variance.

## MAJOR FINDINGS

The mean monthly income was Rs. 1,717.1. A majority of the respondents had semi-pucca houses with one room and a majority used part of the room for cooking purposes. Most of them did not have toilet facilities in the house and many had bathroom as a part of the room. All of them used the community tap as a source of water for drinking and for other purposes, and stored water in earthen pots, cement tanks and aluminium vessels. Respondents collected information regarding health from doctors, relatives, radio, social workers etc. but used to a low extent. Respondents followed fair practices regarding sanitation and curative practice, and followed poor preventive practices. Little less than half of them used sources of treatment to a low extent and the mean expenditure was Rs. 333 per month on health in the past one year. Respondents' education, family income and use of sources of information influenced the practices followed by homemakers. The extent of the use of sources of treatment were influenced by occupation and education, but expenditure was not influence by any of the factors.

***Title: A Study of Food Related Expenditure and Consumption Practices of Selected Manipuri Families***

*Author:* Bijentimala Devi Sapam

*Guide:* Vijaya Lakshmi Yadla

*Year:* 1998

*Keywords:* Food, expenditure, consumption practices

## Introduction

Food is woven in the life fabric of society. It is the largest single item of expenditure. Modernisation and technological advancement have led to a rapid change in the methods of production and communication which are affected on consumption pattern by the families. Each household is individualistic, designing products to fit their own particular requirements. The technologies and fuels used in food consumption activities also vary from place to place and family to family due to the availability of new technology. It is noticed that there is hardly any study which is concentrated in studying various dimensions of food consumption pattern related to not only the expenditure but also practices used for consumption purposes from the economic point of view. So the present study was executed.

## Methodology

A descriptive research design was used and an interview schedule was used to collect the data. Systematic non-random sampling was chosen as the mode for identifying the sample of 80 urban homemakers from two different ward numbers of Imphal, Manipur. For the data analysis, descriptive statistics employed were frequency, mean, standard deviation, and inferential statistics used were coefficient of correlation, F and 't' tests.

## Major Findings

The mean monthly expenditure incurred on cereals was Rs. 984.4 by a majority of the families, for milk and milk products the pulses and meat. It was at highest Rs. 1,014.6 for packed food, bakery products. LPG was the most common cooking fuel. Green leafy vegetables, other vegetables and fish were purchased daily by a majority. Most of the families had all four meals together. A majority of the Manipur families were non-vegetarians. Nutritive value, availability and cost were the major factors considered in meal planning. Most of the families spent 51-60 minutes for lunch and dinner preparation. Traditional types of technologies were used for all tasks related to cooking. A majority of the samples opined that plastics, polythene bags, metal tins and glass tins were harmful to the environment. The age of the spouse, family income, standard adult equivalent and type of family emerged as factors affecting the expenditure incurred on various food groups and other food related expenditure.

*Title: Extent of Awareness, Utilization and Satisfaction of the Customers with the Services of LIC of India*

*Author:* Manisha Sharma

*Guide:* Maneesha Shukul

*Year:* 2002

*Keywords:* Awareness, Utilization. Satisfaction, Customers, Services of LIC of India

## Introduction

Life insurance seeks to reduce the financial uncertainties and to bring about a comparable certainty in case of possible misfortunes- injury and sickness. Life insurance serves as an excellent means of encouraging and even forcing thrift. It serves as a powerful agency which creates and maintains the credit of the insured person, and acts as the best medium of saving. To assess the awareness and utilization of people regarding various policies and services offered by LIC of India and to find out the satisfaction of customers the present investigation was undertaken.

## Methodology

The study was a descriptive research. The sample consisted of 120 customers of LIC, Agra city, selected by systematic random sampling method. An interview schedule was used as an instrument for gathering data. Descriptive as well as relational statistics were used for data analysis.

## Major Findings

The mean age of the respondents was 39.3 years. Nearly half of them were females and postgraduates. A majority of them were employed. Nearly half of them were from joint families and the mean family income was Rs. 31,954.16. Most of them had a medium extent of exposure to the sources of information. The mean amount saved per month was Rs 953.6. Nearly one-third of the respondents had two policies at the time of data collection. The mean face value of the policies was Rs. 245170.9. A majority of the respondents were aware of LIC policies and services to a low extent. All of the respondents considered the advice of the agents. Almost all the respondents were highly satisfied with the services of LIC of India. The statistical analysis indicated that the extent of awareness of the customers regarding services of LIC varied with their education, occupation, exposure to the services of information, sex, family income, numbers of family members and adults in the family.

***Title: Education of Children in Foreign Country: A Multidimensional Study.***

*Author*: Bhavika Shah

*Guide*: Maneesha Shukul

*Year*: 2004

*Keywords*: Education, Children, Foreign country

Abstract:

## INTRODUCTION

Education is a process of human enlightenment and empowerment for the achievement of better and higher quality of life. Higher education in any society as perceived by various authors is of vital importance in the whole education system. The development of higher education in India, in the last five decades, presents a picture of light and shade. A majority of the students go to foreign country to seek education because they get an opportunity for wider choice of courses, cross-cultural experience, global experience, exposure to different language skills, recognition in the job market, and enhancement of social status. The deteriorating quality of Indian education also pushes them to take education in a foreign country. Studying overseas is an expensive business as compared to studying in India. To meet the heavy financial requirements a family needs to manage its own savings, so it borrows from relatives/friends/private parties/ moneylenders, or find a way to obtain loan from banks. Thus, this topics seeks to study the various dimensions, the reasons which influenced the parents' decision to send their children to a foreign country and how much expenditure they incurred on education of their children, as well as to find out what were the problems they faced when they sent their children to a foreign country and how they overcame it. The respondents were parents who sent their children to foreign countries for education within the past one to four year.

## Methodology

The study was descriptive research. The sample consisted of 90 parents who sent their children to foreign countries for education from Baroda. The sample was selected by a snowball technique. The interview schedule was used as an instrument for gathering data.

## Major Findings

The present multidimensional study revealed that the mean age of fathers was 54 years and the mean age of mothers was 51.2 years. More than two-thirds fathers and mothers were graduate. More than half of the fathers and more than one-third of the mothers were in service group. A wide majority of the families had more than four members in the family, and the mean of family income was Rs. 24,289. The mean age of children was 24.3 years. More than two-thirds had males and more than two-thirds children had completed graduation in India. About half of the children had gone to USA for study and more than three-fourths of the children went for postgraduate studies to foreign countries. A majority of the children went for two year courses and a little more than one-third of the children went in the year of 2003. Respondents gave ranks to reasons for their decision to send their children to foreign countries. In descending order the reasons were personal, educational, economic, social and parental. More than half of the respondents considered the "curriculum" while selecting the university. More than three-fourths of the respondents collected information regarding education in a foreign country from friends. Most of the respondents managed the heavy expenditure of education in a foreign country from personal finance. The mean expenditure indicated that the respondents had incurred the highest expenditure on the fees of the university. Less than half of the respondents had incurred an expenditure between Rs. 6,00,000 and 8,00,000. A wide majority of the respondents had a low extent of problems and all of them adopted coping strategies at a low extent. The amount of expenditure incurred by parents on their children's education varied with family income and the country where child was sent for education. There was a positive relationship between problems and coping strategies. The present multidimensional study had clear implications for banks and other families desirous of sending their children to foreign country for education.

***Title: Financial Management Competency of Head of the Family and Family's Financial Satisfaction***

*Author:* Jayshree Pandya

*Guide:* Suramya Joshi

*Year:* 2006

*Keywords:* Financial management competency, satisfaction, families

## Introduction

An individual has to view money as a tremendous source of power for the fulfilment of needs and wants. It is important for every individual to understand the proper use of money. Successful financial management is necessary for the fullest accomplishment of satisfaction in life and it reflects the competency of the money manager in the family. Proper financial management forces a person towards a careful selection of goals and alternatives. It provides an opportunity to practise thrift and substantially increase savings through elimination of wasted expenditure. A wise use of financial management practices by families and individuals helps to improve their financial well-being. The investigator did not come across any considerable amount of research in the area of financial management for the institutions compared to that the families. Thus the present study was undertaken.

## METHODOLOGY

A descriptive research design was used for the present study. The sample of 90 respondents who were head of the family and/or the person involved in the financial decisions was selected from two residential areas of Baroda City, namely, Gorwa and Gotri. Purposive sampling technique was adopted to select the samples. A questionnaire was used for collecting data. Descriptive as well as relational statistics were used to analyse the data. The data were scored, categorised, tabulated and presented in frequencies, percentages, mean and standard deviations for analysing the information. For statistical testing of hypotheses, analysis of variance, 't' test and Pearson's Product Moment Correlation Coefficient were computed.

## MAJOR FINDINGS

It was found that the decision making about the used income was jointly done for investments. For the financial management competencies it was found that 55.06 per cent of the respondents belonged to a moderate level of financial management competencies. A majority of the families had specific financial goals which were considered by the respondents while making the budget. Financial satisfaction was experienced by little more than half of the respondents to a great extent. The statistical testing revealed that the financial management competencies varied with income and family size. The extent of financial satisfaction varied with the type of family. The variation in the economic profile of the family was found due to the education and monthly income of the respondents as well as the monthly income and size of the family.

# 3

# Time and Energy Management

Time and energy are two important human resources available to us, and they must be used properly and not wasted. Homemakers have a lot of responsibilities within the home and outside home, hence they must carefully study how they can improve their methods of work. Work implication is the means of work improvement. Management within homes or in business, has been defined as "the judicious use of means to accomplish an end" which to the home involves a recognition of the human and non-human resources that families use in achieving the desired goals. Two important factors in achieving family goals, time and human energy are limited in amount. In the recent years a major shift has taken place in this direction under the impact of economic poverty, social awakening and technological development. This is projected in the researches carried out in the department.

> ***Title: Time and Motion Study of Meal Preparation in a Home Management House***
>
> *Author:* Aruna Kotecha
>
> *Guide:* Nalini Ogale
>
> *Year:* 1967
>
> *Keywords:* Management of resources, human cost of work, work simplification, time and motion study

### Introduction

Management, whether in homes or in business, has been defined as "the judicious use of means to accomplish an end" which to the home involves a recognition of the human and non-human resources that families use in achieving the desired goals. Two important factors in achieving family goals, time and human energy, are limited in amount. Changes in social conditions with more and more women joining the labour force and changes in the pattern of living make it essential to know how to minimise the human costs of household work.

Work simplification helps for making working hours more productive and for making tasks easier. The real award comes in terms of reduced labour costs, higher production in a given amount of time and better service. Providing food for the family and for the students in a Home Management House is one of the major activities in the daily schedule which requires time and energy input.

It was therefore felt that a study of time and the motion of meal preparation of the Home Management House would contribute toward making the house students' and also homemakers' work methods more efficient and also add to the knowledge of making kitchens more functional in design.

## METHODOLOGY

An experimental study was planned in the Maharani Shantadevi Home Management House of Faculty of Home Science with six pairs of students involved in cooking activities taken as samples. The study was planned to serve two main purposes: (i) work improvement of meal preparation, and (ii) developing a guide for proper location of working areas in the kitchen. Pathway charts and process charts were used to find out the most economical way in terms of time taken, motion used and distance travelled for preparing a meal.

## MAJOR FINDINGS

The change in work methods contributed a total saving of about 13 per cent of the time taken, 36 per cent of the motions and distance travelled; between time and motion, motion and distance and time and distance. The greatest decrease in number of motions was noted in transportation and also in storage and inspection.

***Title: The Amount, Use and Values of Leisure Time of Home Makers***

*Author:* Gyaneshwari Ranawat

*Guide:* Elizabeth Beveridge

*Year:* 1972

*Keywords:* Human and non-human resources, time as a resource, work, rest and leisure time

## INTRODUCTION

Time, an intangible resource, is available in equal amounts to everyone, and it is the use of time which gives it value. During the early centuries, the use of time was very imbalanced. Women had to put in long hours of work at home as they had little equipment. Development of science and technology has played a vital role in transforming their lives, and as a result, the working hours have greatly shortened resulting in more rest and leisure time. By means of scientific management, home makers have been able to simplify their housework so that it takes less of their time and energy and leaves them free for other activities pursued during leisure time which are characterised by freedom of choice. One is free to choose whatever activity prefers. Many of the leisure activities are of temporary interest and contribute little to personal growth.

The other type of activities contribute to an expanding self and provide an opportunity to promote a physical, mental and emotional health. Leisure time activities compensate the tiresome effects of the work hours. Hence to promote recovery is also one of the functions of leisure. The homemaking tasks are not only energy demanding, but their repetitive performance creates monotony and boredom. Therefore, leisure time is an important part of a homemaker's day. One's personality can be enriched through wise use of leisure time. In this study, an attempt has been made to locate the interests of the homemakers, the facilities they would like to have, and when and how much leisure they get. The findings can be used by curriculum planners to plan courses of time management.

## Methodology

A survey method with an interview schedule was used to collect data. Sample for the present study comprised 140 home-makers from three residential localities of Baroda: Alkapuri, Fatehgunj and Pratapgunj through stratified random sampling, i.e., two broad categories: employed homemakers and unemployed homemakers. Categorisation, coding, tabulation and illustrations were used to analyse the data, and t-test and chi-square were used to test the hypotheses.

## Major Findings

All the leisure time pursuits were divided into six categories, namely, physical, social, recreational, intellectual, creative and other activities. Employed subjects had varied occupations, a large number of them were mainly teachers. The leisure time available to the homemakers ranged from one to nine hours.

Of the total sample, two-thirds got three to six hours of leisure hours daily. The mean time available to the employed home makers was 3.22 hours daily and that of unemployed ones was 5.30 hours. The employment status was closely related with the leisure time available to the housewives.

The size of the family, the help available to the homemakers and the number of time saving appliances also affected the time of homemakers, especially that of the employed ones. The activities on which the largest amount of leisure time, about six to 10 hours per week was spent, were conversation, reading, teaching the children and radio-listening. The least time, about one and a half hours, was spent on creative writing and shopping.

The employed homemakers spent a comparatively lesser time than the unemployed homemakers. Leisure time activities were based on interest and time, and they had a liking for reading, movies and songs. The average expenditure on leisure time was Rs. 18.05, mainly on reading materials. The respondents suggested some facilities like hobby centres, short term courses and religions organisations in their locality.

***Title: The Amount and Use of Leisure Time of Rural Homemakers***

*Author:* Lina Mankad

*Guide:* Nalini Ogale, Veena Gandotra

*Year:* 1972

*Keywords:* Leisure time, community facilities

## Introduction

Time is a resource that we share alike, that is, 24 hours a day for everyone. It is an intangible resource. It cannot be saved, stored or accumulated. It has practical acceptance and use. In the time plan for family living, work, rest and leisure need to be considered. Today better equipment and technologies of work have increased an individual's efficiency in work, reduced his working hours and increased his leisure time. Leisure time gives chances to overcome the boredom and limitation of everyday life physically as well as mentally, in shaping an individual's social and cultural values, and directing his energy in proper channels. In rural areas, women go for outside employment but facilities to save their time and labour in household chores, such as labour, saving devices or ready-to-use consumer goods, etc. are not available, nor have they knowledge about such things, besides they cannot afford to buy.

As a result, they put more hours of work at home and so the amount of leisure time they may be getting could be less. The Government and Gram Panchayat have organised a number of programmes for recreation and welfare of rural homemakers such as Mahila Mandal, Library, Adult Education Classes and Sewing Classes. The investigator wanted to know how much leisure time rural homemakers get every day, which are the activities they carry out in their leisure time and how they use the available facilities. The findings could be useful for courses on time management and for community workers, extension students in planning and dealing with rural homemakers leisure time activities.

## Methodology

A survey method was used and the technique employed for collecting data was personal interview with an interview schedule as a recording device. A sample of 100 homemakers was selected from three villages, namely, Timbavadi, Vadal and Kutiyana near by Junagadh city. The facilities common in these villages were library, marketplace and adult education classes. Whereas the variations in the availability of facilities showed that Timbavadi did not have sewing classes, Vadal did not have Mahila Mandal and Katiyana lacked Gram Sevika Training classes. None of these villages had a theatre. The data were categorised, coded, grouped and tabulated and simple frequency, percentages, means and bar graphs were used to present data. Chi-square and t-test were used to test the hypotheses.

## Major Findings

Leisure time available to rural homemakers ranged from one hour to five hours per day. The mean amount of leisure time available to non-employed homemakers was 139.5 minutes per day and for the employed homemakers was 70.5 minutes per day. The paid employed got 61.5 minutes of mean leisure time and the self-employed got 77 minutes of mean leisure time.

The smaller the size of the family the more was the amount of leisure time available per day. Gossiping, stitching, listening to radio, visiting neighbours were the most popular activities. The least popular and time-consuming leisure time activities were singing, drawing, writing, attending *katha*, gardening and going for walks.

The amount of leisure time available to homemakers varied due to the type of family and the age of the homemakers. The range of average expenditure was Rs. 10.65 to 13.50 per month. The greatest expenditure was incurred on activities, such as embroidery, reading and the least expenditure on indoor games and religious activities. The amount of money spent on leisure time was not influenced by an increase in the family income. The community facilities available for their leisure time pursuits were not fully utilised by a majority of the subjects.

*Title: A Study of Time Management Practices of College Students of M. S. University, Baroda*
*Author:* Amita Sharma
*Guide:* Nalini Ogale
*Year:* 1978
*Keywords:* Time management, leisure time

## INTRODUCTION

Time is constant in the life of all human beings. Its use by humans is a major variable. In the traditional society the scarcity aspect of this factor was not felt, hence, very little emphasis was laid on its optimum allocation amongst various activities. In the recent years, a major shift has taken place in this direction under the impact of economic poverty, social awakening and technological development. Time forms the framework in which various activities and work take place. In order to fulfil the demands, time should be well planned, i,e., the best use of what you have to get what you want. Management of time involves the process of decreasing the use of time devoted for a particular work without sacrificing the quality of work. Time used in such a manner that it will mean the most in the attainment of individual and family goals is the real objectives of time management.

Youth in every country is the supreme symbol of strength. Therefore, it is in the interest of the country to pay attention to the specific needs and problems of its youth. The purpose of the study was to collect information about the college students' utilisation of time.

## METHODOLOGY

An exploratory survey method with questionnaires was used to collect data. A total of 300 samples from the first year and the final year class students, both males and females from various faculties of M.S.U. of Baroda were drawn for the study. The data were categorised, coded, tabulated and statistical computation were made to find out the time use pattern and interests of college students.

## MAJOR FINDINGS

The most preferred and strongly held interest of the students were physical (e.g. sports and games, taking walks), literary (e.g. reading magazines and novels), household (e.g. cooking and related activities), social (e.g. gossiping, going to club) and fine arts (e.g. making sculpture, painting and drawing). They had less preference for agricultural (e.g. gardening, farming), technical (e.g. repairing of machines, typing) interests.

The most participated activities of the respondents were personal, educational, physical, literary, fine arts, household, social and religious, and the least participation was in intellectual, agricultural and technical activities. Male respondents were more interested in physical and technical activities, and female respondents had interests for household and fine arts activities.

On working days the mean time spent was between 11 and 486 minutes and on holidays it ranged between 25 and 554 minutes per day for these activities. In the case of recreational activities the respondents participated more on holidays than on working days.

In the case of voluntary service, only one-third of the respondents participated and majority of them spent time up to two hours per week. More male respondents and more first-year students participated in social service. A majority of the respondents were conscious about the importance of time in terms of sense of punctuality, pre-planning of time and proper use of time.

More than 70 per cent of the respondents did not realise the limitation of time. A large number of final-year students were conscious about the importance of time as compared to the first-year students. A majority of the respondents experienced that planning 'always' helped them to finish the work in time.

The respondents were conscious about the importance of time and followed good time management practices. It was noted that as the consciousness of individuals about the importance of time increases, the quality of time management practices also improve.

***Title: A Study of Time, Motion and Physiological Costs of Bed-making Activity***

*Author:* Shubhra Lavania

*Guide:* Nalini Ogale

*Year:* 1979

*Keywords:* Time and motion study, physiological cost of work, energy expenditure, body postures

## Introduction

The house is the physical setting for family living. In a family, mostly the burden of looking after the household jobs lies on the shoulders of the homemakers who have to put in their labour and energies into the accomplishment of the tasks. In recent years, jobs outside the home has increased the demand on the time and energy inputs of the homemakers. To cope up with these responsibilities it is imminent to minimise the cost of the household work. In addition to this, if working conditions at home are poor and the knowledge of homemakers about proper work methods is inadequate then the household work creates a heavy temporal and psychological demand on them. Improper work methods result in poor postures. Very few researches have been reported on the physiological aspects of household activities in relation to energy expenditure heart, rate, body postures and the work itself. Hence the study aimed at an assessment of the physiological costs involved in the bed-making activity. On the basis of that an attempt was made to work out the minimum human resource inputs and maximum achievement in work performance by employing the work simplification method for bed-making.

## Methodology

An experimental study divided into two parts was conducted to determine the time motion and physiological costs of bed-making activity at the two most common levels of work: the floor level and at a height of 18 inches from the floor. The subjects were selected on the basis of their physical fitness, i.e., pulse rate, blood pressure and laboratory testing of haemoglobin level and routine urine test. Seven female subjects of normal health conditions as determined by the medical check-up were selected. The age of the subject ranged from 19 to 22 years. Each subject was asked to make the bed according to her own method at the floor level and on a cot of 18 inches height, and this was considered as the original method. A process chart was made for recording motions. On the basis of the data of the original method, an improved method was evolved by the investigator taking into consideration the work simplification principles of reducing the unnecessary operations and motions, and the revised method was used by the subjects. The oxygen consumption was measured for the consumption of energy expenditure while performing the bed-making activity at the original and improved methods with the help of Kofranye-Michaelio meter with a harness known as the K-M meter which is basically a gas meter for measuring the total volume of expired air during any type of activity.

## Major Findings

The main aim in developing an improved method was to arrive at a method of work which would be efficient in terms of motions used in the activity. The improved method did help to reduce the extra motions used and the total time taken for execution of the task. On an average it requires about five to six minutes. There was also a considerable amount of decrease in the distance walked for the activity indicating that the improved method was a better method of work. In the present study, the estimation of physiological costs of work also reflected that the improved method of work helped to reduce the respiratory, energy and cardiovascular demands on the subjects. The time taken for performance of task differed slightly, i.e., 223.42 seconds at the floor level and 225.4 seconds at 18 inches height. The performance of bed-making task at 18 inches height involved bending and moving; bending and lifting body postures which demanded more respiratory, energy and cardiovascular stresses but this demanded less inputs, maybe due to the combination of different body postures used to execute the task. There was a 28 per cent decrease in the heart rate at the floor level which was due to the change in body postures, i.e. bending was replaced by kneeling which has more advantages, i.e., less energy demands and stress.

**Title: A Study of Use of Time by Homemakers**

*Author:* Kuntal Bafna

*Guide:* Rachael George

*Year:* 1979

*Keywords:* Time as a resource, time management, work rest, leisure time, gainful employment

## INTRODUCTION

Time provides an organising medium for human life – a common denominator within which everyone operates. Some of the characteristics of time are that its quantity remains constant everyday, it cannot be saved but must be used in some way. Different authors have classified time in different ways. Time is one of the major resources in the family life and hence it is essential that it is managed effectively and with satisfaction. A homemaker performs many activities in the course of the day depending on the roles she plays, but no two homemakers would perform these daily activities in the same sequence and consuming the same amount of time for each task. Many homemakers receive help from family members and paid helpers.

The homemaker is primarily responsible for managing the work of the home, and much of her time is required for this. Homemakers do not have sufficient knowledge or information related to the time that can be reasonably spent on particular tasks nor have they proper understanding of this resource which along with other resources like skills, talent, knowledge, ability, etc., can be used to create or substitute other limited resources which in turn can be utilised to improve their well being. Very few studies on the use of time by homemakers are done in India; therefore, this study was taken with a view to have an understanding about the use of time and to gain information related to the average time needed to carry on various household activities and also to find out the various means used by the homemakers.

## METHODOLOGY

A survey method with the use of an interview schedule and time record sheet were used for data collection. Hundred and sixty homemakers with systematic random sampling were selected from four residential areas of Baroda city, namely, Alkapuri, Pratapnagar, Fatehgunj and Sayajigunj as per the convenience of the researcher. Data analysis was done through categorisation, coding and tabulation. The statistics applied were frequencies, percentages, mean, standard deviation, t-test and chi-square test.

## Major Findings

Homemakers made use of paid help especially on a part-time basis and unpaid help to assist in the performance of household activities. Paid helpers spent maximum time on cleaning activities and family members contributed more time on food-related and child care activities. Most of the respondents possessed and used time- and labour-saving equipment, but gainfully employed homemakers were more conscious about its use. The age of the homemakers had influence on the time used and also the employment of the homemaker influenced the use of time. The size of the family, income of the family, education level, stage of family lifecycle were associated with the use of time of the homemaker. In general it was observed that there was not proper balance in the use of time by homemakers in the three general uses, i.e., work, leisure and rest. A majority of the respondents felt that the time at their disposal was adequate to accomplish their activities because of the small size of family, routine work, help received, interest in work, time plans and use of time- and labour-saving devices. The presence of young children, dual roles, mental tensions, large families and no paid help were the common reasons which made them feel inadequacy of time. Food-related activities consumed the maximum time and the least was needed for shopping and management.

***Title: Time Utilisation for Household Work and Its Monetary Value***

*Author:* Renu Chauhan

*Guide:* Nalini Ogale

*Year:* 1981

*Keywords:* Time utilisation, household work, monetary value

## Introduction

The homemaker has to play a major role in getting the household work done. She organises a complicated family schedule regarding meals, work, education, recreation etc. of all the members of the family. Historically household work activities also have not been valued economically, although identical activities have been valued in monetary terms, because most of the household activities do not go through the market system. The money value of household work is usually under-estimated and often work is overloaded. Thus one of the major problems which women face today is their invisibility. A study was thus undertaken to study utilisation of time in household work and estimate its monetary value.

## Methodology

A descriptive research study was undertaken. A questionnaire and a record sheet were used as tools for collecting data. A sample of 300 homemakers, both working and non-working, were selected randomly from nuclear families of high, middle and low income group. The procedures used for data analysis were categorisation, coding, tabulation and statistical analysis; percentages, frequencies, 't'-test, chi-square were used for statistical analysis.

## Major Findings

The homemakers spent the greatest amount of time on food-related tasks followed by the care of family members, care of clothing, house cleaning, miscellaneous tasks an account keeping respectively. The time utilisation on various household tasks by the homemakers decreased with the increase in their age; the size of the family did not have any significant relationship with the time utilisation on various household tasks by the homemakers.

The monetary value of the time utilisation on almost all the household tasks was higher in the case of middle income group except for the care of family members in which the high income group homemakers were ahead of other two groups.

***Title: Development of a Technique for Establishing Time Norms of Household Work of Rural Families***

*Author*: N. Kamalamma

*Guide*: Nalini Ogale

*Year:* 1981

*Keywords:* Time norms, Household work

## INTRODUCTION

Time as a resource is gaining high importance due to the increasing demands on the time of each individual, especially the homemaker. The interest in assessing the time cost of household work and relating it with their money worth is increasing. There is a need to establish time norms of household work at regional and national level. This calls for the development of a good technique for establishing time norms. A study was undertaken to develop a technique for establishing time norms of household work of rural families. For that the study also aimed to survey the time use pattern and determinants of household work of rural families. Time norms referred to the actual average time spent in work by a defined population.

## METHODOLOGY

The research design was descriptive and experimental. As the purpose of the study was to develop a technique for establishing time norms of household work for rural area only the household work was broken into three components: tasks, subtasks and elements. Three major tools of data collection used were interview, observation and simulation. The sample comprised 120 households from selected villages from Gandhigram. The interview was used as a technique for establishing time norm of household work and to gather baseline data for applying the simulation techniques. The respondents were asked to recall and report the tasks performed and time spent on each task. The sample being illiterate, the interview was taken. The time spent was reported taking the signals such as church/schools bells, radio programmes, time of supply of water by authorities, etc. To increase the reliability of the interview it was recorded on a tape recorder as well as by direct investigation, and the reliability coefficient was found to be high between the two. Another technique used for establishing time norms was observation of household work for two days. The non-participant observation was done from 5.30 a.m. to 8.30 p.m. and recorded on sheets. The third technique of simulation was carried out in a created typical kitchen of that region, and four types of typical nine meals were prepared in this laboratory by four workers and four observations were made. The time was recorded by two observers using stopwatch.

## Major Findings

Out of the three methods used for establishing time norms of household work of rural families, interview and observation were used for collecting time use data on household work, and the third method of simulation was used only for food preparation. The interview revealed that household work consisted of food preparation (23.0 hours per week), fetching water (6.9 hours week), physical care of the house (14.4 hours week). The mean was 60.83 hours per week for the total household work which was different for families of different types, sizes and income. The second method of observation revealed that the findings were similar to that elicited by recall while interviewing. The third method of simulation revealed that the time spent in preparing the four typical meals of the group differed. The simple meal required 1.2 hours and the complex one required 2.7 hours on an average. It was concluded that an interview is the most feasible technique for gathering time use data when compared to observation and simulation.

***Title: A Study of Use of Time by Non-working Homemakers and Their Attitude Towards Time Management***

*Author:* Manjula Gulati

*Guide:* Asha Dass

*Year:* 1982

*Keywords:* Non-working homemaker, household work, leisure, attitude, management practices

## Introduction

Time is a resource different from all other resources. It is one of the easiest to measure, but one of the most difficult to understand. Every life has certain demands upon its time – demands which may be met or avoided, enjoyed, accepted or deprived. A housewife has manifold duties. The homemaking tasks are not just energy demanding but productive of monotony as well. Proper utilisation of time can be achieved largely by smooth scheduling of tasks in tune with the flow of time. The attitude of an individual towards time management plays an important role in the proper utilisation of time. It is very important that the homemaker plans events within a given framework, taking into account family preferences, her own preferences and the relative urgency of various tasks.

## Methodology

A survey was done with an interview schedule which included an attitude scale and a time record sheet. The sample consisted of 120 non-working homemakers randomly chosen on the basis of income, age, education, type of family and married lifespan as per the limitations of the study. Four areas of old Delhi were chosen for the study. The data were categorised, coded and tabulated. Chi-square and t-test were used to test the hypotheses.

## Major Findings

Homemakers made use of paid help, especially on part-time basis, to assist in the household activities such as food-related activities, care of utensils, care of house, etc. Most of the homemakers possess time- and labour-saving devices. Most of them got leisure time between 2.30 and 5.30 hours with a mean of 3.51 hours per day. Gossiping, taking walks, worshipping at home, knitting, reading magazines and novels, seeing movies, listening to radio and watching TV were the most common leisure time activities. Planning the use of time, help from servants, small family size, use of time-saving equipment, speed are the factors to develop a feeling of adequacy of time at disposal. A majority of the respondents "sometimes" followed the steps of planning for leisure time whereas more percentage of homemakers "always" planned for work time and followed the step of controlling.

Nearly 30 per cent of them never followed evaluation. Income and education affected the time needed for various activities; whereas there was no effect of age, education and income on management practices and attitudes of homemakers.

***Title: Estimation of Muscular Effort Required for Grinding by Manual Grinders***
*Author:* Neerja Jaiswal
*Guide:* Nalini Ogale
*Year:* 1985
*Keywords:* Muscular effort, manual grinder

## Introduction

Grinding, one of the preparation tasks commonly practised in every home, is reported to be highly strenuous, time-consuming and is disliked task by many homemakers. At the same time it is also injurious to the health of the worker if performed for a longer period of time in an improper manner under unhealthy conditions affecting adversely on the human health and total output of the work. The present study is an attempt to estimate the muscular effort required in wet and dry grinding in two selected postures, and thus identify the most efficient method that involves least exertion by the arm muscles creating a healthy environment of safety for the human welfare.

## Methodology

An experimental study was conducted to estimate the differences in the muscular effort exerted while carrying wet and dry grinding in standing and sitting postures. The female subjects selected for all the three experiments were in the age group of 18-21 years. The data was analysed by computing the mean, percentage, standard deviation, standard error, t-test of mean difference and analysis of variance.

## Major Findings

The areas mostly influenced by the muscular pain during wet grinding were the palm and wrist, and for drying grinding the upper arm and forearm. It was found out that the sitting posture is better than the standing posture during dry grinding as the involvement of muscular strain was comparatively less in it and at the same time subjects also felt tired much later, though the work productivity was observed to be less as compared to the standing posture. The work produced by the arm muscles during wet grinding in the sitting posture was comparatively high. Fatigue also sets in much later and the cumulative muscular load was similar, thus it is reasonable to suggest that when work can be done in sitting posture, the worker may not be engaged in standing posture.

***Title: A Study of Time Utilization Pattern of Married Homemakers Employed in the Public Sector Industries in Baroda***

*Author:* Sheetal Shelat

*Guide:* Asha Dass

*Year:* 1994

*Keywords:* Management of time, balance in work, rest and leisure, time utilisation pattern

## INTRODUCTION

Management plays a vital role in every aspect of our lives. Due to the rapid changes in the life, management has become a necessity in everyday living. Management of time involves the process of decreasing the time devoted for a particular work without sacrificing the quality of work. For a homemaker there must be time for work, rest, sleep with sufficient leisure for living that will keep her emotionally stable and intellectually alert. She organises a complicated family schedule regarding meals, work, education, recreation, etc., of all family members, which sometimes creates monotony and boredom. Therefore, leisure is an important part of a homemaker's day. Women's employment influenced the home life to a great extent. The dual role of a homemaker may sometimes result in ineffective management in the home and in job satisfaction. Therefore, the study was undertaken with a view to understand the use of time, factors influencing time management, problems faced in management of time by working homemakers.

## Methodology

A survey method with an interview schedule and time record sheet were used to elicit the data. The samples were selected purposively and it constituted of married homemakers employed in the public sector as officers. Forty samples from Indian Petrochemicals Corporation Limited and 20 from Oil and Natural Gas Commission of Baroda were selected for the study. The data were presented in frequency, percentages and mean and chi-square and coefficient correlation was used to test the hypotheses.

## Major Findings

The time utilisation pattern of all working homemakers was more or less the same. The time spent by the homemaker in household work was more on a holiday as compared to the working day. She consumed a majority of the time for meal preparation, care of house and care of clothes. All working homemakers possessed the equipment which helped them in managing time. The factors like paid help and family members' help were effective in time utilisation pattern of the homemaker. Regarding time management practices followed by the respondents, all planned their work time and worked according to the planned activities. A majority of the respondents had flexibility in their plans to change and adjust according to the situation. A significant relationship was found between the time management practices and the age of the homemakers, and also with the age of the youngest child. The respondents were aware about the importance of a balance in work, rest and leisure time in their life.

***Title: A Study of Time and Money Use Practices and Problems of Wives of Male Migrants***

*Author:* Reena Gunjal

*Guide:* Maneesha Shukul

*Year:* 1994

*Keywords:* Time, money, practices, problems

## Introduction

India is country of tremendous movement. The flow of migrant in and out of the country also is on the increase. In the case of a man leaving his wife and children behind, the social and psychological consequences are far more complicated.

The impact of family separation due to migration is felt severely by the wife and children on one side and the migrant on the other. It is important to study how migration as a process affects women and households both positively as well as negatively. The wives of male migrants may face various kinds of problems mainly in managing the resources at their disposal. On the other hand knowledge of their problems and practices they follow to manage their resources would add to the knowledge in the field of home management.

## Methodology

A descriptive study was conducted. A questionnaire was used as a tool for collection of data. The sample of the study comprised 90 homemakers selected purposively from some residential areas of Baroda city. The procedure used to analyse the data were categorisation, coding, tabulation and statistical analysis. Data were expressed in frequencies, percentages, mean and standard deviation. To test the relationship between selected variables and practices a coefficient of correlation and t-test were computed.

## Major Findings

The performance of household activity by children and respondents jointly increased after migration. Time use practices of 94.4 per cent respondents were good before migration and for 14.4 per cent respondents better after migration. Money use practices of 51.1 per cent respondents were good before migration which increased to 81.1 per cent after migration. Most majority respondents averagely faced financial problems. The results of testing hypotheses indicated that the time use practices followed by wives of male migrant were related with total family income. After migration the money use practices were found significantly related with the age of the respondents.

*Title: The Study of Time Use, Activity Pattern and Perception of Retired People towards Their Retirement*
*Author:* Kirti Mehta
*Guide:* Maneesha Shukul
*Year:* 1996
*Keywords:* Retirement, ageing, perception toward retirement

## Introduction

Life does not remain static, it continues to change. These changes are natural accompaniment of what is commonly known as aging which affect physical as well as mental structure and functioning. Retirement is a life transition that can be highly stressful. It is characterised by several changes in status, income and daily routine. Further, the phase of retirement marks the end of work and tension, and the beginning of a period of relative leisure and relaxation. People perceive retirement in different ways. For many people retirement is a goal towards which they have been working. The study was undertaken with a view to learn how retired people structure their daily schedule, and what hobbies and interests they have in order to utilise their time properly.

## Methodology

A descriptive survey with questionnaire was selected to collect data. The tool contained a scale to assess the perception of respondents about various aspects of life after retirement. The content validity of the scale was examined by a panel of 10 judges from various fields. Through split-half technique, the reliability of the perception scale was determined and the final scale included 60 statements. The sample included 80 retired people, both teaching and non-teaching staff of M.S.U. of Baroda selected through a systematic random sampling. Chi-square, ANOVA and t-test were used to compute data.

## Major Findings

The study throws some light on the overall perception of retired respondents on various aspects, such as self-image, personal health, financial matters, time use, social activities and relationship in the family. It showed that they had a good perception towards retired life. It was found that teaching and non-teaching respondents spent almost equal time on work, rest and leisure, with more time on leisure. The leisure time activities included religious, physical, recreational activities, hobbies, personal care and miscellaneous activities. In the case of religious activities and hobbies, the difference was observed between teaching and non-teaching retired people.

A significant association was found between occupational status and perception. The time spent on work and rest did not vary due to age, education, occupational status, and personal and family income, but leisure time varied with age group. Since the respondents were from the field of academics, their knowledge, experiences and skills could be really helpful for the people, and experts from home management can help to guide them in proper planning and use of time.

# 4

# Participation in Work at Home

Social, economic and technological development have brought about and will continue to bring about changes in the socio-economic setting of the family. These changes involve attitudinal changes to family obligations, socialisation of children and role of each member within the family. Participation of other family members in household activities reduces the burden of homemaker and decreases her input in many ways. The new opportunities for education and employment in Independent India, the equal legal and political rights to women, are slowly changing the family patterns of living and the traditional conceptions of the role and status of women. A number of studies on the participation of husbands and teenage boys in household activities, the most and least liked household tasks by homemakers, etc. have been undertaken by the department which has been highlighted.

*Title: A Comparative Study of the Participation of Husbands in Household Activities in Baroda and Ludhiana*

*Author:* Inderjeet Bhandari

*Guide:* Nalini Ogale

*Year:* 1974

*Keywords:* Participation, husbands, household activities, attitude.

## Introduction

The new opportunities for education and employment in Independent India, the equal legal and political rights to women, are slowly changing the family patterns of living and the traditional conceptions of the role and status of women, at least in urban areas. These changes have affected the housemaking roles of both men and women and their participation in various tasks at home. This emphasizes the need to know more about the participation of husbands in household activities which varies with certain influential factors. Hence the present study was undertaken to study the extent of participation of husbands in household activities, the reasons and factors influencing their participation, and also to study the attitudes of husbands regarding their participation in household activities.

## Methodology

A survey method was used with a questionnaire as an instrument for collecting data. An attitude scale was developed and its content validity was tested. The purposive sampling technique was used to select the sample of 150 married men, 75 each from the city of Baroda and Ludhiana. The eligibility criteria for selecting the sample were that the respondents should be married and staying with his family and should be from the nuclear family. Data were tabulated and percentage, mean scores, 't' test and Pearson's product moment formula of correlation were computed to analyse the data.

## Major Findings

The respondents participated in all the household activities of planning, selection and buying, preparation, and care and maintenance, though their extent of participation was varied in these activities. The most participated activities by Baroda and Ludhiana respondents were selection and buying, and the least participation was in the care and maintenance activities. For most of the categories of activities respondents participated irrespective of their age and stage of family lifecycle. The wives had impact on an husbands' participation in all the household activities. The respondents from small families participated more than the respondents belonging to large families. The socio-economic status of the respondents influenced their participation to a great extent. Respondents from upper middle class participated more in care and maintenance activities whereas lower middle class participated more in planning, selection and buying, and preparation activities. The respondents whose wives were employed outside the home and without any hired help participated highly in household activities. The respondents with more free time participated more in the activities of planning, preparation, and care and maintenance. Majority of the respondents participated in the household activities with the idea of providing assistance to the housewives in order to maintain good relations in the family. There did not exist much relationship between attitudes and participation of respondents in household activities, except in selection, buying and preparation activities for Baroda respondents.

**_Title: A Study of Attitudes and Extent of Participation of Teenage Boys towards Household Activities_**

*Author:* Sudha Chaudhary

*Guide:* Nalini Ogale

*Year:* 1976

*Keywords:* Attitude, teenage boys, household activities, extent of participation

## Introduction

Social, economic, and technological development have brought about, and will continue to bring about, changes in the socio-economic setting of the family. These changes involve attitudinal changes to family obligations, socialisation of children, and the role of each member within the family. Participation of other family members in household activities reduces the burden of the homemaker and decreases her input in many ways. Since the changes in family structure demand more participation of male members in household work, it would be interesting to know the contribution of boys towards the family living. Therefore, the present study was undertaken primarily to find out the attitude and extent of participation of teenage boys in household work, to identify the factors influencing, and the reasons for their extent of participation in household activities.

## Methodology

A descriptive survey method was used with a closed-ended questionnaire as a tool for collecting data. An attitude scale was constructed, and its content validity and reliability were tested. A sample of 165 teenage boys from three high schools of Baroda were drawn for the present study. The eligibility criteria for selecting the sample were the respondents must belong to the age range, i.e., 13 years to 19 years, they should be staying with their parents / family. The statistics used to analyse the data were simple frequencies, percentage and mean scores. Chi-square test, Pearson's product moment formula of correlation and 't' tests were used to test the hypotheses.

## Major Findings

A majority of the respondents belonged to nuclear families; middle income group; had medium size families with five to seven members; and hired help for the household work was available to them. 'Tidying home' and 'repair and maintenance' were the activities in which a majority of the respondents participated, whereas the least participation was in the 'child care' activity and the activities related to meals. The participation of respondents was found to be influenced by their attitude. They had a positive attitude towards participation in household activities. The reasons that motivated the respondents to participate in the household work were 'love and affection for family members' and 'value of home'. The participation of respondents in household activities varied with their age, type of family and size of family. The income level of the family was found to be an important factor influencing the extent of participation. The respondents participated in household activities irrespective of employment status of the mother, hired help in the family and their ordinal position of the family.

***Title: Homemaker's Contribution to Family Income through Gainful Employment and/or Selected Items of Household Production***

*Author:* Smita Parikh

*Guide:* Veena Gandotra

*Year:* 1977

*Keywords:* Homemakers, family income, gainful employment, household production

## Introduction

Combining home and career is one of the major decisions which married women face today. Industrialisation has played a major role in changing the economic function of families. Production of goods shifted to the factories and the families became more of consuming units than productive ones. Rapid industrialisation also created additional employment opportunities for married women, so more and more women are entering the field of paid employment, to meet their financial need, to raise their standard of living and to gain independence. Although more and more women are entering the field of paid employment, there are a greater number of women who are still working within the four walls of their homes. One should not overlook their contribution to family's income.

## Methodology

A descriptive survey method was used for the present study. The interview schedule was selected as data collection tool. A 100 homemakers (50 employed and 50 non-employed) were selected from Raopura area of Baroda city. The only condition used for selection was that the respondent should be a married homemaker. The procedures used for analysis were categorisation, coding, tabulation and statistical analysis.

Statistical analysis used were frequency, percentages, range, mean, 't'-test and analysis of variance.

## MAJOR FINDINGS

It was found that the family income increased if the homemaker had an outside job. Also it was found that the working women spends extra money for transportation, clothes for work, servants, etc. The employed homemakers had more paid help compared to non-employed homemakers. It was found that the employment status of the respondents did not have much influence on household production as there was not much difference between the contribution of employed and non-employed respondents through household production. There was some difference in the extent of household production by family size and income of the family. The employed homemakers were making dual contribution to family income, both in the form of money and real income.

***Title: A Comparative Study of Indian and Nepali Homamaker's Most and Least Liked Household Tasks***

*Author:* Shanti Basnyat

*Guide:* Nalini Ogale

*Year:* 1977

*Keywords:* Homemaker, household tasks, liked tasks, disliked tasks

## INTRODUCTION

Managing a home requires coordination of a variety of activities and parts of each activity. But many people enjoy performing some tasks, and may have a dislike or hatred for the same task. Since household tasks are so important for smooth functioning of families, it is essential to have more information about the various tasks than the information is available. The present study was undertaken to find out about the liked and disliked tasks, and their characteristics among the two groups, Nepalese and Indian.

The study was limited to the homemakers who have at least one or two children.

## Methodology

For the present study, a descriptive survey method was used with a close-ended questionnaire as the tool for collecting data. The sample for the present study comprised 100 homemakers from Kathmandu, (Nepal) and Baroda, (India). The data collection process was followed by data analysis, including categorisation, coding, tabulation and statistical analysis. Frequency, percentage, mean, median, rank ordering, 't' test, correlation and chi square tests were used.

## Major Findings

Among the Nepalese, there was an equal distribution of nuclear and joint families with large size families. While among the Indian families, the nuclear family type dominated with small size families Hindu religion dominated in both the groups. The tasks performed in both the groups were the same. But most of the liked tasks were performed by homemakers and the least liked tasks were done with the help of servants in both the groups. A majority of the Indian respondents preferred the standing position whereas the Nepalese preferred the sitting position to carry out various household tasks. The most liked tasks, cooking and care of the individual family members were common among the Nepalese as well as the Indians, but they differed in their liking for two tasks; the Nepalese preferred care of house to shopping, which was liked by Indians. Both the groups disliked the tasks of mopping, cleaning utensils and dishes. Characteristics of liked and disliked tasks reported by both the groups were from intrinsic interest, and social or physical situation. Some characteristics were similar among both the groups. On five tasks, i.e., mopping, washing of clothes, ironing of clothes, account keeping and special care of the house, Nepalese and Indians were significantly different about their liking and disliking of these tasks. Only three tasks, cooking, sweeping and account keeping, showed the same rank order for liking and disliking, and it was different for 12 other tasks.

*Title: Time Utilisation for Household Work and Its Monetary Value*

*Author:* Renu Chauhan

*Guide:* Nalini Ogale

*Year:* 1981

*Keywords:* Time utilisation, household work, monetary value

## Introduction

Time devoted to work is usually compensated in money. A major exception is household work. A significant cost of this work to the family is time. Household work is indispensable to the functioning of the family and society. It generally takes place outside the content of the business world, however, and therefore the time spent for it is not normally given a monetary value. Very little investment has been made over the years in this country in upgrading non-market work. The monetary value has not yet been assigned to such productive labour which does not enter the cash economy. Therefore, an attempt was made to investigate the time utilisation in household work and then compute its monetary value.

## Methodology

A descriptive research method was used. The data collection technique used in the survey method were interview and questionnaire and time record sheet. The sample for the present study comprised working and non-working homemakers having a nuclear family, residing in Udaipur city, Rajasthan, drawn randomly. To analyse the data frequencies, percentage, 't' test and chi-square were used.

## Major Findings

The homemakers spend a considerable portion of their time on household work, which amounts to more than what the homemakers generally spend on gainful employment outside home. The food-related tasks were the most time-consuming tasks followed by care of family members, care of clothing, house cleaning, miscellaneous, etc. The homemakers who were non-working and belonged to the age group 21-30 years spend more time than the older group homemakers on various household tasks, hence the monetary value of their work is also greater than these older homemakers. Although homemakers were performing a majority of the household tasks they received some help from family members and servants in household tasks, hence some contribution is made by the family members and servants to the total monetary value of household work. The monetary value of the time utilisation on various household tasks by the homemakers increased as the age of the homemakers increased. But there was a marked decrease noticed as the homemakers reached the age above 40 years. The monetary value of the time utilisation on almost all the household tasks was higher in the case of middle income group except for the care of family members in which the high income group homemakers were ahead of other two groups.

***Title: A Study of Quantification of the Household Work Load***

*Author:* Suman Gehlot

*Guide:* Nalini Ogale

*Year:* 1982

*Keywords:* Quantification, household workload

## INTRODUCTION

The volume of work accomplished and the time devoted to work are usually compensated in money. A major exception to this is household work which is indispensable to the functioning of the family and society. The critical issue in estimating the homemakers' contribution to national income or to the real income of her family is not of determining its market price, but of measuring the real output or to quantify the volume of work accomplished. Thus, an attempt was made to investigate the household workload and to quantify it; thereby work units for specific task were developed according to Indian conditions.

## Methodology

A descriptive research design was used for the present study. The survey method along with the interview schedule and work record sheet was used for collecting data. A sample of 150 homemakers was selected by quota sampling from various residential localities of Baroda city. Statistics used to analyse the responses were simple frequencies, percentages, 't' test, chi-square test and correlation coefficient.

## Major Findings

It was found that the homemakers have a considerable volume of household workload which consumes her time. The homemakers from middle income group have greater household workload than high and low income groups. The total volume of household workload increases with the increase in the size of the family. The families in expanding stage of family lifecycle have more volume of total household workload than the families in beginning and contracting stage. The total volume of household workload is not affected by the employment status of the homemaker or by the availability of help. Only time spent by the homemaker on various tasks is affected by these two factors. Thus, the total volume of household workload is affected by the income of the family, lifecycle stage of the family and the size of the family.

***Title: Domestic Servants: Factors Affecting their Productive Output and Economic Gains***

*Author:* Priti Sharma

*Guide:* Nalini Ogale

*Year:* 1985

*Keywords:* Domestic servants, productive output, economic gains

## Introduction

Household work is indispensable to the functioning of a family and society, and domestic servants bear the 'double burden' of accomplishing household task in their own home and at the place of employment. The critical issue in estimating the domestic servants' contribution to national income or the real income of her family is not of determining its market price, but of measuring the real output or the total volume of work accomplished. The market value of similar services may be used in computing the cost of household activities. The monetary value has not yet been assigned to such productive labour which does not enter the cash economy. An attempt was however made to investigate the productive output and economic gains of domestic servants.

## Methodology

A descriptive research design was used. The survey method was used along with an interview schedule and work, and a time record sheet as a tool for collecting data. Two hundred domestic servants' irrespective of part time / full time or resident / non-resident household workers, were drawn by purposive sampling from various residential localities of Baroda city. Statistics used to analyse the responses were simple frequencies, percentages, 't' test and correlation coefficient.

## Major Findings

The domestic servants have a considerable volume of household workload which consumes her time. The food-related task is the most time-consuming task followed by dishwashing, washing of clothes, buying and shopping, care of family members and house cleaning. The full-time resident servants had greater household workload than the part-time non-resident workers. The time spent and the wages paid in labour market are not indicators of the worth of household work. As regarding the task of meal preparation the domestic servants are better paid and in the case of house cleaning the time spent is lesser than the government fixed timings, and thus the money received is better than the government wage rate. The true cost of household work for domestic servants can be found only if some factors that affect the household work are studied taking into account the real income, apart from the money gains.

***Title: Technology, Women's Task Performance and Quality of Life of Rural Households in Assam***

*Author:* Ruplekha Borah

*Guide:* Nalini Ogale

*Year:* 1991

*Keywords:* Technology, Task performance, Quality of Life

## Introduction

Rural women are responsible for multiple labour-intensive and time-consuming chores, both outside and inside their home. These tasks are laborious and time-consuming because of the rudimentary tools. The drudgery which the rural women suffer can be eliminated to a great extent by adoption of improved technology, and thus their "quality of life" can be improved. A study was conducted to explore the traditional tools/technologies used in the performance of various tasks, to find the extent of adoption of improved technology by rural women for various tasks and determinants for the adoption, to assess their quality of life with reference to the impact of the use of improved technology.

## Methodology

The descriptive research was conducted in the state of Assam. Through multistage sampling the district was purposively selected, block and village were randomly selected and 270 households were selected through systematic random sampling. The data were collected through the interview schedule. Observation of a sub-sample of 27 households was conducted to verify the time-use data reported by the respondents. The tool contained S.E.S. questions to elicit information on time spent on various tasks; availability of leisure time; use of traditional tools, adoption of improved technologies knowledge scale to measure knowledge regarding improved technologies and a scale to find out attitude towards adoption of improved technology. Appropriate statistical tests were applied.

## Major Findings

The mean age of the homemakers was 36 years; one-third had an education till high school and a majority were not employed; a few were self-employed. A majority of the women performed most of the household tasks in which a husband's help was not received. The majority performed most of the agricultural tasks and participated in dairy-related tasks, handloom weaving and sericulture. Rural women possessed an average knowledge regarding improved household technology and exhibited a moderately favourable attitude towards adoption of improved technology. The better the knowledge regarding improved technology, the more favourable was the attitude towards adoption of improved technology. They had comparatively better access to improved household technology. The non-commercial fuel was used. Improved technology for household industry was adopted in weaving but there was no improved agricultural technology available for rural women-dominated tasks. The highest drudgery was felt in the performance of agricultural tasks and the least in the performance of the household industry-related tasks. The socioeconomic status emerged as an important determinant of adoption of improved household technology. The adopters of improved household technology had a better quality of life.

# 5

# Perception Regarding Home Management

Home management, not being a highly popular subject familiar among all its image in the minds of laymen plays a vital role in improving its acceptance as a discipline for study at higher levels. A number of studies have been conducted in the home management department on this topic. The findings of these studies have been presented here in this section.

***Title: A Study of the Perception of Residence Students towards Learning Experiences Provided in the Home Management Residence Course***

*Author:* Kalpana Roy

*Guide:* Veena Gandotra

*Year:* 1979

*Keywords:* Residence course, home management, perception, learning, experiences, students

### INTRODUCTION

Home management provides learning experiences in the environment in which learning can take place by active participation in activities under the guidance of a teacher. Home management residence course is considered as one of the most comprehensive experiences in home science. If the learning experiences provided in the house are perceived clearly and achieved by the students, they will gain more knowledge in a much better way in future. The present study was undertaken to study the perception of respondents' identification of activities, the value placed by students on the residence course, and to compare pre- and post-stay reactions of selected students regarding learning experiences provided in the house.

## Methodology

A survey method was selected and a structured questionnaire was used as the data collecting instrument. Fifty respondents were randomly selected from students who have done the residence course. The data obtained were categorised, coded, scored and tabulated. The statistics used to analyse the data were simple frequencies, percentage and mean scores, and 't' test was used to test the hypotheses.

## Major Findings

A majority of the respondents felt most of the experiences as worthwhile but some enjoyed them while some did not. Managerial activities were identified by a majority of the respondents. The other most identified activities by a majority of the respondents were 'analysing activities in terms of time and energy', 'handling allotted money and planning for party', 'gaining confidence in planning and conducting games' and 'making individual and group decisions'. The type of family, and family income of respondents had an effect on the perception of learning experiences provided in houses. Goals related to the management aspect were perceived at a low level whereas goals related to the recreational aspect were perceived at a high level by a majority of the respondents. A majority of the respondents considered this course as 'equally valuable' as compared to other courses, thereby encouraging other students to take the residence course as an elective. After undergoing the practical experience in the house, there was a slight increase in the perception of experiences and identification of activities by all the respondents.

***Title: Image of Home Management held by Parents of Home Science Students***

*Author:* Jacintha Reddy

*Guide:* Nalini Ogale

*Year:* 1981

*Keywords:* Image, home management, home science, attitude

## Introduction

Home management, not being a highly popular subject familiar among all, its image in the minds of laymen plays a vital role in improving its acceptance as a discipline for study at higher levels. The parents' misconceptions about its learning may often direct students to other branches of home science. So there was a need to assess the image of public on the same area prior to any attempt towards strengthening of the programme. The present study aims at the preparation of all instruments that will help to quantify public image of home management, to assess and establish the profits of the images held, and to seek the variables that are directly associated with the public image of home management.

## Methodology

An exploratory survey technique was found to be the most suitable research design for the present study. A questionnaire was used to collect the data. A scale was formulated and reliability was established; the 'r' value was 0.6. The quota sampling procedure was followed to select 150 parents of the students enrolled in home science faculty. Only those residing in Baroda and who were able to read and understand English were chosen for the study. Of the 150 respondents approached only 100 had returned the completed questionnaires. The data thus collected were analysed by using descriptive statistics like frequency and percentage, and inferential statistics like 't' test and chi-square test.

## Major Findings

The mean age of the respondents was 46.65 years. A majority belonged to the business community and employment in public / private sector; they had education minimum up to high school level. A majority of the respondents had given first preference for food and nutrition while home management occupied only the fourth position. A majority of them had a fairly good image of the managerial, economy and efficiency aspects. More were on the neutral side towards relational and social aspects. Men were better off in their perception than women. There was a significant association between the educational status and the respondents' perception of home management. The respondents had a good knowledge about finance matters where budgeting and record keeping are involved.

***Title: Image of Home Management held by Teachers of Home Science***

*Author:* Mamta Shah

*Guide:* Nalini Ogale

*Year:* 1983

*Keywords:* Image, home management, home science, opinion, attitude

## Introduction

Home management is one of the major areas of home science education. Better managerial ability is installed in learners through fostering of appropriate values, goals, standards and attitudes, and above all the skills required for home management. It is a new discipline that has high relevance to the present day's idea of integrated and multidisciplinary learning for a better living. But often a poor enrolment is noticed in many colleges in this area of specialisation which might be because of the lack of a clear concept of the people about the scope of this subject, its value, etc. Therefore, this study was planned to assess the image of home management held by teachers teaching home management subjects and how the images are influenced by various factors.

## Methodology

A descriptive research design was adopted with the survey approach. An open-ended questionnaire was used to collect the data. The sample was chosen by quota sampling procedure. A list of home science colleges were prepared and then two to five questionnaires were sent to each institution all over India. Of the 140 respondents approached only 42 had returned the questionnaires with relevant information. After the data were collected, they were categorised and tables were made to analyse the data.

## Major Findings

A majority of the respondents who were studied were from the South and North. Almost all teachers belonged to the home management field. All the respondents had education up to M.Sc. level. A majority of them taught the undergraduate courses and were in the teaching career since many years. The most taught courses were housing, equipment, economics and interior decoration. Very few teachers were engaged in field work or attended conferences and seminars. A majority of the respondents opined that courses in interiors and furnishings should be included in the curriculum. Regarding the inclusion of economics in the home management curriculum, respondents felt that it leads to happy living by becoming a wise consumer; they were concerned about the wise use of money resource as well as its utility in becoming conscious consumers. A majority of the teachers felt that home management residence course helps the students in getting practical experience. The teachers' remarks reflect that very few think of management in its real perspective. Most of the teachers felt that home management is useful for attainment of family goals and believe it to be a mental process, and the title should be changed to "family resource management". Most of the teachers expressed their agreement about the consideration of focus of home management on society and community demands of family needs. Cent per cent respondents reported that environment should be considered in viewing the problems in management. The teachers gave emphasis to the decisionmaking process, and resource management as a process of management instead of restricting management to the three-step process of planning, controlling and evaluating.

# 6

# Housing and Furnishing

Shelter is a prime necessity. Before primitive man learnt how to construct a shelter, he sought the protection of natural formations as cave dwellings, in various parts of the world which bear, such testimony. Early man-made shelters were simple shields from the elements, barriers against savage beasts or defences against the human adversities. With the development of civilisation, housing has become more important.

Growth in population, rapid industrialisation, mobilisation of families and increasing awareness of people have emphasized the need and importance of good housing. Good, decent, commodious and adequate housing is one of the basic needs of man.

Besides food and clothing, shelter is required for protection against the natural calamities, wild animals and beasts, and from other fellow beings. Housing is important not only because it provides shelter, but also because it contributes towards physical, psychological and social growth of individuals and families.

According to Chandoke (1974), no dwelling can be called adequate if it does not meet the physical and psychological needs of those living in it. If family life is to be strengthened and preserved, every family must be adequately housed.

A true home provides at least three essentials: a physical shelter for family living, an emotional climate which represents individual differences and encourages positive personal growth, and a setting where good social habits are formed. It is important that families seek housing in which the members experience security, comfort, privacy, self-expression and personal relationship that are sound and satisfying. The importance of housing is emphasized by Benjamin Disraeli (1961). The best security of civilisation is dwelling, and proper dwelling depends more than anything else the improvement of mankind. The house is the centre of a family life, so planning and choosing of a dwelling should be done according to the needs of persons who are to occupy it. The rooms should be so located as to facilitate the essential activities, foster a harmonious life and minister to the privacy and integrity of the individuals living in it. The house should also create an atmosphere of comfort and quiet.

According to Beyer (1958) housing has both economic and social implications because it plays a tremendous role in the economy of a country. Economically, housing is important as a major portion of income of a family is spent on it. It has highly significant social implications because it provides the shelter for our basic unit – the family. Almost every person is affected in his day-to-day living by the kind of house in which he lives.

There is a universal instinct in man, the instinct to own a house. In India particularly, house ownership has some social values and is regarded as a symbol of prestige and status. A man's prestige and status in the society is enhanced, if he possesses a house of his own. But today, for most of the people building a house of their own has gone much beyond their means. The common man has to spend more than his meagre life savings for building his own house. However, group housing is being advocated and offers better avenues for the house building activity on a cooperative basis. The Government of India is relying heavily on the cooperative method to provide adequate housing for a large section of the population. In our country the problem of housing is aggravated by a rapidly growing population, the change from an agricultural to an industrial society, the change in the type of family structure and other changes in culture. Here the housing problem is by no means confined to the urban centres, even rural India suffers from an acute housing problem. Substandard housing is more pronounced in the rural areas, where a major portion of the India population resides. A house can be considered as one of the important factors in the well being of a nation. Therefore research in housing is of paramount importance. Beyer (1960) states that housing research is carried on to fulfil the goal of 'a home and community environment conducive to the healthy growth and development of the family at all stages of the family life'.

*Title: Housing Facilities and Preferences of a Selected Sample of Owners of Houses in Fatehgunj, Alkapuri and Sampatrao Colony in Baroda, Gujarat*
*Author:* Zohra Begum Qureshi
*Guide:* Nalini Ogale
*Year:* 1967
*Keywords:* Housing facilities and preferences

## Introduction

Housing is important not only because it provides a place of shelter, but also because it provides a place of physical comfort and convenience, a place for performing all material functions of family life, and a place which satisfies the spiritual, intellectual and psychological needs of an individual. A house is not merely a shelter with four walls and a roof, but there are other factors which need to be considered for the provision of adequate housing. These factors are general neighbourhood environment, services and utilities, community, facilities, sound structure of the house on its outside as well as in its interior, sufficient space and activities. In order to know whether the houses owned by families are adequate in all aspects and to get an insight into the present conditions regarding housing facilities and the preferences of families regarding various factors of housing, the study was undertaken.

## Methodology

The study was carried out in three localities, viz., Fatehgunj, Alkapuri and Sampatrao colony representing the housing of different income groups. A questionnaire served as a tool to collect data, distributed personally either to the homemakers or to the heads of the families. Thirty-five respondents from

Fatehgunj, 22 from Alkapuri, and 18 from Sampatrao colony were included in this study. Data were analysed by using descriptive statistics such as percentage and mean, and compared locality-wise.

## Major Findings

All the respondents of Alkapuri and Sampatrao colony with their high and medium income respectively had pucca houses built from expensive building materials, whereas many respondents of Fatehgunj with their low income had kutcha or kutch-pucca houses built from less expensive and cheap materials used in roof, walls and floor. Houses in Alkapuri and Sampatrao had roofs of cements, walls of bricks and floor of expensive and strong types of materials while houses of Fatehgunj had roofs of corrugated iron sheets, some had walls of bamboo and mud, and floors of mud.

Income also had its effect on the availability of facilities of open courtyards, gardens and veranda and their preference by the respondents of three areas. A majority of the respondents of all three localities considered it "very necessary". In all three localities respondents had double-storey houses in most of the cases. A majority preferred double-storeyed houses compared to a few respondents of Alkapuri and Sampatrao colony, one-third of the respondents of Fatehgunj who preferred multistorey houses.

The type, size and the stage of family lifecycle showed influence on the respondents' preferences for a certain number of storey in houses. In Fatehgunj the houses were the oldest and almost half of the respondents had made repairs whereas in Sampatrao colony the houses were the newest. The existing direction of most of the houses was north in Fatehgunj area, whereas east was preferred the most, in Alkapuri preference was for north while east was preferred the most; in Sampatrao colony it was west and north but no particular direction was preferred the most. East direction, in general, was preferred the most to get sunlight and breeze and also due to religious beliefs.

Sixty and fifty per cent of the respondents of Sampatrao colony and Alkapuri respectively got 'very adequate', pure and fresh air in their houses as compared to 37.1 per cent of the respondents of Fatehgunj. Income also had its effect on the presence of the number of windows in the houses, the number of rooms, bedrooms and bathrooms available to the respondents of three localities. The highest mean number of rooms, bedrooms and bathrooms was found in the high income group of Alkapuri; and the lowest, in the lowest income group of Fatehgunj. Fewer number of windows in the houses of Fatehgunj were found. Many did not have a single window in their houses.

There was difference in the activity patterns in the houses due to the difference in income. A single room was used for performing some specific activities. The number of rooms available to a majority of the respondents of Fatehgunj were "not sufficient" but they were either "very sufficient" or "sufficient" to a majority of the respondents of the other two localities. A majority of the respondents in all three localities preferred separate a passageway to be "very necessary" or "necessary". Many respondents of Fatehgunj did not have enough storage space in their houses and a majority of them needed more storage space for all necessary things. The mean number of sources of artificial light also showed the same differences as the mean income of the three localities. Only taps were available in the bathrooms in the houses of Fatehgunj as compared to showers, washbasins and taps in Alkapuri and Sampatrao in most of the cases. A larger percentage of the respondents of Fatehgunj than in other two localities were not satisfied with their houses because of insufficient space. Other reasons were lack of specific facilities, the defects of specific features, poor housing conditions, neighbourhood and surroundings.

***Title: House Plan Evaluation Scores, Expressed Satisfaction Scores and Ranking of Values of Homemakers from Private and Government Housing in Chandigarh.***

*Author:* Eipinder Sokhey

*Guide:* Helen L. Wells

*Year:* 1968

*Keywords:* House plan evaluation scores, expressed satisfaction scores, housing values

## Introduction

Since the quality of family life is directly related to the housing in which the family lives, good housing is important because the family is considered to be the basic sociological unit of society. Since the quality of family life is directly related to the housing in which the family lives, good housing is important because the family is considered to be the basic sociological unit of society. Since housing affects and reflects interests, activities and values of individuals and families, the study was, therefore, designed to assess the exiting housing conditions and facilities by use of score sheets for judging house plans, measure expressed satisfaction of the homemakers with their housing, and to obtain a ranking of housing values held by the homemakers.

## Methodology

The sample consisted of 102 respondents representing two housing levels in the city of Chandigarh. Homemakers of government employees living in type VII houses built on plots of 1,000 square yards in sectors 7, 16 and 29, comprised one group of 52 respondents; 50 homemakers living in private houses built on plots of 1,000 square yards comprised the other group. Stratified random sampling was done. The data were collected using the interview schedule. To determine the difference between the two sub-groups of respondents for the difference variables, an analysis of variance was used. Product moment correlation and chi-square were used to determine the relationship among the variables of expressed satisfaction scores, house plan evaluation scores and ranking of housing values.

## Major Findings

The mean score for the total respondents for the total house plan evaluation of the house was 58.80. The total house plan evaluation, scores and the subscores for orientation, circulation, and flexibility were not significantly different for the respondents from private housing and government housing. Sub-scores for landscape and kitchen were significantly different for the two groups at .01 level. Regarding the neighbourhood, a majority of the respondents checked that the population of the area had the right number of people, the houses were built at the right distance from each other, the approach road was of sufficient width and the area was clean. It was further found that the expressed satisfaction scores for the neighbourhood was higher for the respondents from government housing. The mean total expressed satisfaction score for the respondents from private housing was 130.28, as compared to 111.25 for the respondents from government housing. The ranking of values scores were not significantly different for the respondents from private housing and from government housing. Bicycle shops, according to the majority of the total respondents were very convenient while facilities which were not convenient were found to be parks playgrounds. In place of employment, government housing and temples. The scores for the respondents from private housing and for the respondents from government housing were significantly different for total expressed satisfaction score and for each of the sub-scores of expressed satisfaction. The rank order of housing values for total respondents was mental health, physical health, equality, religion, aesthetics, family centrism, leisure economy, freedom and social prestige. Values which ranked higher for the respondents from private housing than for the respondents from government housing were religion, aesthetics and economy; values which ranked higher for the respondents from government housing than for respondents from private housing were family centrism, freedom and social prestige. Statistically, there was no significant difference in scores of housing values based on ranking by homemakers between the respondents from private housing and the respondents from government housing. The expressed satisfaction scores decreased with the increasing age of the house for the respondents from private housing except where the houses were ten years old or more.

There was significant correlation between the total expressed satisfaction scores and the total house plan evaluation scores for the total respondents as well as for the respondents from private housing. For the subscores of house plan evaluation with total expressed satisfaction scores, there was significant correlation for orientation and flexibility for the total respondents and for the respondents from private housing, for the total respondents, circulation was significantly correlated and kitchen was negatively correlated to the total expressed satisfaction scores. There was no significant relationship between the total expressed satisfaction scores and the ranking of housing values, for the respondents from private housing and the respondents from government housing. There was no significant relationship between the ranking of housing values and total house plan evaluation scores for the total respondents.

*Title: House Plan Evaluation Scores, Expressed Satisfaction Scores and Ranking of Values of Homemakers from 100 Government Houses in Chandigarh*

*Author:* Asha Khanna

*Guide:* Helen L. Wells

*Year:* 1968

*Keywords:* Housing plan evaluation, expressed satisfaction, ranking of values

## Introduction

In India, the problem of housing has been very acute. Generally speaking, the existing housing conditions are extremely unsatisfactory. Housing shortage exists among all income groups, and this problem is severe, especially among the low income groups. Housing for comfortable living should provide space for the family's daily activities, as well as for the personal activities of each member of the family. As the size, income and composition of the family change, the housing needs and facilities of the family also change.

The housing problem in India can only be successfully alleviated after recognising the existing conditions and determining the preferences of various classes of population regarding housing. In view of the above-mentioned factors, the study was undertaken to determine the adequacy of, and the satisfaction with, the housing facilities provided by the government in Chandigarh.

## METHODOLOGY

A random sample of 100 homemakers consisted of 50 homemakers from low income group and 50 from high income families, residing in 11 type, 6 type and 5 type government houses, respectively, in Chandigarh city. For data collection, the interview schedule was used, which contained questions regarding background information of the family, expressed satisfactions of the housewives regarding their houses, the community facilities, house plan evaluation checklists and ten value definitions. Data were analysed using descriptive and inferential statistics, such as mean, percentage, correlations and analysis of variance.

## MAJOR FINDINGS

The respondents from the high income group were more satisfied than the respondents from the low income group with the neighbourhood facilities of distance of houses from each other, density of the area and cleanliness of the neighbourhood and the respondents from the low income group were more satisfied than were the respondents from the high income group with the approach road to their house. The mean scores for the house plan evaluation were higher for the respondents from the high income group than for the respondents from the low income group. The scores for the total house plan evaluation and for the sub areas of House Plan Evaluation (orientation, landscape, circulation, flexibility and kitchen) were significantly different for the respondents from the two levels of government housing. The respondents from high income group obtained higher mean scores on expressed satisfaction than the respondents from the low income group.

Analysis of variance showed that the total satisfaction scores with the house for the respondents from low income group and the high income group were significantly different at .01 level of significance.

Physical health and mental health were ranked first and second respectively for total respondents as well as for respondents from the low and high income group. The number of persons in the household and the education of the homemaker had no direct relationship with the expressed satisfaction scores, for the respondents from both the categories of housing. The total expressed satisfaction scores and total house plan evaluation scores were significantly correlated at .05 level of significance. The value of mental health was the only one significantly correlated with the total house plan evaluation at .01 level of significance. The values of leisure and aesthetics were the only ones significantly correlated with the total expressed satisfaction scores at .05 level of significance for the respondents from the high income group. The scores of sub-areas of house plan evaluation of orientation, landscape, circulation, flexibility and kitchen were significantly correlated with scores of one or more sub-areas of expressed satisfaction of physiological, psychological, protection against contagion and protection against accidents. Mental health, equality, leisure, family centrism, aesthetics and religion were the values that were significantly related with scores of one or more sub-areas of expressed satisfaction.

***Title: A Study of the Housing Values of a Select Group of Married Men and Women Residing in the City of Baroda***

*Author:* Sukhvarsha P. Khanna

*Guide:* Vijay Taneja

*Year:* 1970

*Keywords:* Housing values, married men and women

## INTRODUCTION

The study was primarily undertaken to gain an understanding in developing various techniques for measuring the housing values held by the respondents, also to determine whether there is any relationship between the housing values held, and certain background characteristics of the respondents. The study also found out whether there is any difference in determining the values of the respondents by different techniques of eliciting data.

## METHODOLOGY

A survey research was adopted. An interview method was considered most appropriate. On the basis of the pilot study and some retrospective thinking an interview schedule was designed. Five techniques were used for eliciting the housing values, viz., graphical rating technique, Thurstone's scale paired comparisons technique, Likert technique or the summated rating scale and rank order technique. The sample was drawn from two residential localities of Baroda city, namely, Oil and Natural Gas Commission colony and Electrical and Mechanical Engineering colony.

### Major Findings

Findings revealed that the background characteristics of sex and age influenced the holding of the values of economy and external convenience. No association between the background characteristics, and the values of family centrism and internal privacy were found. No conclusions could be drawn for the values of aesthetics, external privacy and internal convenience as the interactions of the background variables were also found to be significant. Out of the ten analysing techniques, six of them ranked the values of economy as first, however it was ranked second by the paired comparison and rank order technique.

***Title: An Evaluation of the Cooperative Ownership Housing Societies in Baroda***
*Author:* Anjana Katwala
*Guide:* Nalini Ogale
*Year:* 1976
*Keywords:* Evaluation, cooperative ownership housing societies

### Introduction

The cooperative housing societies in private sector help in providing the houses to the people, and thus are some help to the government in solving some of the housing problems. The study was mainly designed to know, to what extent the houses provided by the cooperative housing societies fulfil the needs of occupant families. The study identified satisfactory and unsatisfactory features of the housing based on the opinions of homemakers, evaluated the house plans in relation to (a) the activities carried out by the occupant families and (b) the minimum space standards for specific features in the house.

## Methodology

The study was based on the selected house plans from some of the existing cooperatively built housing societies in Baroda. The sample consisted of 36 homemakers, six from each of the selected six types of house plan. To collect the data an interview schedule and observation sheet were devised by the investigator. The pretesting of the questionnaire was done with six homemakers and one house plan before finalising it. The data were collected by the personal interview by the investigator. Evaluation of the house plans was done by observations about the selected features of the house. The information included in the interview schedule was coded, recorded on code sheets and analysed. The results were reported in terms of frequencies, means and percentages. The information on each selected feature of the house was compared with the minimum or recommended space standard in terms of either more than the recommended standard, equal to the recommended standard or lower than the recommended standard in order to see the adequacy of each feature of the house. The working heights were judged on the basis of the possible normal, maximum and minimum reaches of the homemakers.

## Major Findings

All the six types of plans contained the living room, the bed-room, the kitchen, the bathroom, the verandah, and the store room. Except for the F type plan all the other types had a second bedroom. A courtyard was present in only A, B and C types. Only the D type plan had a dining room, and was found to be the largest in the total sq ft area among all the types. A majority of the homemakers were satisfied with the sizes of different rooms, dimensions of the working centres, location of certain features and traffic routes, ventilation, amount of daylight and artificial light, and storage space in all the rooms of the house. For most of the activities, the bedroom and the living room were used mostly by a majority of the families. Sizes of different rooms were found adequate in all the six plans. The dimensions of working centres and the size of passages were found to be inadequate in most of the house plans. Locations of certain features, such as mixing, cooking and sink centres were found to be adequate in all the types of the plans. Traffic routes were found to be clear and safe. Hence, they were adequate for the circulation within the rooms and between the rooms.

The size of doors were found adequate in most of the rooms, except in the storeroom in all the types of plans. The dimensions were less by 3 sq ft to 8 sq ft than the recommended size of door of the storeroom in these five types of plans.

The size of the windows were found to be more than adequate in most of the house plans for most of the rooms. The cross-ventilation was also found in most of the rooms of the six house plans. Hence the good ventilation was provided in all the types of plan. In all the types of house plans the amount of artificial light was found to be inadequate in most of the rooms. The wall cabinet and the base cabinet dimensions were found to be equal or more than recommended dimensions for all the rooms in all the types of plans. Hence, storage space provided to the occupant families was enough to store the needed household articles in all the rooms of the house.

It can be concluded that though the homemakers living in cooperative housing societies were satisfied with all the selected features of the house yet in reality certain features were not found to be satisfactory when evaluated on the basis of the specified standards. Of the six features four features were found inadequate or not up to the standard. These features were working centres, orientation, daylight and artificial lighting. Education, employment status, extent of exposure to the sources of information of the respondent and the total monthly family income significantly affected the awareness of the respondents regarding fire safety facilities.

***Title: A Study of Housing Values and Satisfactions of Rural Houseowners***

*Author:* Renu Saini

*Guide:* Nalini Ogale

*Year:* 1978

*Keywords:* Housing values

## Introduction

The study explored the housing values held by the rural people, measured the respondents' expressed satisfaction with the house in which they were living, and the relationship between the housing values held by respondents and their expressed satisfaction.

## Methodology

For the present study, a survey method was used with an interview schedule as a tool for collecting data. Thurstone and Chave technique was used for measuring the aesthetics, economy, external privacy, external convenience, family centrism, internal privacy and internal convenience. The housing value developed by Khanna in 1970 was further modified by the investigator for three more housing values, namely, social prestige, health and religion, and was used for eliciting the values of the respondents. Twelve statements were finally selected under each housing value. For eliciting the responses to these scales, all the statements under each value scale were read out to the respondents, and they were then asked to indicate which of these expressed their views. An expressed satisfaction score sheet was also made consisting of 41 statements for measuring satisfactions of the respondents with their present housing conditions. The data were collected by personal interviews. The collected data were then coded, categorised for tabulation and statistical analysis. Statistics used to analyse the responses were simple frequencies, means, correlation and analysis of variance. One hundred and fifty heads of the families from the two villages of Bhatinda district of Punjab, namely, Khenuana and Jida were drawn as samples for the present study.

## Major Findings

The value of internal convenience was ranked first and economy was ranked the lowest among the ten values. It was also found that respondents varied in holding each of the housing values. It was found that there was a variation in the ranking of the housing values of respondents from low, middle and high income groups. In the low income group internal convenience held first rank while external convenience, religion and economy held last three ranks. Internal privacy held the first rank for middle income group while religion held the last rank. The high income group respondents gave internal convenience first rank while economy got the last rank. Illiterate respondents gave the first rank to internal convenience and religion held the last rank. A high education group gave the first rank to internal privacy and the last rank to external convenience.

***Title: A Study of Housing Facilities Provided to Government Employees and Evaluation of Those Plans***

*Author:* Vipla Mehta

*Guide:* Salma Nadvi

*Year:* 1979

*Keywords:* Housing facilities

## Introduction

Government provides housing accommodation to its employees in view of the scarcity in the private sector of proper houses, within the paying capacity of the employees. Planning of government houses is a more complex job as it has to be flexible to satisfy the general needs of not only one family but many who stay in the house during their service period. The present study was undertaken with a view to throw some light on the housing facilities provided by the government to its employees. An evaluation of the house plans was also done.

## Methodology

A descriptive research design was adopted A closed-ended questionnaire along with a plan evaluation sheet was used for collecting the data. For the purpose of the study plans were taken in original from the Ministry of Planning, Delhi. Twelve plans from four different types of quarters provided by the government for railway employees, M.E.S. employees and C.P.W.D. employees were taken, and three houses from each type of quarter were visited to make the sample of 36 families. For the evaluation of house plans, a sheet with minimum recommended standards in each area to be evaluated was prepared on the basis of literature available, and previous research findings on different features and other sources, like I.S.I. standards, etc. This was then given to engineers and architects, and suggestions given by more than seven out of 10 were taken into consideration and plans were evaluated on those basis, as up to standard, below standard and above standard. Bar graphs were drawn to compare with the recommended standards.

## Major Findings

The study found out that the housing facilities provided to the government employees is quite adequate. C.P.W.D. houses had the highest built-up area and were built in a row form but planning of MES houses was better as the were more compact and semi-detached while the railway houses were multistorey. The window area in all the rooms was above the recommended standards while the amount of daylight in the kitchen of all the houses from four types of quarters was found inadequate. Very few houses had the recommended orientation of some of the rooms. Findings revealed that the depth of the storage cabinets was not up to standard in different rooms and hence the storage space was less. M.E.S. houses had most efficient plans.

Certain facilities, like the vegetable market, police station, post office, and fire protection were found to be not conveniently located for a majority of the families. But other services and utilities, like water supply, disposal of garbage, bus facilities and other public conveyances were satisfactory for a majority of the houses. Room sizes of type I and II quarters were felt adequate by the respondents even though these houses have smaller rooms. Regarding neighbourhood location, the feeling of respondents from all types of houses was satisfactory. Evaluation showed that some of the rooms were not cross-ventilated, which reflects the ignorance of the respondents regarding cross-ventilation. Evaluations further showed that cabinets were not spacious. A majority of the respondents reported dissatisfaction regarding storage space.

***Title: A Comparative Study of Existing Housing Conditions and Sanitary Facilities in a Slum and Government-Aided Low Income Housing Colony and their Effect on the General Health of the Homemakers.***

*Author:* Asha Kaul

*Guide:* Asha V. Dass

*Year:* 1981

*Keywords:* Housing conditions, sanitary facilities

## INTRODUCTION

Housing in the modern concept includes not only the physical structure providing shelter, but all the immediate surroundings and the related community services and facilities. Since environmental sanitation is one of the factors responsible for the present unhealthy status of the people, the study was designed to know the existing housing conditions, sanitary facilities and its effect on the health of the homemakers.

## METHODOLOGY

A survey method was adopted for conducting the study. Using an interview schedule the data were collected by the personal interview and observation from one hundred homemakers from two areas, namely Tulsiwadi slum of Karelibaug and Savatnagar colony at Harni Road, Baroda. Systematic sampling was done by selecting every sixth family for inclusion in the sample. In this way, fifty families from each area were selected. The collected data were statistically analysed using simple frequencies, means and chi-square test.

## MAJOR FINDINGS

None of the houses of both the areas were puacca. All houses in housing board were mixed, made up of brick, mud plaster walls and asbestos roof while a majority (72 per cent) in slums were kuccha with mud walls and thatched roofs. Lighting and ventilation were poor in a majority of the houses in both the areas.

The sanitary conditions around the house were very poor in slums as compared to the housing board. Bathroom facilities were not provided in both the areas while flush type latrines were only provided with no proper water facility. Poor hygienic habits were observed, especially in slums due to lack of pipe water supply and proper drainage.

A significant relationship between the housing conditions and the health of the homemaker was found in the case of both the areas (Chi-square cal = 9.84 for housing board and 12.3 for slum). It was also seen that the people of the housing board were less prone to certain diseases like malaria than the people of slums because the surroundings of the slums were full of stagnant water near the houses which was a breeding place for the mosquitoes. With respect to certain aspects like water supply, drainage facility, bathroom and toilet facilities the housing board colony was slightly better off than the slums. Thus the study stressed on the need for more attention by the higher authorities towards these areas in order to provide them with the basic necessities of life, if not more, in order to lead a healthy life.

***Title: A Study of the Existing Housing Conditions and House Plans as Related to the Selected Household Activities of Rural Households of Jammu and Kashmir State***

*Author:* Rainu Dhar

*Guide:* Veena Gandotra

*Year:* 1981

*Keywords:* Housing conditions, houseplans, household activities

## INTRODUCTION

The study examined the existing housing conditions and house plans in relation to (a) total built-up area of the houseplot (b) type of house, (c) orientation, (d) lighting (e) ventilation (f) entrance of the house, (g) sanitary conditions (h) drinking water facility and (i) storage facility. The opinion of homemakers was also taken regarding the convenience of space utilised by them for different activities.

## METHODOLOGY

A descriptive study using a survey design was conducted in two purposively selected villages, namely, Galwadaychak and Halqua of Jammu district of Jammu and Kashmir state. Data were collected from a sample of 100 families using the interview schedule through the personal interview method. Statistics used to analyse the responses were simple frequencies, means and median.

## MAJOR FINDINGS

The findings of the study revealed that only one-third of the total families had adequate built-up area for their houses. Houses were single-storeyed in a row form, having an entrance through the compound. A majority of the houses (83 per cent) had adequate sized kitchen while a few of them had a verandah and a bedroom. Only 16 per cent of the houses had electricity, while the rest were using kerosene lamps. Houses were mostly kuchha and ventilation was given the least importance, as no ventilators were provided with only a few houses having windows. The sanitary facilities were very poor with no latrines, covered drains, arrangement for the disposal of garbage. Separate water supply was absent, and there was hardly any proper storage place. The respondents stored in mud vessels and on the floor of the room also. No fixed place was kept for animals. Dissatisfaction was reported mainly regarding storage space, less rooms, open kitchen as it was in the compound in all the houses. Respondents wanted to have more storage space, a roof for the kitchen and addition of rooms.

***Title: A Study of the Impact of Age and Income on the Preferences of Homemakers for Soft Furnishing Materials***

*Author:* Sadhan Sagar

*Guide:* Asha Dass

*Year:* 1983

*Keywords:* Age, income, preferences, homemakers, furnishing materials

## Introduction

Furnishing materials are simple home equipments which can be changed frequently and one possesses a number of sets for each room. They look and feel softer than any other material, and are differently textured, brightly coloured and richly patterned. Furnishing materials are durable and also expensive consumer goods which people buy rarely. Hence, it needs to be selected with ample amount of care. While selecting furnishing materials one considers its colour, texture, print, durability and its appearance, and in addition to these, the current fashion, the cost, the maintenance required by the material and, above all, the preferences of an individual and the family members are taken care of. Therefore a homemaker requires to be aware of various tastes and preferences of all cozy appearance through effective furnishing. His/her duty is to provide a happy, orderly atmosphere within the home, where members can find place to rest and share their experiences.

## Methodology

A descriptive research study was conducted. A questionnaire was used as a tool for collecting data. The sample of the study comprised 120 homemakers out of which 60 belonged to high income group and 60 to middle income group selected by purposive stratified random sampling technique. The data were categorised, coded tabulated, and t-test was used to test the relationship.

## Major Findings

A smooth texture was preferred for bedspreads because of the appeal which gave the feeling of spaciousness. Mainly light colours were preferred by a majority of the homemakers; mainly natural designs were preferred for all the furnishing items, and they were washed fortnightly, monthly and six-monthly by both income groups. Mainly the material that was in fashion and had beauty was given top priority. It was found that there was no difference in the attitudes of homemakers as per the income but as regards the age it had an influence on the homemakers.

***Title: Development of Low Cost Interior Plans of Masters Bedroom for Selected Families of Baroda***
*Author:* Sangeeta Shukla
*Guide:* Salma Nodvi
*Year:* 1988
*Keywords:* Lowcost interior plans, master bedroom

## INTRODUCTION

As most of us face the problem of choosing interiors within a limited budget which satisfy one's needs, the present study made an attempt to devise low cost interior plans for bedrooms according to the respondents' choice with available furniture, furnishings and accessories in the market, budget and the space available in the household.

## METHODOLOGY

A research design for the present study was experimental-cum-descriptive in nature. A sample of 60 families was a collected by random sampling for the survey. For the case study sample of 10 families was selected on the basis of purposive sampling belonging to A and B type houses. The development of a model interior plan was limited to the existing dimensions of the bedroom, the budget of the respondents, the availability of furniture, furnishings and accessories. Results were reported in terms of frequency, percentage and mean. Spearman's rank correlation test was executed to find out the sex-wise difference for colour preference.

## MAJOR FINDINGS

The study found out that annual redecoration budget does not increase with the increase in income but it depends upon furnishing goals and values which differ from individual to individual. A high positive relationship was found between sex and colour preference. The colour trend was towards cool colours, like blue and green but ivory, beige and tints and shades of white were also popular for bedrooms. Light blue was liked the most by husbands and wives. For furnishings, a majority of the respondents liked cotton and its variety with restrained and bold floral patterns. Vertical stripes, diagonal stripes, dots and circles were other favoured patterns for furnishings. Soft and smooth, sleek and woven were the preferred textures. On the basis of the survey findings, low-cost model interiors plans were developed which could to be passed onto the dealer and manufacturer of furnishing materials, furniture and soft floor covering so that consumers could be guided in the proper direction to implement these information in their decorative plans.

***Title: A Study of Housing Facilities and Problems of Residents of Flats in High Rise Buildings***

*Author:* Falguni Gandhi

*Guide:* Nalini Ogale

*Year:* 1992

*Keywords:* Housing facilities, highrise buildings

## Introduction

The present study compared the plan layout of selected flats from high rise buildings in Baroda with the Baroda Municipal Corporation Specification related to: adequacy of space, ventilation, lighting, privacy, availability of lift and vehicle parking space. The facilities provided in the flats related to water supply, drainage system, storage facilities, lift, garbage collection and removal, vehicle parking, recreation facilities were also assessed, and the problems faced by the occupants were identified.

## Methodology

Data were collected through an interview method from 90 families, 40 from the inner city area (I C), 23 from Fatehgunj (f) and 27 from Alkapuri (A) area. Respondents comprised both owners and the tenants having flats with two rooms / three rooms plus the kitchen.

## Major Findings

The area of the flats varied in two-room and three-room plus kitchen types. For one bedroom and living room flats the sizes of the rooms were larger than specified by the Baroda Municipal Corporation standards. Flats had adequate natural light and ventilation. About 55 per cent were satisfied with regard to privacy and with the planning of rooms in relation to circulation and exterior privacy. Almost all of them had sufficient vehicle parking space in all the areas. All the complexes had an open terrace but only 21 per cent families had a safe height of balcony. There was adequate water supply for household activities along with borewell facility for supplementing municipal water supply. About 18 per cent respondents were facing dampness in their flats while a majority (61.11 per cent) of the respondents were facing strong breeze. About 68 per cent had fire protection facility. A majority of the respondents expressed that they were satisfied with their housing conditions. Seventy-seven per cent respondents reported that they get good security in high rise buildings. Disadvantages specified were noise which was the highest in the inner city and the lowest in Alkapuri area. Eighty per cent had faced lift failure and there was not much difference in the reports of these groups. About 49.84 per cent were satisfied with the physical features of the house; 55.26 per cent were satisfied with the existing facilities of high rise building while 49.52 per cent were satisfied with the safety features.

***Title: Responses of Residents of a Selected Middle Income Group Housing Colony of Rajasthan Housing Board in Kota City***

*Author:* Indu Shrivastava

*Guide:* Rachael George

*Year:* 1993

*Keywords:* Housing colony, middle income group

## Introduction

The study was undertaken with a view to get acquainted with the opinions of people regarding the basic housing condition. On the basis of these opinions conclusions could be drawn regarding the defects of public housing. Thus, suggestions could be made about remedies to overcome the drawbacks in the houses built by the housing board.

## Methodology

A survey design was adopted. An interview schedule was used for data collection administered personally by the investigator. The data were collected from "Mahavir Nagar", a middle income housing board colony of Kota city, built in 1977-78, having 100 housing units. Each occupant household referred to in the present study as a family was included in the study as a sample. The data were analysed using simple frequencies, mean and standard deviation.

## Major Findings

The study found that a majority of the housewives were satisfied with the space-in-use in the case of the kitchen, bathroom, verandah and dining room. Rest, relaxation and entertainment activities, conversation, newspaper or other light reading, listening to music, making handicrafts and entertaining day-to-day guests were activities pursued by families in their housing. Bedroom, dining room, drawing room and verandah were the spaces used by a large number of families for varying purposes. A majority were highly satisfied.

Each family chose the space according to its convenience putting various rooms for multipurpose use. The master bedroom was used in a majority of families for children's routine study while the second master bedroom was used for working out creative assignments. For storing kitchen items like small utensils, big utensils, dairy products, semi-perishable goods, the kitchen was the primary area used in almost all families and nearly almost all families were satisfied with the space in use. Modifications were made by the households in all the rooms as well as in verandas. The modification made in the drawing room included: converting the room into bedroom, adding storage cabinets, replastering the room. Seventy-four per cent families modified bedrooms by adding storage cabinets. In the kitchen, working platforms were raised (13.5%), cupboards were added (38.9%) while in the bathroom and W.C. modifications done were adding of storage cabinet, or converting the area into another room. Nearly 53 per cent of families studied, held housing goals, and mostly they held only one goal. The goals held by families included adding one more storey, building another house (17 per cent).

***Title: Status of Existing Interior in Drawing Rooms of Residential Buildings***

*Author:* Shalini Chandra

*Guide:* Rachel George

*Year:* 1994

*Keywords:* existing interior drawing rooms, residential buildings

## Introduction

The study ascertained the status of selected components of existing interior in the drawing rooms of residential buildings, identified the main decision maker for the arrangement of the same and the factors underlying the choice. The knowledge and attitude towards the interior decoration of the decision maker responsible for the arrangement of the interior space was also determined.

## Methodology

A descriptive research design was adopted. A sample of 120 families, 60 each from two residential areas, viz., Pratapgunj and Alkapuri which house both middle and high income families, was selected, using a purposive random sampling questionnaire-cum-observation schedules. Data were collected with the help of a questionnaire-cum-observation schedules. The housewives acted as the respondents of the study and they reported on family data also wherever necessary. Knowledge test and attitude scale were also developed. Data were analysed using both descriptive (mean, frequency, percentage, standard deviation) and inferential statistics (analysis of variance and coefficient of correlation).

## MAJOR FINDINGS

The study revealed that females were the main decision makers in most of the families pertaining to the arrangement of the interior of the drawing room. In most of the families the drawing room was a separate room with an area ranging from 159 to 199.9 square feet. Regarding the furniture pieces three- seaters, upholstered chairs, centre tables and peg tables were found to be common in most of the families. A showcase was available in a majority of the cases. Potted plants and flower vases were popular accessories. Most of the families had monochromatic colour schemes (one colour used) in their drawing rooms with both smooth and coarse textures.

Regarding the floor treatment marble was used by a majority of the families. Both plain and patterned surfaces were used in most of the families. Regarding the colour scheme, accessories and furniture, in most of the cases the wife was the key person involved in selection and arrangement. Cost, colour and durability were the most common factors in the mind while buying paints, curtains, furniture and accessories. Tints / shades of yellow existed as well as those desired by most of the families.

By and large, a majority of the decisionmakers revealed a fairly high level of knowledge on interior décor. Most of the decision makers had a favourable attitude towards interior decoration. The calculated 't' values revealed that the difference in the means of quality of existing interior by decision makers' occupation was significant at 0.01 levels. The walls and ceiling, furniture accessories and lighting in a majority of the families were rated as 'fair' while the floor was rated 'good'.

Most of the families entertained two guests daily and it was reported that in almost all cases the housewife and / or husband received and entertained the guests. The furniture for seating was found to be sufficient in most of the families as it could be seen that 59.2 and 60 per cent families never needed to pull out chairs from other areas or stand respectively.

***Title: A Comparative Study of the Housing Conditions of non-Beneficiaries and Beneficiaries of a Select Low Income Housing Scheme in Aizawal, Mizoram***

*Author:* Marina Zohruailiani

*Guide:* Rachel George

*Year:* 1995

*Keywords:* Housing conditions, low income housing scheme

## INTRODUCTION

In India, housing has become a problem due to the rapid growth of population, industrialisation and urbanisation. A number of positive measures have been initiated by the government to bridge the gap between housing supply and demand. Various social housing schemes have been introduced to help people in general and the economically weaker sections (EWS) in particular. The present study evaluated the functioning of one such low income housing scheme known as 'The State Housing Scheme for Low Income Group' introduced in Mizoram during the year 1972-73 by the Mizoram government against the guidelines of the implementing state agency. The housing conditions of non-beneficiaries and beneficiaries were also compared.

## METHODOLOGY

A descriptive survey method coupled with the experimental design was adopted. A multistage purposive sampling technique was used for the selected of the locale of the study which were Tuikual Vaivakawn and Chawnpui. Through a systematic random sampling technique, a sample of 70 families, 35 each from the list of beneficiaries and non-beneficiaries, was selected. The interview schedule-cum-observation checklist and field measurements were used to collect data. Interviews were also conducted on various officials of the state housing scheme which included the Director, Deputy Director, Executive engineer, L.A.D. (Local Administrative department) Housing Technical Wing, who were the officers to approve and check the proposed house plan made by the loanee, at the time of application for the loan. Data were analysed using descriptive statistics (frequency, percentage, mean and standard deviation) and inferential statistics (canonical correlation analysis and coefficient of variation).

## Major Findings

The analysis of the exterior housing conditions as a whole revealed that a majority of the respondents in both the cases had used appropriate materials for construction of their houses. A majority fell in the category of less than recommended standards in regard to plinth level, and a majority had placed various rooms in the wrong location and therefore were not as per the recommended orientation.

Beneficiaries were in a better position with regard to the number of room, sizes of rooms, density of occupancy, ratio between window and floor area, and space per occupants.

The mean number of rooms for the beneficiaries was three rooms and had a separate bathroom kitchen and living room arrangement whereas the mean number of rooms was two for the non-beneficiaries with an arrangement of separate bedroom with kitchen-cum-living accommodation.

The sizes of all the various rooms were found to be bigger than the recommended sizes. Regarding the evaluation of housing schemes, it was found that only certain rules were complied, like the mortgage of land and production of land settlement certificate, and disbursement of loans while none had insured their house and only a few complied to the requirement of producing estimated cost of the house, its plan and production of income certificate.

The officials had reported that all the rules were complied by, except the insurance of the house. The coefficient of variation and housing conditions scores also revealed that there was a significant difference between the housing conditions of the two groups and that beneficiaries had better housing conditions as compared to the non beneficiaries.

***Title: A Study of Satisfaction Expressed by Aged towards Their Existing Condition of House and Type of House***

*Author:* Hina Baria

*Guide:* Veena Gandotra

*Year:* 1997

*Keywords:* Existing condition of house, type of house, satisfaction, aged

## Introduction

As housing is an important source of continuity in the lives of most older people proper housing exercises a profound influence on people's health. It is essential to give special needs, physical, economic, socio-psychological and recreational. The greatest drawback of such mass housing is the social distance between the designers and the users of the housing which sometimes result in poor 'fit' between the users and their housing. The study was therefore undertaken to measure the satisfaction expressed by the aged towards various factors of housing condition and the type of house along with their preferences.

## Methodology

A research design was the descriptive type. A survey method was used to collect the data using the interview schedule. Purposive sampling was done. The selected sample comprised 120 respondents, i.e., 30 males and 30 females—those residing in apartments; 30 males and 30 females—those residing in tenements from Fatehgunj, Pratapgunj, Akota, Harni Road, Nizampura, Sama Road, EME road, Gotri, Alkapuri, Productivity Road, Old Padra Road, and Karelibaug located on the outskirts of Baroda city. 't' test was used for judging the significance of independent variables of house-type, sex, living arrangement, family type, family income, education and duration of stay. The analysis of variance was also applied to test the relationship between the selected personal variables and the satisfaction expressed.

## Major Findings

A majority were in the age group of 60-65 years and more number of the aged in the 71 and above years category were living in tenements. A majority had low level education, a joint family with 3-4 adult members and 1-2 children, depending on their children for finance, more in the case of women. Almost all the respondents lived in their own house and over 38.3 per cent were living since five years. A majority were having two bedrooms. Most were provided with a separate bedroom, a separate beds (94.3 per cent) and personal cupboards (83.3 per cent) but very few had separate toilets and baths. Most of them were satisfied with cleanliness, quiet and peace, spaciousness in the community, location of community services and facilities, site density, roads and street layout, housing design. A majority of the sample were living nearby religious places and dispensaries. They had proper windows and ventilators, accessible cupboards, proper lighting and balcony, safety precautions like grills over doors and windows, houses which faced the wind direction and were fully ventilated. A majority wanted the aged in their neighbourhood, were not bothered by common areas and lived their lifestyle as Indians. Everybody was satisfied with the security inside the house as compared to security provisions in the housing scheme in which case less number of respondents were satisfied. A majority preferred their house to be in the interiors away from service zones to face private space and near religious place. A majority viewed their present house as "good". Testing of hypothesis revealed that the more lower educated aged were satisfied. Satisfaction scores revealed that a majority of the respondents were averagely satisfied. Income also influenced one's level of satisfaction. The higher the income, the more were the facilities obtained resulting in satisfaction.

***Title: A Study of Occurrences of Household Accidents and Knowledge and Practices of Homemakers Regarding Household Accidents***

*Author:* Reema Chaurasia

*Guide:* Maneesha Shukul

*Year:* 1996

*Keywords:* Accidents, occurrences of accidents, knowledge, practices of homemakers, household accidents

## Introduction

Though the house is considered as the safest place, it is a dangerous place as well. A homemaker is the key person who selects the household tasks, supervises various household activities and establishes the safety rules. To perform this effectively, safety education should be given to homemakers so as to minimise the damage / loss of human resources of the family. In order to impart safety education it is essential to know the level of knowledge of the homemakers regarding safety and the safety practices they follow to prevent accidents that lead to certain social and economic implications, and affect the individual as well as the society. Therefore, the present study was undertaken to find out the frequency of occurrences of household accidents, knowledge of homemakers regarding safety and practices related to safety against accidents at home.

## Methodology

The present study was a descriptive survey method. The data were collected by the interview schedule having a summated rating scale. Content validity and reliability were established for the scales through split-half method. The correlation values for knowledge scale was r=0.75 and for practice scale was r=0.65. The purposive sampling technique was used to select the sample. The criterion for selecting the sample was only those houses where household accidents have occurred in last two years. A total of 90 homemakers were interviewed from five slums of Vadodara city taking 18 respondents from each slum. Data collected were coded and tabulated. Mean, standard deviation and percentage were applied to describe most of the information. Analysis of variance, 't' test and coefficient of correlation were computed to test the hypotheses.

## Major Findings

A majority of the respondents were illiterate, unemployed, belonged to nuclear families and had semi-pucca house. The various household accidents occurring at home as reported by the respondents were "falls due to inability of clear vision", "burns due to spilling of hot liquid", and "electric shock due to putting finger in the bulb holder'. A majority of the respondents had average knowledge regarding household safety, and two-thirds of the respondents had average practices regarding household safety. The knowledge of the homemakers regarding household safety was not influenced by their age, education and occupation whereas practices were influenced by only the educational level of respondents. No relationship was found either between the knowledge and practices nor between the knowledge and occurrences, and practices and occurrences of household accidents. The number of household accidents varied due to family income.

***Title: Appraising the Existing Fire Safety Facilities and Awareness of Residents Regarding the Same in Multistoreyed Residential Buildings***

*Author:* Neelam Shekhawat

*Guide:* Maneesha Shukul

*Year:* 1998

*Keywords:* Fire safety facilities, multistoreyed residential buildings

## Introduction

Fire is the major cause of accidental deaths in the home. In the fast developing cities the home accommodations are changing from single units to multistorey apartments. Such residential structures are no doubt beneficial in accommodating a large population in a limited space, but also increased the danger of fire accidents. Almost all fires are preventable and therefore all buildings should essentially have a well developed fire safety system. The residents should be well aware of fire fighting systems. Keeping in mind the above-mentioned, the investigation was carried out to study the existing fire safety facilities in the selected multistoreyed residential buildings, and to assess the awareness of the selected homemakers, who were residents of the select buildings about fire safety facilities in multistoreyed buildings.

## Methodology

A descriptive research design was adopted. A systematic random sampling was done to select a sample of 208 respondents from 62 multistoreyed residential buildings in Node (Fatehgunj, Pratapgunj) and other areas (Alkapuri and Old Padra Road) of Vadodara city. The selected buildings had their safety certificate issued between January 1987 and December 1997. An observation sheet and an interview schedule were used to find out the availability of fire safety facilities and the awareness of the resident homemakers, respectively. Both the schedules were developed as summated rating scale, based on the specification of the general development regulation act of Vadodara Municipal Corporation. The census of 80 per cent among the judges was taken as a yardstick for inclusion of the statement in the final tool. The reliability coefficient for the scale was 0.72. t-test was applied to find the difference in the fire safety facilities and F-test was applied to find the difference in the awareness of the respondents due to the difference in age, and education total monthly income.

## Major Findings

On the analysis of the data it was found about 77 per cent buildings obtained moderate scores on the scale regarding the availability of fire safety facilities. It was further found that the availability of staircase, emergency exit and electricity facility was the best and those of fire life, fire alarm and safety signs were of the poorest extent. It was found that 44 per cent of the respondents were unemployed and 54 per cent had moderate exposure to the source of information. Nearly 53 per cent respondents had a total monthly family income less than or equal to Rs. 10,000. On the total awareness scale 49 per cent respondents obtained moderate scores. Awareness regarding fire hydrants, sprinklers and extinguishers was the lowest and that regarding lifts, liftmen and watchmen services was found to be highest. The testing of hypotheses revealed that the availability of fire safety facilities was significantly different by their area of location and year of certification. It was also found that age, education, employment status, extent of exposure to the sources of information of the respondent and the total monthly family income significantly affected the awareness of the respondents regarding fire safety facilities.

***Title: A Study on Consideration of Vastushastra in Housing Design***
*Author:* Divya Lakhani
*Guide:* Veena Gandotra
*Year:* 1999
*Keywords:* Vastushastra, housing design

## Introduction

The importance of Vastushastra in housing can be judged by the fact that it lays down principles for the orientation of buildings with the aim of creating healthy living environments. Therefore the study was undertaken to find out the place of Vastushastra in factors considered while choosing a house and the attitude of people about Vastushastra. The existing level of knowledge of people about Vastushastra was also ascertained.

## Methodology

A descriptive research design was adopted and a survey method was used. The interview schedule was employed to collect the data. The data were supplemented with the qualitative analysis of the existing floor plans from Vastushastra point of view by use of an observation sheet. A sample of 120 respondents was selected using the purposive random sampling. The data collected were coded and categorised. For data analysis, descriptive and relational statistics were frequency, percentage, mean, standard deviation, co-efficient of correlation and t-test.

## Major Findings

Findings revealed that a majority of the respondents, i.e., 66.7 per cent had a lower level of knowledge about Vastushastra while 33.3 per cent of the respondents had a moderate level of knowledge. Respondents from the service class scored more in the knowledge test than those from the business class. A majority (55.8%) of the respondents had a neutral attitude towards Vastushastra. Findings revealed that the evaluating criteria given more importance by the respondents were the adequate size of the house, with enough number of rooms, affordable cost, etc., and less importance was given to the consideration of Vastushastra. The maximum number of house plans scored 20-29 in the house plan evaluation checklist. Occupation and income of the respondents were found to be significantly correlated with their attitude towards Vastushastra. People with a higher income had a favourable attitude towards Vastushastra. Similarly, people from the business class had a favourable attitude than those from service class towards Vastushastra. A positive correlation between the knowledge of the respondent about Vastushastra and his education was found. The attitude of the respondents their knowledge about Vastushastra had a direct correlation with the application of Vastushastra in their housing design.

# 7

# Consumer Studies

The consumer is the backbone of any economy. He is the key to almost all the economic activities. The importance of consumer education cannot be neglected. Today's market is globalising having complex products, latest technology and advanced sales techniques. Consumers are moving towards a changed lifestyle and thereby making the market also very complex. Also the choice making of today's consumers in this changed state of affairs has also become very difficult. Intelligent consumers in the market get help in making their choice through advertisements brands, labels, packages, quality marks and trademarks. The advertisements also affect the consumers tremendously. Also the consumers face a variety of problems in the market. To deal with this many studies have been undertaken regarding the use of the advertising media, buying behaviour and attitudes of consumers, opinion, brand preferences, knowledge, utilisation of goods, etc. Though there has been considerable progress in research in the area of consumer studies, there is still a long dark way ahead for researchers to throw light upon. The psychological field is highly complex and we need to examine all aspects. Also, booklets and print matter can be developed for the consumers so that they can be enlightened and made aware of their rights and responsibilities, and also about redressal mechanism.

***Title: Awareness of Consumer Responsibilities***

*Author:* Miriam John

*Guide:* Nalini Ogale

*Year:* 1974

*Keywords:* Awareness, Consumer Responsibilities

## Introduction

Consumers in India need to safeguard their own rights and interests and contribute to the progress of the country. This is possible only if they know their responsibilities. Consumer protection and actions depend on effective and widespread consumer education which would make the consumer enlightened about their rights and responsibilities, and make them intelligent consumers. Consumer education must be an integral part of curriculum for formal education. To make it very relevant, the existing level of knowledge of consumers about their responsibilities and rights must be studied. With this background the study was undertaken to find out the awareness of consumer responsibilities, their knowledge about commonly used consumer terminology, to identify the factors impeding the execution of consumer responsibilities.

## Methodology

The research design was descriptive survey. The questionnaire contained direct and indirect ways to find out awareness about consumer responsibilities. Nine problem situations explaining nine responsibilities were framed having three solutions reflecting complete, partial or low awareness. The respondents were asked to select any one of the given solutions and give reasons for that. The scale was subjected to establishment of validity and reliability. A sample of 132 people was selected purposively from two schools of Delhi.

## Major Findings

The age of the respondents ranged from 15 to 75 years income ranged from Rs. 100 to Rs 3,500 and education ranged from high school to postgraduation. A majority were gainfully employed. A majority of the respondents were females. A large percentage of respondents had a high awareness of consumer responsibilities, but had partial awareness of consumer terminologies. It was found that even though respondents did have an awareness of responsibilities, there were certain factors that impeded the execution of these responsibilities. These factors were thrift, trust in sales persons, fear of consequences, etc. The Chi-square revealed a significant association between the income and the awareness of the consumer responsibilities; the age and the awareness of the consumer terminology, and between the consumer responsibilities and the consumer terminology. Consumer education will have to find the means of overcoming, factors of hindrances, which prevent people not only from being knowledgeable but also conscientious in their behaviour and deeds.

*Title: Food Buying Habits of Lower Income Group Families in Baroda City*

*Author:* Saroj Patel

*Guide:* Nalini Ogale

*Year:* 1975

*Keywords:* Food buying habits

## Introduction

Food management is one of the most important jobs in the home. The trend of food we buy is determined by habit, cultural background, dietary knowledge, income and relative prices, there are many factors which influence the selection of stores and food for the family. A study was planned to explore the buying habits of low income families, to assess the factors which influenced the food buying habits and to find out the problems faced by the families in buying food.

## Methodology

A descriptive survey method was used. An interview schedule was used as a tool for collecting data. The total sample comprised 100 homemakers selected through random sampling from low income families in four residential localities in Baroda city. Data were analysed and reported by descriptive statistics, such as mean, average and percentage.

## Major Findings

The homemaker was the actual buyer for the food in the family. Homemakers took independent decisions in all the areas of buying food except in financial matters. The varieties of pulses and vegetables increased with the increase in the income. For the actual selection of food, "availability of money resources" and "availability of the product" in the market were the most important factors. Homemakers preferred rationing stores and independent stores for the groceries and miscellaneous items, vegetable markets for the vegetables, food hawkers for the fruits, and cooperative stores and independent stores for milk. More importance was given to the "credit facilities", "lowest price", "fixed price" and "location of the stores" for the selection of store. Family income, age and education of the homemakers had a direct influence on collecting information about products, and in the selection of bulk buying of seasonal produces. Various problems faced by low the income group homemakers were "adulteration", cheating by the shopkeepers in terms of "price and weights", "fluctuation of price" and "shortage of food products", in the market. The buying habits of low income group homemakers were seen to depend more on income, education of the homemakers, age of the homemakers, availability of the product in the market than the "likes and dislikes of the family members" and nutritional requirements of the family members.

***Title:* A Study of Advertising Media used by Housewives in Selection of Soaps and Detergents**

*Author:* Asmita Bhatt

*Guide:* Veena Gandotra

*Year:* 1975

*Keywords:* Advertisement, media, soaps, detergents

## Introduction

Advertising is recognized force and has become an integral part of our modern civilization. Advertisement benefits consumers, as it helps them to select goods at competitive price that may be available in the market. Sometimes it misguides the consumers by giving false and inadequate information about the product qualities. Manufacturers provide information about the product availability, its qualities, price, uses and so on to the consumer by using various advertising media, suitable to that particular product. The present study was undertaken to find out the advertising, media commonly used by the housewives in the selection of soaps and detergents, most and least approved characteristics of advertisements and opinions about advertisements in general.

## METHODOLOGY

Survey method along with an interview schedule was used for the present study. A systematic random sampling method was used in the selection of sample. From the house numbers collected from Sayajigunj ward office, Baroda. Every fifth house was taken. The total sample constituted of 100 middle income group families. The data were coded, tabulated and analysed in frequencies, means and percentages.

## MAJOR FINDINGS

Majority of the respondents were housewives (86%) had some college education (48%). The mean age was 36.4 years. Housewives were the decision makers regarding the selection of soaps and detergents (68%). The commonly used brands of detergents were 'DKT', 'Surf' and 'Rin', while the washing soaps were '501' and 'Sunlight'. In the case of toilet soaps 'Lux', 'Hamam', 'Rexona', 'Jai' and 'Lifebuoy' brands were commonly used by the respondents. Advertisement was not the only aid taken (56%) but other factors were also considered by the housewives in selection of soaps and detergents such as: economic appeal (86%), past experience (75%), friend's advice (56%), liking for the product (64%) and availability of the products (52%). Newspapers, cinema slides, posters, retail shop display were the four most frequently used advertising media used by majority of the housewives as sources of information. Respondents showed greater interest in audio-visual media. The most approved characteristics of advertisements included information regarding use and quality of product, economy appeal, clarity and simplicity of written message, gift offer and bargain price offer. Most of the respondents felt that advertisement prompts one to try new things, gives useful information about the product, while some respondents felt that advertisements encouraged impulsive buying, increased the cost of the product, are unreliable and mislead the consumers. Newspaper and radio advertising media were used by the respondents regardless of their age, while to use of other advertising media varied with different age groups of the respondents. Newspaper, periodicals and magazines, cinema and posters were the most common advertising media used by the respondents regardless of their education level.

***Title: A study of Homemakers' Buying Behaviour and Attitude towards certain Marketing Practices in the City of Baroda***

*Author:* Veena Bhatia

*Guide:* Kamala Srinivasan

*Year:* 1977

*Keywords:* Consumer, attitude, buying behaviour, marketing practices

## Introduction

Consumers have an important and significant role to play in the proper functioning of an economy. The Indian market is more producer-oriented than consumer-oriented. Exaggerated and misleading advertisements, short weights and measures, and adulteration of foods and drugs are becoming rampant. Various measures have been taken to protect the interests of the consumers. There have been serious attempts to create consumer awareness towards the existing marketing practices. Now consumers are slowly becoming aware of their rights and responsibilities. This is an opportune time to study the current attitudes towards marketing practices of different segments of consumers and their influence on the buying behaviour. Hence the present study was undertaken.

## Methodology

A survey method was used with a structured type questionnaire as the tool for collecting data. Content validity and reliability were established for attitude scale and descriptive rating scales. The r-values were 0.74 and 0.65 for attitude and descriptive scale, respectively. A random sampling technique was followed to select one hundred and twenty homemakers from six wards of Baroda city. The raw data were categorised and coded for statistical analysis. Descriptive statistics like measures of central tendency and 't' test of pooled variance, chi-square test and Pearson's product moment formula were used to test the hypotheses.

## Major Findings

A majority of the respondents read advertisements through published media (67%). More than half of the respondents made joint decisions (55%). A majority of the respondents had a positive attitude towards marketing practices (90%), and the influence of attitude was also exhibited in their buying behaviour. A majority of the respondents had a positive attitude towards marketing practices and their buying behaviour. Product quality in terms of packaging and brand name also served as a guide to ensure good quality. About 95 per cent of the respondents had a positive attitude towards consumer responsibility, and it also reflected in their buying behaviour. Income and education had a significant, influence on the formation of a positive attitude. Income and reading advertisements had a significant influence on the buying behaviour. The conclusion which could be drawn from the research in the present-day advertisements served as a reliable guide for the selection of the product for the sample population. A small percentage of the respondents had a negative attitude towards consumer responsibility. They felt that it was impossible for consumers to check trade malpractices. Most of the families belonged to nuclear families (75%), had medium to small size family (91%), nearly half were in the age group of 18-35 years and were graduates (73%), and belonged to middle income group (70%).

***Title: A Study of Homemakers' Opinions Regarding Two Brands of Refrigerators***

*Author:* Rita Singh

*Guide:* Asha Dass

*Year:* 1977

*Keywords:* Opinions, refrigeration, homemakers

## Introduction

Refrigeration is an important and helpful way of preservation of perishables, and for the attractive, appetising appearance of fresh, cooked and frozen foods. There are different brands of refrigerators available in the market. The consumer, after taking a decision to purchase a refrigerator, goes to the market as a novice, has a particular budget in mind, feels completely at a loss as to which brand to select. The investigator was curious to know the various selection factors considered by the homemakers while purchasing refrigerator. Further it was also thought worthwhile to compare two brands of refrigerators by their various costs, to study opinions of the homemaker in regard to material, construction, operation, safety features, servicing and methods used for the care of the refrigerator, and also to assemble suggestions for further improvements in the refrigerator.

## Methodology

A survey method with an interview schedule was used for the present study. A purposive sampling technique was used to select a sample of 100 families from various localities of Baroda city. Fifty of them possessed a Godrej refrigerator and the rest possessed Kelvinator refrigerators. The statistics used to analyse the data were simple frequencies, percentages and mean scores.

## Major Findings

A majority of the respondents purchased their refrigerator with full payment of cash. Though all the refrigerators had guarantee period, it differed according to the brand. Most of the respondents purchased a refrigerator according to the size of their families, popularity of the brand, spaciousness, material used, smoothness of operation (i.e., without noise) and reliability of the retailer. The price of Kelvinator was higher than that of Godrej. Not much difference was found in the installation cost and operation cost of both the refrigerators. Most of the repairs in both the brands were done after the guarantee period. Respondents of both the brands were not satisfied with the outside enamel finish as it got scratched very soon. Another prevalent complaint was the fungus growth and breeding of cockroach on and around the gasket. Most of the respondents were satisfied with the outside design, shape and opening and closing device of the door. Most of the respondents faced difficulty in removing the ice tray from the freezer and releasing the ice cubes from the ice tray. Most common problems faced by homemakers while cleaning the Godrej and Kelvinator refrigerators were "difficulty in cleaning (i) cracks and crevices, (ii) dirt collected in hollow parts of the shelf" and "(iii) the sharp corners". All the owners of Kelvinator brand felt the need of stabiliser as no such inbuilt facility was provided. Most of the families were satisfied with the services provided by the manufacturer and dealer in terms of workmanship and promptness.

***Title: A Study of Consumer Experiences towards Electric Iron and Blender in Terms of Their Utility***

*Author:* Mamta Saxena

*Guide:* Asha Dass

*Year:* 1980

*Keywords:* Consumer, consumer experiences, utility

## Introduction

Home activities in Indian homes are very time-consuming and tiring because many essential time- and energy-saving appliances are not available. Proper selection, use and care of the appliances are essential to get the maximum possible benefit from it. The electric iron and blender are appliances commonly found in most families. The appliances made by different manufacturers differ, in some or other aspects in their construction and design. The present study made an attempt to find out the different brands and types of the electric iron and blender possessed by the families, their extent of use, reasons for purchasing them and factors that were considered in their selection.

## Methodology

A survey method along with an interview schedule as a tool were used to collect the data. Through a purposive sampling method, a sample of 100 nuclear families, possessing the electric iron and blender of Indian make were drawn from Baroda city. The data collection process was followed by data analysis including categorisation, coding, scoring, tabulating and statistically analysing by using frequency, percentages and means.

## MAJOR FINDINGS

The majority of the respondents came from small families, were below 40 years of age, and were unemployed. The main reason for purchasing the appliances was to save time and energy. The availability of the spare parts, brand, material and finish, construction and size were the main factors considered during the selection and purchase of these appliances. Bajaj was the most popular brand among families and many of the families had automatic irons. The weight of all the irons ranged from 1.5 to 3 kilos. Slanted bakelite handles were provided in all the irons. The sole plate, made of cast irons, was narrow at one end in all the irons. Hot, linen, cotton, wool, silk, rayon and nylon were the sequence of fabrics mentioned over the thermostat knob. None of the irons had the specified two-metre cord. Families were dissatisfied with the shape of the handle in Murphy non-automatic irons. Families were not aware of the use of the grooves in the sole plate. Heel rest and heat control knob were found as satisfactory parts of the iron. Families reported that Murphy non-automatic irons took a long time to get heated. Most families had difficulty in cleaning the sole plate and ironing big garments with a short cord. All the families owning automatic irons wanted a good quality heating element, and suggested that a section on the care of the iron should be added to the instruction booklet. The most popular brand of blenders was Sumeet. The instruction booklet and one-year guarantee were provided with all the blenders. Families were not satisfied with the dry grinder capacity in the blender. Sumeet's dome cover was prone to cracking because of its fixing method. Families were dissatisfied without the handle in the container and with the push button type speed control. Only the dry grinding blade was used by most families for all purposes. Families found difficulty in pouring liquids without a guiding lip, and in cleaning the fixed blades. It was suggested that the guarantee period should be increased.

*Title: Effect of Selected Factors on the Quality of Buying Practices of the Consumers*
*Author:* Meera Agarwal
*Guide:* Nalini Ogale
*Year:* 1983
*Keywords:* Economic function, production, consumption, buying practices

## INTRODUCTION

Family continues to perform certain functions in spite of many social, economic and technological changes that are taking place. One of the main functions that used to be performed by the family was economic function which constitutes production as well as consumption. Buying to be effectively done must be based on a thorough knowledge of the needs of those for whom the goods are purchased, qualities and prices of goods in the market and their relation to use. The efficiency of consumer buying is affected by several factors. The study was planned to explore the buying practices of the consumers and the effect of certain factors on these practices.

## METHODOLOGY

A survey method with a questionnaire was used to collect data. The total sample was 158 respondents drawn through a selective sample keeping in mind that they knew English and had some formal education. The data were, and tabulated and analysed in terms of frequencies, percentages, t-tests and coefficient of correlation.

## MAJOR FINDINGS

A majority of the respondents did not have any specific information in consumer economics through either formal or informal education. In most of the families, the major buying decisions were taken by the husbands and the actual buying was done by the husband and wife. Consumers had satisfactory buying practices and partial awareness of common consumer terminologies. Age and income affect the quality of buying practices, i.e., the older the consumer the better the buyer, and the richer the consumer the more careless the buyer. There was no relationship between the awareness of common consumer terminologies and the quality of buying practices. The awareness has to be raised to the levels of responding, valuing and integrating information in making decisions and buying. In order to achieve competence in buying, the consumers have to be taught in the art of actual buying.

*Title: A Study of Advertisement and Advertising Media Considered by College Girls in the Selection of Cosmetics and Their Attitude towards Advertisement*

*Author:* Biraj Desai

*Guide:* Veena Gandotra

*Year:* 1983

*Keywords:* Consumer, advertisement, media, students, attitude, cosmetics

## Introduction

Cosmetics are a part of every girl's daily grooming routine. The advertisements play on their psyche and invite the attention to the product. Advertisements benefit consumers, as they it help them to select goods at competitive price that may be available in the market. It also helps the consumers to overcome old habits and stimulate them to want new products. Sometimes advertisements also misguide the consumers by giving false, inadequate information about the product qualities. Most of the advertisements have emotional rather than rational appeal. Many research studies have been undertaken to measure the effectiveness of advertisement. While a few have been undertaken on the advertising media used by housewives in the selection of different products. The present study was undertaken to determine the place of advertisement in relation to selected factors in the selection of cosmetics by college girls. Further specific objectives drawn included an assessment of the frequency of exposure of college girls to different advertising media, their opinions regarding the existing characteristics of advertisement and their attitude towards advertisement in general.

## Methodology

A survey method was used and data were collected by means of a questionnaire and an attitude scale. The reliability of the scale was 0.82. A purposive sampling technique was used to select a sample of 120 respondents from final year undergraduate and post-graduate courses from different faculties of the M.S. University of Baroda, Baroda. The data collected were coded, tabulated and analysed in terms of frequencies, percentages, means and coefficient of correlation.

## Major Findings

A majority of the respondents used more than one brand of powders, while in the case of creams and shampoos a majority used one brand only. Advertisement was not only the aid taken, but other factors like 'manufacturer's reliability' and 'economy' were considered in the selection of cosmetics. Students were highly exposed to the media, like cinema slides, short feature films, hoardings, periodicals, retail shop displays and magazines. They took a great interest in these media and were able to recall different brands of powders, creams and shampoos. Newspaper advertisements were never used as a source of information by a majority of the respondents. Students were aware of the deceptive characteristics of advertisements in the field of cosmetics and hence did not totally base their selection of cosmetics on advertisements but gave more importance to other factors. Most (65%) of the respondents had a positive attitude towards advertisement. The higher income group respondents gave a lower rank to advertisement as a factor in comparison to other factors. Respondents who had a positive attitude towards advertisement ranked advertisement lower than those who had a negative attitude. A high positive relationship was found between the interest taken by the respondents in each advertising medium and use of each advertising medium for getting information.

*Title: Image of Women in the Media: Viewpoints and Attitude of Cross-section of Females of Baroda City*

*Author:* Chand Rumu

*Guide:* Kamala Srinivasan

*Year:* 1986

*Keywords:* Women, image, attitude, media

## Introduction

Media constitute a very powerful tool which can bring any change in the society, shaping attitude and values as well as behaviour. As per the media, a woman is considered best suited at home to perform her usual role of a housewife and a mother. Thus, it is possible that damaging and misleading notions of female characteristics and capabilities are perpetuated in men and women through the media. This issue needs proper attention. The higher educational institutions can play a significant role to curb this trend of portraying women in the media in a non-progressive or stereotyped role, and see to it that the media is used properly for portraying the progressive or modern role of women. Thus, the present study was undertaken to study the opinion and attitude of the sample of women respondents, regarding the image of women in the media, and relate them with the demographic and socio-economic characteristics of the sample.

## Methodology

A descriptive research design was selected, using the survey method for the present study. A close ended / structured questionnaire was used as a data gathering instrument. An attitude scale was constructed and reliability was calculated through the split-half technique, and the 'r' value was 0.91. Three strata of women, i.e., students from final year undergraduation and above, employed women and full-time housewives formed the sample of the study. A purposive sampling technique was used to select the sample. The total sample comprised 120 respondents, 60 belonged to students, 30 employed women and 30 full-time housewives. Descriptive statistics used for analysis of data were frequency, percentage and measures of the central tendency while hypotheses were tested by using the analysis of variance and 't' test of pooled variance.

## Major Findings

*Eves Weekly* was popular among readers of the weekly magazine, *Femina* among readers of the fortnightly magazine and *Readers Digest* among readers of the monthly magazine. The maximum sample read *Times of India* newspaper. Full-time housewives topped the list of members in a club. Cent per cent watched TV serials. 'Rajani' TV serial topped the list with cent per cent viewers and also took its first position from the point of view of projecting a positive image of women. Most of the full-time housewives found advertisements as sex-oriented. In the case of the opinion of respondents regarding the depiction of women in Indian films and TV commercials the percentage of negative views were relatively more, and students and full-time housewives were highly displeased with the image of women portrayed in Indian films and TV commercials. With respect to the attitude scale, a relatively higher percentage revealed a positive attitude. The respondents felt that the use of the female body as a mere decoration or as an attention-getting device which diminishes women's self-esteem and ignores other aspects of their personality and potentials, should be discouraged. Occupational status and readership level emerged as determinants of opinion scores whereas the readership level and frequency of TV watching emerged as determinants of attitude scores.

***Title: Determinants of Women's Awareness of Legal Rights and Coping Behaviour in Redressal of Their Problems***

*Author:* Chitra Mahajan

*Guide:* Nalini Ogale

*Year:* 1990

*Keywords:* Women awareness, Legal rights, Coping behaviour, Problems

## Introduction

Women in India suffer from a variety of social and economic disabilities which prevent them from exercising their human rights and freedom in society. During the last few decades, a number of legislations have been passed with a view to ensuring equality of status and opportunity for women. Therefore, it is important to find out how far women are a ware of the radical changes in the law and to assess their knowledge about their rights related to property, marriage and dowry.

## Methodology

The descriptive survey methodology with the case study method was adopted to study the research problem. The interview technique was used to collect the information. For the selection of sample, the purposive sampling method was used. The sample was confined to 150 women of Delhi city from two selected localities. Fifteen case studies in total were done. Five cases from each of three areas were included, which were divorce, dowry and property. For the purpose of data analysis correlation and t-test were used.

## Major Findings

The sample shared the dominance of nuclear families. The number of children in 70 per cent of the families ranged from 1 to 2. It was revealed that 90 per cent of the respondents were married and 6 per cent were widows. About 3 per cent were single and the remaining two respondents were divorced. A majority of the respondents were young or middle aged, literate, followed. Hinduism and were not gainfully employed. The mean income of the family was Rs. 175. Regarding the extent of awareness about the existence of the legal rights it was revealed that 38 per cent of the respondents had a medium extent of awareness and about 35 per cent had a high level of awareness. It was found that age, education and employment were the key determinants of the extent of awareness. Existence of property right and right of divorce was commonly known among the women respondents. From the case studies certain emerging trends in coping styles were identified. The better educated victims took legal measures for solving their problems. The respondents with a higher extent of awareness showed a positive style of coping, hence it was concluded that victims generally reported of having action-oriented styles, that is, positive styles.

*Title: A Study of Milk Consumption Pattern of Households and Homemakers views Regarding Baroda Dairy Milk versus Vendors' Milk*

*Author:* Bharati Sawant

*Guide:* Kamala Srinivasan

*Year:* 1991

*Keywords:* Milk, consumption, consumption pattern, consumer

## INTRODUCTION

A household's consumption of goods and services depends on individual preferences. Buying food involves the selection of so many different items and is done so often that many people, in addition to families, are concerned with it. Among the food items, the importance of milk is well known. Milk is considered as a complete food. Milk supply in urban areas is met by dairy as well as private vendors. There are many consumers who prefer milk from vendors to that of the pasteurized milk supplied by Baroda dairy. This study attempted to determine the milk consumption pattern of sample households, in terms of the type of milk consumed per month, the quantity, expenditure incurred per month, and the significance of the impact of various demographic and socio-economic characteristics on milk buying practices.

## METHODOLOGY

A descriptive study was planned along with an interview schedule to collect the data. The total sample comprised 120 homemakers belonging to three market segment areas with a purposive deliberate sampling, viz., Shiya baug (low income), Makarpura (middle income) and Motibaug (high income). The data were subjected to a statistical analysis by using frequency, percentage and measures of central tendency and dispersion. Chi-square and 't' test of pooled variance were used for testing the hypotheses.

## MAJOR FINDINGS

The income level of families, the mean size of families and the joint family type showed a positive relationship. Significant mean differences in the income of households as well as family were found between income classes. The educational level of the spouse and the occupational status were significantlyassociated with the income class. An inverse relationship was found between the income class and the wife's gainful employment. There was a positive 'income effect' on milk expenditure between income classes. Vendors' milk dominated over dairy milk for the overall sample households. The share of mean milk expenditure by three income groups substantiated Engels' law of consumption. There was a significant mean difference of milk intake between income classes during ordinary days, festivals, rituals, social functions and an emergency situation. The opinions of respondents significantly related to the income level of the households. Vendors' milk scored high for the hygienic factor and Baroda dairy milk scored high for other three factors, viz., availability and accessibility, economy and product attribute. There was cent per cent awareness regarding new information packaging material, brought out by the Baroda Dairy. The existing sizes were found satisfactory by a majority of the respondents. The comprehension level of the qualitative information inclined with the income class. There was a significant association between the number of children, the education and age of the homemaker, the income of households and the type of milk consumed whereas the size and type of family, the number of children, the household income and the quantity of milk purchased were significantly associated. There was a significant association between the source from which households purchased the milk and their views.

***Title: Households' Purchase Behaviour, Brands Preference and Performance Evaluation of Two Competing Brands of Refrigerators – A Segmentation Analysis***

*Author:* Alpa Vora

*Guide:* Kamala Srinivasan

*Year:* 1991

*Keywords:* Consumer, brand, performance, preference, purchase behaviour, refrigerator, equipment

## Introduction

Different kinds of household equipment, which can considerably reduce drudgery and improve work productivity, have become a boon to homemakers, a especially in the urban region. The challenge facing modern families is how to make wise use of resources to make wise choices in the marketplace that reflect their real needs and desire. Producers of different household equipment like refrigerators may not be aware of the changing needs of the families and satisfaction desired by them from consumer durable goods. The present investigation was undertaken to study the buying behaviour of the sample households, an awareness regarding the nature and type of facilities available in the selected brands of refrigerators, and to assess the satisfaction of homemakers regarding their refrigerators with a view to build a valuable database for refrigerators, producers and promoters' use.

## Methodology

A descriptive research design was selected, using the survey method for the present study. A precoded and structured interview schedule was used as a data gathering instrument. A purposive sampling technique was used to select the sample of 60 households from each ward, of which 30 households were having Voltas refrigerator and 30 households were having Kelvinator. Descriptive statistics such as mean and standard deviation were computed to interpret the tables, and 't' test of pooled variance and chi-square were used for testing hypotheses.

## Major Findings

There was a significant relationship between the educational level of homemakers and the timing of the purchase of the refrigerator, the source of information and family members involved in decision making regarding the purchase of the refrigerator. Income class and the size of the refrigerator had a significant relationship. A greater percentage of middle income class took advantage of off-season as well as discount sale purchase. Most of the respondents had come across TV advertisements and found them most popular. There was a significant relationship between the education level of homemakers and their views regarding the kind of advertisement. Most of the homemakers were satisfied, only 2.5 per cent were not satisfied with their purchase decision. Most of the homemakers found television advertisement useful and it affected their decision while purchasing their refrigerator. Income class and the mode of purchase were significantly related to each other. 'Look' and 'cooling power' took the first ranking for Voltas and Kelvinator refrigerators, respectively, by the users of the respective brands. Voltas took the first position followed by Kelvinator, Godrej, Volga and Allwyn.

***Title: Extent of Awareness, Utilisation and Satisfaction of the Customers with the Services of LIC of India***

*Author:* Manisha Sharma

*Guide:* Maneesha Shukul

*Year:* 1992

*Keywords:* Awareness, utilisation, satisfaction, customers, services of LIC

## Introduction

Life insurance has become an important part of everyone's life all over the world. LIC of India has diversified its business by creating various subsidiaries, such as LIC Housing Finance and LIC Mutual Fund. Though people have been taking advantage of LIC of India it is essential to know the quantum of utilisation of various services and policies offered by it. At the same time there is also a need to find out the awareness of people regarding policies and services provided by LIC, and to find out the satisfaction of customers with LIC of India.

## Methodology

A descriptive research design was used for the study. An interview schedule was used for data collection. From the list of 500 claimants, 120 were selected through systematic random sampling. They were the customers of LIC who made claims and had one more policy at the time of data collection. The sample was from Agra city.

### Major Findings

A majority of the respondents had a low and medium extent of awareness regarding LIC policies and services. A wide majority of the respondents had low utilisation of policies and services provided by LIC of India. A wide majority of the respondents were highly satisfied with their services. The extent of awareness, utilisation and satisfaction were influenced by education and family income amongst all the selected variables. Apart from this, the extent of awareness was influenced by their occupation, exposure to the sources of information, sex and number of adults in family. The extent of the utilisation was also influenced by their exposure to the sources of information, sex, the number of adults the number of policies and the extent of awareness. A positive relationship was found between extent of utilisation and satisfaction. The extent of awareness and utilisation were found to be positively correlated with each other.

*Title: An Exploratory Study on the Diffusion and Uses of Video Cassette Recorders – Opinions of its Impact, Perceived Changes in Lifestyle and Consumer Satisfaction – A Segmentation Analysis*

*Author:* Sejoo Maheshwari

*Guide:* Kamala Srinivasan

*Year:* 1992

*Keywords:* Consumer, diffusion, video cassette reorders, lifestyle, opinion, satisfaction

### Introduction

Communication media like television, radio, newspapers, films contribute largely to bring a change in human behaviour. Television and video are innovations that are widely used to create awareness, knowledge, entertainment, trial and adoption. TV and video are powerful media of mass communication with the capability to create revolutions in ideas and processes of social transformation in developing societies like India. However, not many statistical data are available on different aspects of VCRs in households in India, such as family life, impact on children, changing opinions, purposes of VCR use, brand preferences, complaints of consumers and so on. Hence, the present study was undertaken to study the impact of VCR on family interaction and lifestyle, influence on children, compare the brand preferences, and identify the consumer satisfaction of quality and performance of different brands of VCR.

## Methodology

A descriptive research design was selected, using a survey method, for the present study. A precoded questionnaire-cum-interview schedule was used for data collection. The multi-stage sampling method was adopted for the selection of video cassette libraries and for the selection of samples. Two different localities in Baroda city were selected to stratify the income group levels of sample households, using the random-cum-purposive sampling procedure. A sample of 40 households each from different areas consisted of the total sample of 80 households. The data were analysed in terms of measures of central tendency, and measures of dispersion. For testing the postulated hypotheses, 't' test of pooled variance, chi-square test and Spearman Brown's rank correlation test were used.

## Major Findings

The educational and occupational status of the families owning VCRs was high. Most of the respondents were graduates and postgraduates. The income levels of the two area segments were found to have a wide difference which was found statistically significant. VCR viewing householders were found to be progressive minded and modern with traits of adaptability. The socio-economic status of the families also emerged as a variable influencing upon the outlook of the families and their lifestyle. 'Entertainment' and 'to watch at convenient timings' were highly motivational factors for purchasing VCRs. VCRs were used mostly for the purposes of watching movies and recording TV programmes. Entertainment expenditure was felt to have increased after the introduction of VCR. The high income class showed less influence of VCR in their family life than the middle income class. Parents were concerned about satisfying their children's desires for video viewing opportunities and preferences. The VCR adopting households were found to be progressive, modern and outgoing, and liberal in behaviour in all aspects including control on their children. There was a great degree of consumer satisfaction on the quality and overall performance, repair and after-sales services. Families have positive views on the changing communication technology and they try to adopt themselves to the new social set-up. Owning a VCR had no impact on their work schedule and their family life.

***Title: A Study to Assess Knowledge, Utilisation and Satisfaction Expressed by the Consumers Regarding Telecommunication Services***

*Author:* Anjana Palkar

*Guide:* Veena Gandotra

*Year:* 1995

*Keywords:* Consumer, telecommunication services, satisfaction, knowledge, utilisation

### Introduction

Telecommunication has expanded at a high speed during the recent years, and has become a common and easily accessible means of communication. In India, the telecommunication network is a monopoly of the government, and thus its quality and prices could be regulated. A study was undertaken to find out the services provided by the department of telecommunication, and to assess knowledge, utilisation and satisfaction of homemakers regarding these services.

### Methodology

An exploratory-cum-diagnostic research design was selected for the study. A survey method was thought to be the best. The interview schedule was employed to gather data. The knowledge scale was tested for its reliability and validity. The reliability coefficient for knowledge test was found to be 0.78. A purposive random sampling technique was used to select 110 respondents.

Data thus obtained were coded and categorised. For data analysis, descriptive and inferential statistics employed were simple frequency, percentage, mean, standard deviation and canonical correlation analysis.

## MAJOR FINDINGS

A majority of the telephones were personally subscribed and most of the respondents' families possessed telephones since last 14 years or less (90%). The various services provided by the department of telecommunication were found from the department itself. Most of the respondents obtained moderate scorers on the knowledge test regarding the awareness of the services provided by the department of telecommunications. The average utilisation of telephone was found to be 367.3 units and the cost for the same was Rs. 72. Telephone was used mostly by all the members of the family, but there were some services which were not utilised by the respondents' families most of the times. Respondents were quite satisfied with some services like 'morning alarm', 'time', 'postal enquiry' and 'directory inquiry'. Problems while installation and related to the instrument and repairs were faced by a majority of the respondents' families. For solving the problems, most of the time respondents approached the exchange and gave oral or written complaints. There existed a relationship among the independent variables, like age, education, occupation, family income, mode of ownership and category, on the dependent variables, like knowledge regarding the services, utilisation of them and satisfaction gained from the use. The type of exchange had no relationship with the extent of the problems.

***Title: Consumer Preference and Perception of Attributes of Toilet soaps in Relation to Advertisement and Experience***
*Author:* Minal Trivedi
*Guide:* Rachel George
*Year:* 1995
*Keywords:* Consumer, advertisement, Attitudes, perception, experience, toilet soaps

## INTRODUCTION

The Indian consumer, both in urban and rural areas, now has much more purchasing power. With the explosion of new products in the market, choice making for consumer item is becoming more and more difficult. Producers try to sell their products through deceptive advertisements. A review of literature revealed that many studies have been undertaken to measure the effectiveness of advertisement. A few have been undertaken to study the effectiveness of different media. But very little effort has gone to assess consumer preference and perception in relation to advertisement in the area of toilet items. Hence, the present study was undertaken to determine the buying practices related to toilet soaps, exposure of consumers to mass media, to ascertain respondents' opinion towards advertisements, consumer preference, and perception of the attributes of toilet soaps before and after using the brand of toilet soap purchased due to the influence of advertisements.

## METHODOLOGY

A descriptive research design with the survey method was selected for the study. A questionnaire schedule was employed to gather data. The preference and perception scales were used which were standardised and their reliability co-efficient was 0.76 and 0.83 respectively. A purposive random sampling technique was used to select a sample of 112 housewives. For data analysis descriptive and inferential statistics employed were frequency, percentage, means, standard deviation, co-efficient of correlation and analysis of variance. Wherever significant F values were obtained 't' test was applied.

## MAJOR FINDINGS

A majority of the respondents used toilet soap cakes of various brands under the influence of advertisements. Monthly bulk purchase of toilet soaps was made by a majority of the respondents since it was most convenient to them. Most of the respondents purchased toilet soaps from retail shops and departmental stores due to shopping convenience and habit of purchasing from a single point. Importance was given to the composition of the product of information on the package by a majority of the respondents. Quality was ranked the highest by the respondents while buying soaps. Most of the respondents considered brand name more frequently than other factors. Television was the most useful media and the most preferred one by most of the respondents. Most of the respondents felt that advertisement makes shopping easier by providing comparative information though they were aware of the deceptive characteristics of the advertisements. They were highly influenced by the advertisements. Most of the respondents looked for the presence of a moisturiser when they bought the soap. Most of the respondents wanted to stick to the preferred brand even if other cheaper brands and gift offers were available. The most preferred soap in the first preference was E Vita, and Camay was purchased under the influence of advertisements. There existed a negative correlation between the consumer preference to toilet soap and age, education of the housewife, size of the family and income of the family. There existed a negative correlation between the perception on attributes of toilet soaps and the age of the housewife and a positive correlation between the perception on attributes of toilet soaps and influence of advertisement media.

***Title: A Study of the Buying Process Undergone by Families for the Purchase of an Automatic Washing Machine***

*Author:* Shailee Mehta

*Guide:* Asha Dass

*Year:* 1996

*Keywords:* Buying process, washing machine, automatic washing machine, consumer equipment

## INTRODUCTION

Domestic work in Indian homes is very time-consuming and tiring. Homemakers spent on an average about six hours a week on washing clothes which is a heavy job and which consumes much energy of the worker. It is being slowly replaced by the mechanical servant washing machine. Availability of many brands of washing machines in the market makes the buyer to think on what to buy to suit the family's needs and wants. The buying process involves steps of related and sequential stages. Hence, to study the buying process perceived by families for the purchase of fully automatic washing machine, the present study was undertaken. The study also attempted to find the problems faced by homemakers regarding the washing machines they owned.

## Methodology

A survey method was used with an interview schedule as a tool for collecting the data. A purposive sampling technique was used to select the sample of 120 respondents from Alkapuri of Baroda city. Data collected were coded and tabulated. For statistical analysis descriptive statistics of mean, standard deviation and percentage were applied. A canonical correlation analysis was applied to test the hypotheses postulated.

## Major Findings

A majority of the respondents were graduates and from nuclear families. A maximum number of respondents had bought IFB-BOSCH, TVS and Videocon washing machines during 1993 to 1995. THe husband was the decision maker in the purchase, in a majority of the cases. Various factors which influenced respondents to identify their need to own a washing machine were 'non-availability of services', and inefficiency of services by majority of respondents followed by saving time and energy, frequent guests, convenience and poor quality of washing by hand. Exposure to advertisements through various media also played an important role in identifying the need to own a washing machine. The need for recognition led the respondent to other three important steps of buying process, i.e., information search, evaluation of alternatives and purchase decision. The information they collected was maximum in regard to price, capacity, durability, brand, design, construction, convenience features and safety features while in evaluation of alternatives step, most of them considered brand, capacity, durability, convenience and safety features. A majority of the respondents preferred capacity, durability and brand as the most important attributes while giving their final preference. There was a great correlation between the importance given to product attributes and the preference given to product attributes. Most of the respondents of all the brands were satisfied with the operational cost of the washing machine in terms of electricity, water and detergent consumption. The problems faced by a few respondents were hand-wash to clean collars of shirts, more water consumption and cannot put coloured clothes with white clothes. There was a good relationship between the preference given to product attributes, and personal and family variables.

***Title: A study to Assess Knowledge, Utilization and Satisfaction Expressed by the Consumer and Their Problems Regarding Railways***

*Author:* Umrana Shaikh

*Guide:* Veena Gandotra

*Year:* 1996

*Keywords:* Consumer, knowledge, utilization, satisfaction, railways, problems

## Introduction

Railways is the principal mode of transport for freight and passengers. It plays an integrating role as people move across the country for business, sightseeing, pilgrimage, education, etc., and bring together the people of far-flung states. There are some problems which are faced by an average railway user. The consumers are not aware of the various facilities available for their benefit. An analytical approach to consumerism emphasizes data collection to help understand the consumer's needs and behaviour. It provides essential facts on which improvements can be made. The study was undertaken to find out the consumers' knowledge, extent of utilisation and problems faced regarding the facilities provided by the railways.

## Methodology

An exploratory research design was used. The survey method was selected and an interview schedule was employed for data collection. A knowledge scale was prepared and its reliability established. It was found to be 0.83. A total sample comprising 120 respondents, 40 each from three income groups, were randomly selected. The data thus tabulated were further analysed in terms of simple frequencies, percentage distribution, mean and standard deviation. Chi-square test and coefficient of correlation were used to test the hypotheses.

## Major Findings

A majority of the respondents were travelling sometimes but had a moderate level of knowledge regarding the facilities provided by the railways. Some facilities which were utilised by most of the respondents (50 to 70%) were making reservation in advance, making inquiry on telephone regarding train schedule, use of retiring rooms and dormitories, licensed posters, pantry cars and buffets. However, there were many facilities which were never utilised, like vigilance organisation, tourist cars, Indrail passes, concessional facilities, use of safe deposit lockers, wheel chair facility. The one facility which was used by all respondents was booking ticket in advance. Many of the respondents were satisfied with the various facilities that they utilised, like tourist cars, concessional facilities for various purposes, Indrail passes, making reservation bed roll facility, etc., while inquiry on telephone, rail travellers, agents, retiring rooms etc. were the facilities with which they were not satisfied. Many problems were faced by the respondents at the railway station, such as latrines and bathrooms being dirty, good and hygienic food not available, announcements regarding platform numbers and train timings not given clearly. The problems faced by passengers during a journey in the train were improper provision of light, fan, water and latrines, reserved, berths occupied by unreserved passengers, insufficient police protection, no proper coach numbers, etc., the knowledge of respondents varied with their education and the income of the family, while utilisation of services was affected by income, education and occupation of the respondents. The satisfaction of services was found to be not significantly related to the selected variables. The problems faced by respondents had a significant relationship with age, education, occupation and income of the family. Further knowledge had a positive relation with utilisation but not with problems. Utilisation has a significant relation with satisfaction but not with problems. So finally it could be concluded that if the knowledge of the respondents increases, utilisation also increases, and it leads to an increase in satisfaction and decrease in problems.

***Title: A Study of Opinion of Consumers towards Department Store and the Products Purchased***

*Author:* Aditi Vats

*Guide:* Maneesha Shukul

*Year:* 1997

*Keywords:* Opinion, consumers, department store

## Introduction

Marketing starts with the consumer and ends with the consumer. Various retail outlets satisfy the consumers' demands on buying goods. Today's consumers find it convenient to buy from 'one-stop-shop', i.e., the department store where various products are kept under one roof to meet the consumers' numerous needs. Several factors are affecting the store patronage. Being a new retail outlet, it was considered important as well as interesting to know the opinion of consumers regarding the department stores. Hence, the present study was undertaken to find out the products purchased and the frequency of their purchase from department stores, the opinion of consumers about the department stores, and to study the relationship between the opinion of the consumers about the department stores and selected variables.

## Methodology

The present study was a descriptive survey. An interview schedule was used as a tool for data collection. Content validity and reliability were established for opinions. The reliability coefficient of correlation value was 0.61. A systematic random sampling was followed to select a sample of 120 respondents from two department stores, i.e., Pkds and Kalpataru in Baroda city. The data were analysed by using the descriptive and inferential statistics. The descriptive statistics applied were frequency, percentage distribution and measures of central tendency. Pearsons product moment coefficient of correlation, F test and 't' tests were the relational statistics that were applied.

## Major Findings

More than half of the respondents were graduates and females. Most of the respondents purchased the items monthly and had good opinions about 'store location', 'store design and physical facilities', 'merchandise' offered in department store, 'advertising and sales promotion'. On the whole most of the respondents (64.20%) had a good opinion about the department store. The opinion of male and female respondents were not significantly different. The opinions of the respondents differed according to the age and total family income. It was negatively associated with age but positively associated with income. However, the opinions of the respondents regarding store did not vary due to their education and occupation. The respondents of Kalpataru had a better opinion about the store than those of Pkd's.

***Title: A Study of Information Search Behaviour of Consumers Involved in the Purchase of a Vehicle***

*Author:* Vibha Bhargava

*Guide:* Veena Gandotra

*Year:* 1997

*Keywords:* Consumer, vehicle, information search behaviour

## Introduction

Mobility is a fact of modern life, and to cope up with it, more people own vehicles today. Purchasing a vehicle is an expensive financial responsibility. The average individual family feels this and therefore a wise selection of the vehicle requires thought and effort in the decision-making process which in turn is governed by information search. Thus, the present study was undertaken to find out the information collected by respondents regarding the attributes of vehicles and financial agencies disbursing loans, to find the information sources used for collecting information regarding vehicles before making the purchase, to determine the order of importance of information sources as considered by the respondents, and to assess the information search behaviour of consumers involved in the purchase of a two-wheeler and a four-wheeler.

## Methodology

A descriptive research design was selected for the present study and the survey method was used. An interview schedule was employed to collect data. A stratified random sampling technique was adopted to select a sample of 60 two wheeler owners and 60 four-wheeler owners. For data analysis the descriptive and relational statistics employed were frequency, percentage, mean, standard deviation, co-efficient of correlation, analysis of variance and 't' test.

## Major Findings

A majority of the purchasers of two wheelers as well as four-wheelers paid in cash and self-financed their purchases. 'Driving comfort', 'technology', 'pick up' and 'fuel efficiency' were the high ranked attributes of vehicles considered by the respondents when they went for a purchase. Regarding the attributes of sources of finance, 'fast clearance', and 'rate of interest' at which loan was offered were the attributes considered most relevant by the respondents.

The respondents relied more on personal and experiential sources as compared to commercial and public sources for collecting information before making the purchase. Nearly half of the respondents for two wheelers, four wheelers as well as the total sample had good information search behaviour while the other half had poor information search behaviour. There was no difference in the information search behavior of respondents involved in the purchase of two-wheelers and four-wheelers. Age was the only variable influencing the information search behaviour. There was no significant relationship between the income, level of education and employment status, and the information search behaviour of the respondents.

***Title: A Study of Frequency and Use of Convenience Food and the Opinion of Users and Non-users towards It***

*Author:* Sonal Bhavsar

*Guide:* Veena Gandotra

*Year:* 1998

*Keywords:* Convenience food, Opinion

## Introduction

Convenience foods are those products in which all or a significant portion of their preparation have been transferred from the consumer's kitchen to the processing unit. The use of convenience foods has increased due to many reasons, one of the prime one being 'time and energy saving' component. Increasing number of convenience foods are available in the market; some are comparable with home made products. A study was conducted to find out exactly the frequency of use of convenience foods the opinion of user and non–user homemakers towards convenience food.

## Methodology

The research design was the descriptive survey. Two departmental stores were purposively selected. A list of customers who were users and non-users of convenience food purchase/not purchased from these stores was prepared by visiting the stores for two hours in the evening (rush hour) for three days. From the list thus obtained 120 users and 120 non-users were identified, and from them 60 users and 60 non-users were considered as the sample. The data were gathered through an interview as literacy level was expected to be varied. The tool contained an opinionnaire about convenience food which was subjected to establishment of validity and reliability (split half). Coefficient of correlation, $x^2$, ANOVA and t-test were applied to test the hypotheses.

## Major Findings

A little less than half of the non-users of convenience food were in the age group of 45-55 years whereas users were from 25 to 35 years. A majority of the total sample had a medium level of education and most of them were employed. The total monthly family income ranged from Rs. 5000 to Rs. 15,000. Amongst the use Rs of convenience food more than half of the respondents in 25-35 years group having a medium educational level and employed, used the convenience food more frequently. The opinion about convenience food revealed that more than half the users as well as the non-users had a satisfactory opinion. Age was significantly associated with the frequency of use and age and employment were associated with the opinion towards convenience food. All the respondents opined that the end product was not the same as the picture given on the packet.

***Title: Eating Out Practices of Families and Expenditure Incurred on them***

*Author:* Jalpa Majmudar

*Guide:* Veena Gandotra

*Year:* 1999

*Keywords:* Eating out practices, expenditure

## INTRODUCTION

The taste and habits of people keep on changing from time to time. The most significant change is in eating-out habits of people, which has led to a fast growth of the hotel industry. A number of fast food centres have developed everywhere. It is rightly said that today is a fast food generation, no wonder, that now-a-days investors have made forays into the food business by opening chains of restaurants and hotels. People nowdays simply go to eat out because they like having fun and adventure which eating out provides. It has become a way of celebrating occasions with friends, relatives, colleagues or family members. During the past several decades, the number of women who have joined the labour market, is steadily increasing. The time constraints faced by these women and the extra cash they bring to the family could be the motivating force of their eating out more frequently. Thus the present study was planned to gain an insight into the factors underlying eating-out practices of families and find out the expenditure incurred by families on eating out. Also an attempt was made to study the effect of selected variables on eating-out practices of families and the expenditure incurred on them.

## METHODOLOGY

A descriptive research design was adopted for the present study. An interview schedule was used to collect data. The sample was purposively selected from two areas of Baroda, namely, Race Course and Fatehgunj where most of the fast food centres are located. A sample of 30 respondents in each strata, i.e., employed and non-employed homemakers, were selected from a list of families identified in both the areas. Thus a total of 120 respondents were selected.

## MAJOR FINDINGS

A majority of the homemakers belonged to the age group of 36-45 years, and a nuclear family with a family size of 2-4 members. The respondents generally belonged to an income group of Rs. 15,001 to Rs. 30,000 but among the families belonging to non-employed group, nearly 50 per cent belonged to the group income of below Rs. 15,000. Breakfast was the meal generally taken at home. Nearly three-fourths of the respondents did not take lunch outside. Dinner was the meal that the family preferred to take outside. Most of the respondents ate out just for a change and nearly half of them ate out because they liked the taste of food.

Another popular reason for eating out was festivals and also occasions like birthdays and anniversaries. With regard to the characteristics of the type of place of eating it was found that elders preferred places which were clean and hygienic while children liked places where the taste of food was good. Nearly three-fourths of the homemakers ordered Punjabi food when they ate outside, probably because a majority of the respondents were Gujarati. Children liked Chinese food when they ate outside. Nearly all of the respondents ate icecream at ice-cream parlours or restaurants.

With regard to packed food it was found that nearly half of the respondents ordered packed food so that they could eat in the comfortable and informal surrounding of their homes. Employed homemakers ordered packed food when they were tired and non-employed ordered when they had guests. However for picnics nearly three-fourths of the respondents bought food from outside but they did not go for picnic very often. A majority of the respondents ate out on birthdays and anniversaries and nearly half of them preferred to eat out on Diwali and Dussehra festivals. Nearly three-fourths of the respondents in both the groups spent below Rs. 500 per month on eating out; very few spent more than Rs. 1000 on eating out. The data on expenditure on various types of food revealed that the highest expenditure was on Punjabi food for all family members. The mean expenditure on non-vegetarian food was generally made by husbands. The children spent the maximum on Chinese and fast foods. The results of the test conducted revealed a significant relationship between the employment status and the frequency of eating out, i.e., employed ate more frequently than the non-employed.

With regard to relationship between expenditure and selected variables it was found that age and the employment status of the respondents affected the expenditure incurred on eating out. With regard to the meals it was found that as the age of the homemakers increased the expenditure on eating breakfast out increased but eating dinner out decreased.

***Title: Purchase Behaviour of the Families with Reference to the House***

*Author:* Ruchi Tandon

*Guide:* Veena Gandotra

*Year:* 1999

*Keywords:* Purchase behaviour, families, house

## Introduction

Housing is one of the basic necessities of life next to food and clothing. It needs no emphasis that it constitutes one of the major requirements of the people, and it assumes a special significance in the vast changing socio-economic conditions. Housing and physical environment are defined by three simple measures which are dwelling conditions, the fraction of income spent on housing and the degree of satisfaction expressed with the house. Hence every family wants to purchase or invest in a house.

## METHODOLOGY

A descriptive research design was used. The sample size was 120 respondents and the samples were collected from Akota area of Baroda city. The sampling procedure for the study was "snowball method". Interview schedule was used as a tool to gather the data for data analysis, descriptive as well as relational statistics were used, namely, frequency, mean, coefficient, of correlation, t-test and F-test.

## MAJOR FINDINGS

A majority of the respondents wanted to own a house for economic security, freedom to live and to meet the growing needs of the family. Most of the respondents had seen the cost of the house in relation to the mode of payment and also analysed the costs and benefits of owning a house. The respondents gathered the information from various sources, like family members, relatives, friends, etc. The evaluating criteria were availability of electric supply, cost, water supply, quality of construction, privacy, facilities, etc. Most of the respondents, in spite of carrying out intensive search, were not highly satisfied with their choice. The husband's income was significantly related to the satisfaction. Also, the husband's education and information search behaviour were significantly related. The information search behaviour was also significantly related in the satisfaction.

***Title: Knowledge and Utilisation of Food Products with Standardisation Marks and Awareness Regarding Prevention of Food Adulteration Act 1954***

*Author:* Bhavna Gupta

*Guide:* Vijaya Lakshmi Yadla

*Year:* 1999

*Keywords:* Knowledge, utilisation, food products, standardisation marks, awareness, Food Adulteration Act

## Introduction

The quality control and checking of manufactured goods, although existing on paper, is not prevalent in practice. Adulteration of edible articles has assumed such proportions today that the consumer is constantly exposed to the danger of the health hazards resulting from consumption of such articles. It was with a view to fighting this menace of adulteration that the Prevention of Food Adulteration (PFA) Act was enacted and standard marks were given to various food products enabling the consumer to have a choice of choosing food items that are safe and pure for human consumption. Keeping these things in mind the present investigation was undertaken to assess the knowledge and utilisation of food products with standardisation marks and awareness about PFA.

## Methodology

A descriptive research design was used. A questionnaire was used to collect data. The sample of 80 respondents was selected through accidental sampling technique from Pratapgunj and Karelibaug areas of Baroda city. Descriptive statistics employed were frequency, percentage, mean and standard deviation while inferential statistics employed were coefficients of correlation and analysis variance.

## Major Findings

A majority of the respondents purchased white fats, mustard powder, sugar and jaggery with Agmark, while most of the frequently purchased items with ISI were Swiss rolls, candies, toffees, cakes and jelly sweets. Chutneys, fruit boxes, onion and ginger paste with FPO marks were purchased by a majority. Most of the respondents purchased products bearing ISI marks to prevent health hazards, and even if purchases were made by servants, it was made sure that it had standardisation marks. Most of the respondents knew that imprisonment was given to the manufacturer if adulterated food caused injury to health and when food weighed less than the prescribed weight. The testing of hypotheses revealed that the older and highly educated people have more knowledge about food products with standardisation marks. The unemployed and those living in joint family were more knowledgeable about food products. The high income group uses less of the products with these marks as they don't have time, and depend on paid help. The highly educated and old people and those living in a joint family are aware of the PFA Act in comparison to their counterparts.

***Title: Development and Impact Assessment of Educational Programme on Wise Buying***

*Authors:* Ami Shah

*Guide:* Neerja Jaiswal

*Year:* 2001

*Key words:* Wise buying, Educational programme, Impact assessment

## Introduction

An educated and well-informed consumer is an asset to any society. A person can attain the attributes of a good consumer through consumer education which is a prerequisite for the success of consumerism. Consumer education is needed in India because of the sharp diversity in attitudes, awareness and spending habits of Indian consumers in rural and urban areas. The Indian consumers do not get the best value for money as they lack accurate information, mainly due to ignorance and illiteracy about consumer rights and responsibilities. Thus the need of the consumer is well realized. A study was conducted for the development and impact assessment of educational programme on wise buying. It also aimed to study functioning, activities and educational programmes done by the consumer organization of Mumbai metropolitan city.

## Methodology

The research was descriptive as well as experimental in nature. A pre-validated interview schedule was used as a tool to collect the data from consumer organizations. A questionnaire was used to collect data from 108 homemakers as respondents, who were members of a Mahila Madal (Women's Club). An educational programme on "Wise Buying" was developed through slides shown on the computer and accompanied by live commentary. The awareness of respondents was assessed prior to and after the administration of the educational programme. The awareness scale about "Wise Buying" consisted of 17 stories/situations with two options for answer – one correct and the other incorrect way of buying. The scores obtained by each respondent were considered to decide the extent of awareness.

## Major Findings

The information about consumer organization in Mumbai revealed that they were NGOs: they had their own publications: they used a variety of media for consumer redressal activity followed by educational campaigns. Based on the feedback from these organizations, an educational programme on "Rights and Responsibilities" and "Redressal Methods" to be imparted through the electronic media was developed and tested for its effectiveness on 108 member homemakers of one of these NGOs. Most of these homemakers were between the age of 26 and 35 years, majority were educated up to 10$^{th}$ standard; they were not employed; and belonged to low income group. The respondents had low exposure to sources of information which had led to a low score on the awareness scale for 'wise buying' before administration of the educational programme. The educational programme consisted of a lecture and a slide show on the computer followed by a live commentary. The educational programme consisted of four stories developed by the investigators, covering all the principles of "Wise Buying", having suitable illustrations developed by the artist. The respondents awareness before and after the exposure to the educational programme differed significantly as revealed through paired t-test. The study revealed a need of consumer education.

***Title: Bank Services: Awareness, Utilisation and Customer Satisfaction***

*Author:* Namrata Singh

*Guide:* Neerja Jaiswal

*Year:* 2002

*Keywords:* Bank services, awareness, utilisation, customer satisfaction

## Introduction

Customer service is the most important aspect of the banking operations. Prompt and efficient service with a smile will develop good public relations, reduce complaints and increase business. The most important requirement for financial institutions like commercial banks is to understand and anticipate a customer's needs. Thus the prime function of banks is the creation and delivery of customer-needed services in a customer-satisfying manner. Banking being a service industry, the success of a bank will naturally depend upon the range and quality of services offered. With all the changes taking place in the financial marketplace and the increase in the competition, it becomes apparent that more attention must be given to customer service and customer satisfaction. In India the field is yet to be explored to a greater extent which motivated the investigator to conduct such a study.

## Methodology

The research was descriptive in nature. The study comprised 100 respondents, 50 each from the State Bank of India and the Bank of Baroda (BOB), selected purposively from Agra city. The survey method was utilised to collect the data. The data were analysed by employing descriptive (mean and percentage) as well as relational statistics (ANOVA, Scheffe's test, 't'-test and regression analysis).

## Major Findings

Awareness regarding the various bank services offered by the banks was found to be good among the respondents of both the banks. Utilisation regarding the various bank services revealed that deposit schemes were more utilised by the BOB respondents whereas the rest of the services the special deposit schemes, advance schemes, retail lending and other services were more utilised by SBI respondents. Miscellaneous services of the bank were almost equally utilised by BOB and SBI respondents. Most of the respondents of both the banks were satisfied with the services provided by their banks. The majority of the respondents did not face problems while operating their banks. The statistical findings depicted that the awareness and utilisation of the respondents engaged in service were significantly better than the respondents engaged in business. Respondents under the income range of ≤Rs. 10,000 had more utilisation and satisfaction related to bank service. Awareness regarding bank services was found to be much influencing factor for satisfaction.

***Title: Services Provided by Tours and Travel Agency: A Study of Consumer Satisfaction***

*Author:* Nipa Mehta

*Guide:* Veena Gandotra

*Year:* 2002

*Keywords:* Services, tours and travel agency, consumer satisfaction

## Introduction

The tourism industry in this country has gradually become highly competitive. Today people travel in groups for social, religious and economic reasons. With the advent of modern means of transportation and communication, travel for pleasure has become feasible, attractive and within the reach of many people. Package tours are cheaper than the individual tours, and there is no botheration of any kind of booking or reservation. The consumer behaviour also has undergone changes. Today, the consumer is educated and well informed. The present research was undertaken to study the consumer satisfaction from the services provided by the tours and travel agencies.

## Methodology

A descriptive research design was used for the present study. An interview schedule was used for collecting data. The sample comprised 60 families who had undertaken national level tours, 30 families who had undertaken local level tours, and 30 families who had undertaken international tours The target group for the present study was families who had been on package tours in the past six years. Data we collected through the snowball method. The procedure used to analyse the data were categorisation, coding, tabulation and statistical analysis.

## Major Findings

Mostly people plan the package tours once in a year. Many of the respondents did not have the benefit of LIC. Most of the people chose the package tour because of no botheration of anything, also the package tours were well planned. Most of the tourists had good experience and they were satisfied with the services provided by tours and travel agencies and also in relation to the money spent for package tour. Some of them wanted improvement in all the facilities, such as the quality of food, the time for sightseeing must be increased, the hotel should be clean and cheaper, etc. Most of the agencies planned the tour during Diwali and summer time because of the availability of holidays. The South is less hot during Diwali and the weather is quite pleasant in the summer time in hill stations. It was found that the frequency per year of national, local level tour was more than the international level tours. Most of the agencies tried to fulfil the tourist demands and tried to decrease the complaints. The age of the respondents, the number of adults, and the type of family affected the problems faced by tourists. It was found that when the number of adults increased the satisfaction level decreased. Also the satisfaction was less with more expensive tours than economy tours.

***Title:* Extent of Impact of Selected Television Programmes on Homemakers' Management Practices as Perceived by Them**

*Author:* Richa Tyagi

*Guide:* Asha Dass

*Year:* 2003

*Keywords:* Impact, television, management practices

## Introduction

Television, the powerful medium of communication, is a product of the ongoing modern communication revolution. It commands bigger influence than any other media on the perceptions, emotions and the outlook of the masses. The impact of television on the society is often compared with the effect of "water dripping on a stone steadily, imperceptibly eroding old values and attitudes in favour of new ones". Also in relation to women, television has assumed critical significance in shaping and reshaping the attitudes of them. It is more true in the case of a developing society like India, where women, till recently, were kept away from outside influences through the iron curtain of traditions. Television for her to explore as various women-based programmes are telecast, which talk about spiritual, physical, intellectual, emotional and social development that help them to become perfect homemakers, and provide time for entertainment and relaxation. Hence, the present investigation was undertaken to study the extent of the impact of select television programmes on homemakers' management practices as perceived by them, keeping the following objectives in mind.

## Methodology

A descriptive research design was used. An interview schedule was used to collect data. The sample of the study comprised 120 full-time homemakers of Vadodara city selected through a purposive sampling technique. Frequencies, percentages means, S.D. were computed. Relational statistics like ANOVA, Chi-square and co-efficient of correlation were used to test the relationship between selected variables.

## Major Findings

A majority of the respondents were from the middle age group, and were graduates. Most had their monthly family income ranging between Rs. 10,001 and Rs. 20,000 and had middle-sized families which were at the expanding stage of their family lifecycle. The extent of viewing select television programems was moderate. It was found statistically that no age group, education level, monthly family income and stage of family life -cycle of homemakers had any impact on televiewing practices of homemakers, while the extent of viewing varied only with various family sizes. As the family size increased, the extent of viewing select television programmes decreased. Thus, it could be said that homemakers having large-sized families spend more of their time housework than on a television as the number of family members were more than small-sized families. The availability of TV for watching may also be a reason in a large-sized family. Msot of the respondents reported that they mainly watched television to gain information for self-entertainment and also to learn new ideas to decorate their home. The extent of the impact of select television programmes on homemakers' management practices was reported to be moderate. The homemakers' cooking practices were found to be influenced most by viewing cookery-related programmes. It could be said that the extent of viewing influenced more of cooking practices of the homemakers due to their own inclination towards cooking. Also, statistically no relationship could be traced between the extent of viewing and the impact of select television programmes. The extent of improvement made on homemakers' management practices indicated a positive association with the extent of viewing select television programmes. Moderate improvement was found in homemakers' management practices. The extent of impact had a significant relationship with regard to the extent of improvement made by select television programmes.

*Title: Nature, Extent of Use and Opinion Regarding Impact of Computer by Families: A Comparative Study*

*Author:* Vinita Bhardwaj

*Guide:* Neerja Jaiswal

*Year:* 2003

*Keywords:* Extent of use, opinion, impact of computer, families

## Introduction

The computer is one of the most powerful forces in society today. It is used everywhere, whether it be a home or an organisation. It is widely used in European countries. The Indian families too have come into the mainstream with its increased personal computer usages. Even for the average middle class family a computer is an asset and a means of acquiring its share of information. The computer plays a very important role in developing the skills among the family members. Indepth reviving of literature has highlighted that the computer as an object of investigation has been explored to a greater extent outside India. Many computer-related studies which have been conducted abroad and in India focused on children primarily. But the investigator did not come across the single study on the use of computer-especially in Indian homes. This made her motivated to conceptualise the present study.

## Methodology

The present research was descriptive in nature. The total sample size of 240 comprising 120 husbands and 120 wives from 60 families each of Delhi and Baroda were selected purposively. The survey method was used to collect the data. The data were collected by personal interview of the respondents on a pre-validated and pre-tested interview schedule. The data were analysed by employing descriptive methods of mean and percentage as well as relational statistics (ANOVA, Scheffe's test, 't' test, paired 't' test and chi-square test).

## Major Findings

The women and men in Baroda city were found to be comparatively younger than the women and men in Delhi. Most of them were graduates. The husbands belonging to Baroda had a slightly better educational level than those in Delhi city. It was also found that their educational level was comparatively higher than the wives. Most of the wives were housewives in both the cities, and in the case of husbands, more number of husbands of both the cities were involved in service. Respondents from Delhi were economically better off than those in Baroda. Most of the families were nuclear in structure, but the number of joint families were found to be higher among the respondents of Baroda than those in Delhi. Most of the husbands belonging to Delhi and Baroda were found using the computer outside the home as compared to the wives of both cities. Most of the families in both the cities had assembled computers. Almost all the families of Delhi and Baroda owed a computer at home. The families of both the cities own their computer personally.

Availing internet subscription through Dial-up was found to be popular among the families of both the cities. Most of the respondents were using computers for personal purposes only. City-wise analysis showed that more number of families from Baroda were using computers for personal and commercial purposes compared to those in Delhi. Of all the computer users "searching in world wide web" for educational purposes, "watching movies" and "listening to music" for entertainment purposes were found to be popular uses of computers among the families of both the cities. The extent of the use of computer was found to be comparatively low among the husbands, wives, children and families of both the cities. Husbands from Baroda city had a more favourable opinion regarding the computer, on education, entertainment, information, economic, health and miscellaneous aspects than those in Delhi. In the case of wives also, the wives from Baroda city had a more favourable opinion on education, entertainment, information economic, health and miscellaneous aspects than those in Delhi. The wives Delhi city a more favourable opinion of information and miscellaneous aspects than those in Baroda.

The statistical findings depicted that age, education, occupation computer training type, income of family and use of the computer outside the home, did not make a significant impact on the extent of use and the opinion of wives regarding the impact of computers. There was a variation in the extent of use of the computers with husbands' age and occupation that was mainly business. The extent of the use of the computers varied with the nature of the use of the computers.

***Title: Extent of Awareness, Utilisation, Problems and Satisfaction of Customers Regarding Services Provided by Two Domestic Airlines***

*Author:* Vandana Mahore

*Guide:* Asha Dass

*Year:* 2003

*Keywords:* Awareness, utilisation, problems, satisfaction, customers, services, domestic airlines

## Introduction

Air transport to India is primarily used for passenger transportation, and hence it has a very important role to play in the development of domestic travel in India. The present study was conducted in Vadodara which is one of the high growth rate cities of Gujarat. It lies in the outbound traffic belt and has a very cosmopolitan character. It is connected by Indian Airlines and Jet Airways flights with Mumbai and Delhi. In today's industrial society, the time at the disposal of a traveller is very limited. A leisure traveller may have only a few weeks while the business traveller can afford to spend only a few days.

Consumer psychology is as applicable at present in the travel industry as in any other service industry and thus the consumers like to maximise the returns of their spending. Hence, the objective of the airline industry should be to make an attractive promise, and a valid obligation to provide proper transportation for customers. The cynosure of the industry is customer/traveller. His need, his satisfaction should be the ultimate goal of the airline industries as their prices are to highest compared to other modes of travel.

The collected review of literature gave an insight about the importance of air travel in economic development and a very scanty data has been found in this field till now in India. Since this area has been less explored in Indian conditions, the present study was undertaken. The extent of awareness, utilisation, problems and satisfaction were expressed by the customers regarding services provided by two domestic airlines during their travel from Vadodara to Mumbai and Delhi.

## Methodology

A descriptive research design was used. An interview schedule was used for gathering data. The snowball method was used as a sampling technique. Data were collected from 55 respondents from Indian Airlines and 55 respondents from Jet Airways, thus a total of 110 respondents were taken. The data were analysed employing the descriptive as well as the relational statistics. 't' test, F-test and coefficient of correlation were used to analyse the data.

## Major Findings

The study revealed that mot of the respondents belonged to the middle (35-50 years) and old age (above 51 years) groups, were graduates and were occupied in service and business/professions. The family income of most of them was less than Rs. 30,000 per month. Nearly half of the respondents had travelled seven and more times to Mumbai and one-three times to Delhi in the last two years. Most of them had travelled in the economy class. The main purpose of travel for the majority of the respondents was job related and business. Most of the respondents from both the airlines had medium extent of awareness regarding services, and rules and regulations of the airlines. Almost all of the respondents from both the airlines had utilised services to some extent. A wide majority of the respondents from Indian Airlines and nearly half of the respondents from Jet Airways were least satisfied with the services, while almost one-fourth of them from Indian Airlines and nearly half of them from Jet Airways were moderately satisfied with the services provided by the airlines. Nearly 40 per cent of the respondents from both the airlines faced the problems to a low extent. Apart from this no significant variation was found in the extent of awareness, utilisation, problems and satisfaction with respect to selected personal and family variables of the respondents for both the airlines. The extent of satisfaction and utilisation were found to be positively correlated with each other. No relationship could be traced between the extent of satisfaction and the extent of awareness and problems faced by the respondents regarding the services provided by the airlines.

***Title: Development and Testing of Efficacy of the Educational Programme on the Knowledge of the Homemakers Regarding Food Adulteration, Health Effects and Redressal Mechanism***

*Author:* Shilpi Sharma

*Guide:* Sangeeta Patel

*Year:* 2003

*Keywords:* Educational programmes, knowledge, food adulteration, health effects, redressal mechanism

## Introduction

The education regarding food adulteration its health effects, and redressal mechanism is needed in India because consumers are lacking information. The position of the Indian consumers is weak as the market works against their interests. They are exploited at each step. This way they do not get the best value for their money, mainly because they lack accurate knowledge about food adulteration, its health effects, the detection methods, standardised marks and redresssal mechanism and also are ignorant about their consumer rights and responsibilities. Voluntary organisations, government institutions, education institutions and business leaders who can undertake the job of consumer education in India too are scarce or they do not work as required. Hence, there is an urgent need to initiate efforts to make the consumer knowledgeable, well informed, well educated so that they become more intelligent, strong and skilful in curbing the exploitation on their own. Also, it is essential to make them aware of the consumer rights and responsibilities, and the whole redressal mechanism to fight against the malpractices used by the manufacturers. It cannot be denied that the educated and well informed consumer is an asset to any society. There is hardly any effort made on the development of the educational programme regarding food adulteration, health effects and redressal mechanism which motivated the investigator to undertake the present investigation.

## Methodology

A descriptive research design was used. A questionnaire was used to collect the data. The sample of the study comprised 90 respondents. A video cassette was chosen as a tool for the preparation of the educational programme.

## Major Findings

The mean age of the respondents was 37.12 years. The mean size of the family was 4.88. About two-thirds of the respondents belonged to nuclear families. The newspaper was the most popular source of information on food adulteration, health effects and redressal mechanism. Most of the respondents had a high level of knowledge about food adulteration, health effects and redressal mechanism. More than one-third of the respondents scored low on the knowledge score. Most of the respondents frequently faced adulteration of milk. None of the respondents had fought any case for food adulteration. Most of the respondents did not face health hazards after consuming the adulterated food items. Food poisoning was a health hazard faced by a little less than one-half of the respondents. In the light of the findings it can be concluded that age, education, exposure of respondents to varied sources of information did not cause any variation in the existing level of knowledge of the respondents about food adulteration, health effects and redressal mechanism. There was a significant increase in the level of knowledge about the homemakers scoring low on the knowledge test prior to the administration of the educational programme. Hence, this proved the high efficacy of the educational programme prepared and administered on the homemaker with a low level of knowledge about food adulteration, health effects and redressal mechanism. The level of knowledge of these respondents had increased a little after a period of one month. It can be concluded that the background characteristics of the respondents, like age, education, occupation and their exposure to different media, did not have an effect on the level of knowledge of the homemakers about food adulteration, health effects and redressal mechanism.

***Title: Brand Preference, Satisfaction and Environment Friendly Behaviour of Home Science Students Regarding Use of Two-wheeler Vehicles***

*Author:* Maya Raut

*Guide:* Sangeeta Patel

*Year:* 2003

*Keywords:* Brand preference, satisfaction, environment friendly behaviour, two-wheeler

## Introduction

Two-wheelers are getting popular with increasing urbanisation and industrialisation. The market for two-wheelers has undergone a change in their structure with focus on fact efficiency, riding comfort, safety, power and style. Very few people are aware of environmental impact of vehicles they use. The study was thus undertaken to know brand preference, extent of satisfaction experienced, and care and maintenance practices of home science students. An attempt was also made to assess the environmental-friendly behaviour of the respondents.

## Methodology

A descriptive survey was carried out on a sample of 140 students of the faculty of home science. The sample was chosen systematically from a list of 300 students. The sample comprised 70 home management department. students and 70 from other departments. A questionnaire was used to collect the data. The reliability and content validity of the tool were established.

## Major Findings

The students belonged to small size families with a mean income of Rs. 15,232.14 and were in age group of 19-20 years. Nearly half of the total sample possessed TVS scooty, one-fourth had Kinetic and Bajaj scooters. The respondents chose, the brand themselves in more than half of the cases. The mean cost of the vehicle was Rs. 27,362.43 and the mean expenditure was Rs. 359.50 on petrol and Rs. 38.1 on repairs. The students got information from TV and newspaper advertisements and booklets. One-third asked for a trial run. The extent of exposure to media revealed a lower level. The selection factors considered by the respondents were ease of operation, self-image, value for money, good pick-up, ease of maintenance and auto start. Satisfaction was experienced with regard to comfort in ride, stability, foot space, visibility from side mirrors, movement of handle, locking facility and power of vehicle. They were also satisfied with the initial pick-up, changing of battery, soft and comfortable seat, ergonomic design, weight of vehicle hand grip, quality of finish and horn of the vehicle. The mean score on the extent of satisfaction did not vary with age, education and family size but varied with income and exposure to media. Most of the two-wheelers scored a medium level on the care and maintenance score. The students also scored a medium level on environment friendly behaviour and it did not vary with age, education income and exposure to media, while sight variation was seen in relation to the size of family. The extent of satisfaction did not vary with the brand, and it was also not related to their environment-friendly behaviour.

***Title: A study on the Extent of Awareness, Use, Satisfaction and Problems Faced Regarding Cellular Phone and Cellular Service***

*Author:* Reena Rao

*Guide:* Neerja Jaiswal

*Year:* 2004

*Keywords:* Extent of awareness, Use, Satisfaction, Problems, Cellular phone

## Introduction

Telecommunication is an essential part of daily life. A new trend of communication through cellular phone and cellular service acts as catalysts in India's planning efforts to bring about a rapid, purposive, positive and significant change in the development of the country and people. Thus the present study was planned with the objectives of studying the extent of awareness, use, general satisfaction experiences and problems faced by the respondents regarding cellular phone and cellular service.

## Methodology

The present descriptive study comprised 120 respondents selected in four phases from Baroda City of Gujarat, India. The study was limited to the ones who owned and used "Nokia" cellular phone with "Hutch" cellular services for two years or more. The interview schedule was used to collect data. Descriptive and relational statistics, such as frequencies, percentage mean, t-test and coefficient of correlation, were computed for statistical analysis.

## Major Findings

A majority of the respondents were unmarried, highly educated and employed, with service as their nature of employment, and having a personal income range of Rs.5,000 and less per month. A majority belonged to the nuclear family, enjoying the single status. Almost a majority of them used the cellular phone because of its "Convenience of use'. They preferred to use the "Nokia" brand of phone due to its ease in operation and "Hutch" cellular service due to its faster services. A majority of them used the prepaid card. The extent of awareness regarding the cellular phone functions and services was moderate, the extent of use was low; the extent of satisfaction experienced by the respondents regarding the purchase of cellular phone was moderate. The extent of problems faced by the respondents were at a medium level but the extent of problems were low. The respondents differed significantly in their extent of awareness and use regarding cellular service due to stages of family lifecycle. They also varied significantly in their extent of use of cellular phone due to their nature of employment. The extent of satisfaction was effected due to the educational level and employment status. The extent of problems were affected by family income. There existed a correlation between the extent of awareness and the use of cellular phone; the extent of awareness and the problems experienced; and the extent of use and the problems faced. There was a significant relationship between the extent of satisfaction and the extent of awareness and problems, and also between the extent of awareness and problems of cellular service.

***Title: Level of Knowledge, Extent of Problems Faced and Satisfaction Experienced by the Customers Regarding Home Loan Facilities***

*Author:* Vidhu Bhatnagar

*Guide:* Suramya Joshi

*Year:* 2005

*Keywords:* Knowledge, problems, satisfaction, customers, home loans

## Introduction

There has been a phenomenal growth in the demand for housing both in quantitative and qualitative terms due to an increase in population. There are various housing loan facilities and schemes provided by the financial institutions to meet this growing need. The present study was designed with the objective of assessing the knowledge of the head of the family regarding available home loan facilities, to assess the extent of problems faced, the satisfaction experienced by customers, and to establish the association between selected variables under study.

## Methodology

The present study had a descriptive research design and a questionnaire was used to collecting data. A sample of 120 home loan borrowers from two select finance companies, viz., ICICI Housing Finance Company and BOB Housing Finance Ltd. of Udaipur City was used. A systematic random sampling technique was used to select the respondents. Data were analysed and frequencies, percentages and mean standard deviations were used. 't'-test and correlation were used to test hypotheses.

## Major Findings

A majority of the respondents belonged to the age group of 41-50 years and they were postgraduates with income ranging between Rs. 10,001 and Rs. 15,000. They were engaged in the government service. Most of the respondents had correct knowledge about various sources from where loans could be obtained. They were aware of criteria for getting loans, documents and formalities required to get loans and the process involved in getting loans. The problems experienced were incorrect information, poor response, and correspondence with the housing finance company. Some faced problems due to the chargeable rate of interest during the process of sanction and disbursement of loan. A few reported problems due to inadequate sanction of the loan amount. Findings related to satisfaction reveal a high level of satisfaction. A few were unsatisfied with the changeable rate of interest and pattern of correspondence. They were satisfied with the terms for which the loan was provided and the tax rebate on loans. They were also satisfied with the doorstep service. The results of hypotheses testing revealed that the knowledge of respondents varied with the level of education. The problems faced varied with the education, income, type of house and amount of loan. Satisfaction varied with level of knowledge education, income and amount of loan. A positive association was also between the extent of satisfaction and the availed loan; and the level of knowledge and availed loan. The extent of satisfaction was negative associated with the extent of problems faced by the respondents.

> ***Title: Extent of Awareness among the Homemakers Regarding Consumer Protection Act, Consumer Rights and Responsibilities and Attitude towards Consumer Movement***
>
> *Author:* Neha Bhasin
>
> *Guide:* Suramya Joshi
>
> *Year:* 2005
>
> *Keywords:* Awareness, Consumer Protection Act, consumer rights, attitude, consumer movement, homemakers

## Introduction

With the rapid industrialisation and fast technological development and advancement, the market has become complicated and complex for consumers. In today's market consumers are cheated every day. To protect the them government has passed some laws, and also some rights and responsibilities are declared for them so that they can protect themselves from exploitations by manufacturers and sellers. Consumer education imparted through effective formal / non-formal ways can prove to be of vital importance to enlighten the consumers in this context. Hence an attempt was made by the investigator to assess the awareness regarding the Consumer Protection Act and consumer rights and responsibilities, and regarding the attitude towards consumer movement among the selected group of homemakers as respondents.

## Methodology

The study was descriptive in nature along with an attempt to create awareness among the respondents through implementation of the need-based awareness programme. A questionnaire was used for collecting data. The sample of 120 homemakers from Officers Colony, ONGC Township of Ankleshwar was selected by systematic random sampling technique. Descriptive statistics such as frequency percentage, mean and SD were used, and to study the relationship between the variables 't' test, ANOVA and coefficient of correlation were computed.

## Major Findings

A majority of the respondents purchased their convenience goods from fixed shops. A majority of the respondents purchased convenience goods monthly and shopping and specialty goods occasionally. A little more than two-third of the respondents utilised services from private sectors and nearly two-thirds of utilised services from public sectors.

A majority of the respondents sometimes experienced incidents of malpractices. Many of the respondents did not take any steps to avoid hassles and their family members also discouraged them. A majority of the respondents had good buying practices and had a neutral attitude towards consumer movement. More than two-thirds of the respondents had a low level of awareness regarding the Consumer Protection Act, and consumer rights and responsibilities. Based on these they were exposed to the awareness programme through posters and leaflets.

A remarkable improvement was found. Results of statistical analysis revealed that the buying practices of the homemakers varied with the education level and not with any other variable. The attitude towards consumer movement and the extent of awareness regarding the Consumer Protection Act varied with age, education, employment status and size of the family. The extent of awareness varied with age, education and employment status. A positive association was found between buying practices and the extent of awareness regarding the Consumer Protection Act, and consumer rights and responsibilities; also between the attitude and extent of awareness regarding the Consumer Protection Act, and consumer rights and responsibilities.

*Title: Opinion and Extent of Use of Electronic Media for Purchase of Goods and Services by Families*
*Author:* Tejal Barot
*Guide:* Maneesha Shukul and Sarjoo Patel
*Year:* 2006
*Keywords:* Opinion, use, electronic media, purchase, goods, services, families

## Introduction

There is a revolution taking shape about how people shop, and the advent of the internet is changing the business done electronically at a very fast pace. Gone are the days of pushing heavy shopping carts up and down the airless, loading up with weekly groceries, dragging tired and reluctant children's behind, driving home amid heavy traffic, unloading and then reloading kitchen cupboards and fridge.

The convenience is at the heart of what fundamentally drives the demand for the the electronic media—internet. Electronic shopping saves time and promises lower prices. However, in our Indian society this type of online purchase is found to be very rares especialy in small towns and non-metropolitan cities. The Indian families too have come into the mainstream with increased personal computer and internet usage. But now it has become the need to investigate the use of electronic shopping, especially in Indian homes, to find out the most frequently used goods and services actually purchased and their opinion regarding electronic shopping.

## Methodology

The present research was descriptive in nature. The total sample size comprised 120 respondents of Baroda city. A auestionnaire was used as a tool for data collection and it was prevalidated. The sample was selected through the purposive sampling methods and data were analysed by employing descriptive as well as relational statistics (ANOVA, t-test and correlations).

## Major Findings

A majority of the internet users were found to be students and officers. The study revealed that a higher number of respondents purchased services for product information, banking, job seeking and matrimonial compared to goods. The goods were very rarely purchased by the respondents whose frequency varied from daily to once-a-year. A wide majority of the respondents had a very favourable opinion regarding the electronic media goods and services. A relationship was found between the opinion of the respondents and the extent of use of the electronic media for the purchase of goods and services.

# 8

# Environment

Environment is the sum total of all conditions and influences that affect the development and life of the organisms. It includes the quality of air, portability of water, adequacy of light, sound and temperature levels and the extent of pollution affecting the environment. Very few people realise that they are polluting the environment. They feel that one person cannot cause pollution but they forget that when numerous such "one persons" think the same way that pollution results. Research studies have focused on the quality of indoor environment in the household with emphasis on the kitchen which is the workplace in the home. The researchers have looked into the quality of air, water, sanitation, light, sound level and temperature levels in the kitchens. Knowledge scales and environment quality scales have been used along with laboratory tests and field tests of air and water samples. Thus both subjective and objective assessments have been made. The results reveal that the quality of air under certain conditions is poor, water samples have shown pollution levels above the prescribed limits, lighting is inadequate and temperatures are high, especially in summer, and in poorly ventilated kitchens. Sound levels vary with the locality but are still not a very serious problem.

***Title: An Exploratory Study of Sound Levels in Homes***
*Author:* Seema Sharma
*Guide:* Nalini Ogale
*Year:* 1984
*Keywords:* Noise / sound pollution, environment, effects of noise, sound levels.

## Introduction

Literally sound is that which can be heard. In our daily lives we hear numerous sounds, out of which some do convey some meaning to us and are pleasant to the ear while others are unnecessary and annoying. Today the latter type seems to be increasing, leading to noise pollution. Noise is the responsible factor for disturbing the general peace of the environment. Noise is not only harmful to health but it also interferes with many of our daily activities, like sleeping, conversation, reading, concentrating, etc. One can not perceive any harmful effects of noise but in the long run, it is found to be responsible for various adverse effects. A study was undertaken to explore the sources and levels of sound, how people react to sound and what measures they take to control noise in the home.

## Methodology

An exploratory survey method with a questionnaire and observation were used as techniques for gathering information. Sampling was selective in value, 180 samples were selected from noisy, not so noisy and quiet localities of Baroda. Sound levels were measured using a sound level meter. The data were coded and analysed in terms of frequencies, percentages, mean, median, t-test and Pearson's product moment correlation.

## Major Findings

Sources of noise varied from locality to locality. Traffic was the major source of external noise, and crying and shouting were the major sources of noise inside the home. Noise caused the maximum disturbance to sleep. Use of architectural acoustics in order to control noise was not very prevalent while constructing houses. Use of soft furnishing in order to absorb sound was quite common. Closing of the door and windows helped to reduce the sound level inside the house. It was found that the sound level decreased as the distance from the source increased. The sound level measurements showed that washing of clothes, water running in bathrooms, call bells produced high levels of sound in the home.

*Title: A Study of Knowledge, Sanitary Practices and Opinion of the Housewives Regarding Air and Water Pollution*

*Author:* Jasvir Kaur

*Guide:* Veena Gandotra

*Year:* 1984

*Keywords:* Knowledge, Sanitary practice, Opinion, Air and water pollution

## Introduction

The industrialization, urbanization and ever-increasing population have polluted the basic amenities of life, namely, air, water and land. Preservations of the delicately balanced ecological system is in the interest of mankind. The family plays an important role in this. The decisions taken by families in relation to the use of natural resources affects the environment at large. Since housewives are the chief executives in the home, they only can help in controlling pollution, at least at the home level by their good sanitary habits. Such habits can be inculcated in their children so that future citizens can assume their share of responsibility in pollution control. A need was felt after reviewing the relevant literature for conducting a study to find out the knowledge, sanitary practices and opinion of housewives regarding air and water pollution, so that they could be educated to reduce pollution.

## Methodology

The research design was descriptive in nature and data were collected through a survey of 120 households by interviewing of the housewives. The interview schedule consisted of questions to elicit required information as per the objectives of the study, and contained rating scales to find out the practices of sanitation and hygiene, knowledge about controlling air and water pollution. The knowledge test was subjected to validation, item-analysis, establishment of reliability through split half method. Stratified random sampling was followed to select the sample. From three localities stratified on the basis of sources of air pollution and from each locality, 40 households were selected randomly as sample. The coefficient of correlation and t-test were computed to test the hypotheses.

## Major Findings

The mean age of the housewives was 35 years; more respondents were graduates and postgraduates, a wide majority were not employed and were married. About one-third of respondents had an income ranging between Rs. 1,500 and Rs. 2,099 per month. A little less than half belonged to the second high socioeconomic group. A majority of the respondents had "fair" housing conditions. The mean fuel used for cooking was gas and most of them stored drinking water in 'mud pots'. A wide majority of the respondents had a "medium level" of knowledge about air and water pollution and had "fair" sanitary practices. Most of the respondents had a favourable opinion regarding controlling air and water pollution. A positive relationship was found between the socioeconomic status and knowledge as well as sanitary practices. The study revealed a need to enhance the knowledge of people so as to reduce air and water pollution in and around houses.

***Title: A Study of Various Practices of Homemakers and Bacteriological Quality of Drinking Water Stored in the Vessels of Different Materials***

*Author:* Manju Taneja

*Guide:* Asha V. Dass

*Year:* 1986

*Keywords:* Quality of water, bacteriological quality, materials for storage, disinfecting quality

## Introduction

Water is one of the basic necessities of life. It has many uses, like households, agricultural, public, industrial and many other purposes. Drinking water must be safe to drink, i.e., free from chemical substances and microorganisms which might be dangerous to the health of the community. It should also be cool, pleasant, clear, colourless and devoid of a disagreeable taste or smell. If it is not pure, it will lead to various water-borne diseases, which will cause various health hazards to the consumer. It is a common belief that the water quality improves with the storage in the vessel of different materials, which act as the disinfectant, i.e., killing of the microorganisms. The study was carried out to find out the use and reasons of various materials and practices of use of vessels of various materials for storing drinking water. Experiments were conducted to find out the bacteriological quality of drinking water stored in the vessels of different materials.

## Methodology

The research design was descriptive-cum-experimental, and for survey method, the interview schedule was used. A simple random sampling method was used and the sample consisted of 100 homemakers of three residential areas of IIT Kanpur Campus. For experimental work, i.e., to study the bacteriological quality of drinking water with respect to metal / material of the vessel used for storing drinking water, a multiple tube fermentation technique was used. The materials studied were copper, brass, stainless steel, earthenware and plastic.

## Major Findings

The various materials used for the storage of drinking water at home were copper, brass, stainless steel, plastic, earthenware, galvanised iron bucket and water filter. The use of these materials was affected by the monthly income of the respondent's family, whereas religion did not have any effect on the material used. The frequency of filling the water was dependent on the size of the family. All the respondents were filling, covering, storing and taking out drinking water from the containers in hygienic conditions. Copper had the highest disinfecting quality, then were brass, earthenware, stainless steel, and plastic had the least disinfecting quality.

*Title: Assessment of Performance of Candle Water Filters for Water Purification*

*Author:* Deepa Bhatnagar

*Guide:* Asha V. Dass

*Year:* 1986

*Keywords:* Physical, chemical and bacteriological quality of water, water filters, water borne diseases

## INTRODUCTION

Water can be classified as clean, polluted or contaminated. Clean water is one which is at all times free from pollution and contamination for human consumption, as determined by laboratory analysis, sanitary survey and continued uses. Polluted water is one which has suffered impairment of physical qualities, through the addition of substances causing turbidity, colour, odour or taste. In India only 12 per cent of people get clean drinking water. Disinfection of water is an ideal way to check contamination and avoid health hazards. Filteration is the most convenient and effective process at the domestic level, and several kinds of commercial filters are available in Indian market with a claim to producing bacteriologically safe and clean water. This study was taken to test the performance of the candle water filters available in Baroda by examining the physical, chemical and bacteriological quality of the drinking water.

## METHODOLOGY

The research design of the present study was experimental-cum-descriptive, and a questionnaire was used for data collection. Purposive sampling was done to collect the information from hundred households from Baroda city who had water filters and used it regularly. Experiments were conducted to test the physical, chemical and bacteriological quality of the water. Colour, odour, pH, hardness and turbidity were tested before and after filteration by candle water filters. For bacteriological test the coli form bacteria was chosen as an indicator of faecal pollution, and multiple tube fermentation test was carried out. Physical and chemical composition were studied by standard methods. The data were coded, tabulated and presented in terms of frequencies, means and percentages, and coefficient of correlation was calculated. For the experiments mean, percentage, t-test and chi-square were calculated.

## MAJOR FINDINGS

A majority of the respondents used water filter for more than five years. The capacity of water filter was not dependent on the family size. The main reasons for purchasing water filters were water-borne diseases, and the motivating factors were friends, relatives and neighbours. Most of the respondents had knowledge that water filters filtered the bacteria present in water, and most of them were satisfied with the performance of water filters. Water from Municipal Supply was colourless and odourless. Turbidity was removed by the candle water filters which is the only true claim made by the manufacturers. The pH of the water was not changed by the candle water filters. Filters were not able to remove hardness and bacteria present in water, thus the claims made by the manufacturers were proved to be false. Thus, though the use of candle water filters is increasing in urban areas, they do not alter the hardness, pH and bacteria count; therefore, some disinfectants should be used to make the water bacteria-free.

***Title: A Study on Environmental Conditions of Domestic Kitchens***

*Author:* Jayeti Singh

*Guide:* Salma Nadvi

*Year:* 1986

*Keywords:* Environment, environmental conditions or quality, environmental pollution

## INTRODUCTION

The environment is the aggregate of all social, biological, physical or chemical factors which comprise the surroundings of man. The deterioration of environmental quality has posed a serious problem under the ever-increasing population and of the industrialising society. The environment in the kitchen is affected by certain features such as the quality and quantity of lighting and ventilation, various pollutants due to fuels, noise due to different equipments and method of storing water. The healthy environment also depends upon the sanitation practices used by homemakers. In order to bring out more information the study was undertaken to find out the sources of environmental problems and levels of environmental pollution in the domestic kitchens.

## Methodology

The research design was experimental-cum-descriptive in nature and the interview schedule with the observation sheet was used to collect data. The sample comprised 120 domestic kitchens from different localities of Baroda city. To measure the level of environmental pollution in domestic kitchens, experiments were carried out in relation to water pollution, air pollution and heat stress in 20 kitchens only. The bacteriological test was carried out with MPN index to find out the level of pollution in drinking water. The level of air pollution was found out by measuring the gaseous pollutants like hydrocarbons (methane-$CH_4$), carbon monoxide (CO) and oxides of nitrogen (NOx) because gas was absorbent. Sterilised bottles were used to collect the air (gas) sample from the kitchen and analysis was done with gas chromatograph and spectrophotometer. A simple mercury thermometer was used for measuring heat stress in the kitchens. Categorisation, coding, frequencies, percentages, mean were used to analyse the data.

## Major Findings

The mean income was Rs. 1,750.6 and respondents lived in apartments and bungalows. The mean kitchen size was 6.92 sq. mts. Most of the respondents felt that they had sufficient ventilation. None of the kitchens were dusty or smoky. Respondents felt discomfort due to over-crowdedness, ill-ventilation and high temperature. Most of the kitchens had sufficient natural and artificial lighting. Very few of them used dustbins. Kitchen walls were light coloured in most of the kitchens and were getting dirty because of the light colour and the rough texture. Almost less than half of them had a separate storeroom while most of them had wall and base cabinets in the kitchen. Most of them did not get disturbed by noises. They had municipal water supply in the kitchen and they stored water in earthen pots, metal and plastic vessels. They used a plastic or cloth strainer and only a few boil the water. The finding of the experimental work revealed that there was no general trend obtained for the gaseous pollutants with respect to the type of fuels. An air analysis showed that the level of methane was within permissible limits, whereas, carbon monoxide and oxides of nitrogen levels were high. The bacteriological analysis of drinking water showed that 20 per cent samples did not come in the standard limit. Because of the good ventilation less number of respondents had discomfort as the kitchen temperature was balanced.

***Title: Assessment of Microenvironment Conditions in Selected Households and the Extent of knowledge of Homemakers with Regard to Pollution***

*Author:* Rachana Ramdas

*Guide:* Veena Gandotra

*Year:* 1988

*Keywords:* Micro-environmental conditions, knowledge regarding pollution, sanitation practices

## INTRODUCTION

The human activities aimed towards economical development has led to serious environmental problems. The environmental contamination has become a threat to the continued existence of many plants and animal communities of the ecosystem and may ultimately threaten the very survival of the human race. The environment, inside the home is affected by various aspects of environment such as the quality and quantity of ventilation and lighting, heat stress, noise produced by different equipments, activities, method of storing water and sanitation practices used by the homemakers. In order to bring about more information regarding the environmental aspects in the kitchen and bedroom the study was undertaken to assess the level of pollution, to find out sources of pollution, knowledge of respondents regarding pollution, etc

## Methodology

The research design was descriptive-cum-experimental in nature. A survey method with the interview schedule and observation sheet was used to collect data. An experimental design was used to assess the quality of the environment and the aspects covered were water, noise, lighting and heat stress. The study covered the domestic kitchens and bedrooms from three localities of Baroda city. The sample comprised 30 randomly chosen households from three areas, i.e., IPCL Township, railway station area and Fatehgunj slums. To measure the level of water pollution, a bacteriological test was carried out on the water samples with M.P.N. test. The sound level meter was used for measuring the sound levels in the kitchen and the bedroom. A simple alcohol thermometer was used to measure the temperature in the kitchen and the bedroom. A light meter was used to measure the intensity of illumination in the kitchen and the bedroom. The data were categorised, coded, tabulated and presented in frequencies, percentages, range and mean. Coefficient of correlation, t-test and chi-square were used to test the hypotheses.

## Major Findings

Kitchens in railway and Fatehgunj areas were small in size and kitchens in IPCL township were according to the standard size, whereas bedrooms in Fatehgunj area were below the standard size and in railway area and IPCL township were of adequate size. In Fatehgunj slums, most of the kitchens and bedrooms lacked ventilation; here the respondents used wood and kerosene as fuels. In the railway station area and in IPCL Township kitchens gas was used as fuel. In most of the kitchens discomfort was felt due to inadequate space. There was sufficient lighting in a majority of the cases in railway and IPCL Township areas. They used to dispose kitchen waste in an open area or in a large bin outside. A majority of the respondents were disturbed by the noise in the kitchen and bedroom due to vehicular traffic, and sound-absorbing materials were not used by them. Experiments showed that most of the water samples in all three areas were polluted. The noise level was recorded above the tolerance level in railway station area and noise levels were below tolerance level in Fatehgunj slum area and IPCL Township area. The temperature levels were above the recommended level in all three areas. The illumination level was found to be poor or adequate. In Fatehgunj area and railway station area, the respondents had a low level of knowledge regarding environmental pollution, and in IPCL Township area, a majority of them had high knowledge. A positive relationship was found between the knowledge of respondents and the quality of environment in home.

***Title: Assessment of Micro-environmental Conditions of Selected Household Kitchens in Three Areas of Delhi***

*Author:* Veerbala

*Guide:* Veena Gandotra

*Year:* 1990

*Keywords:* Environmental pollution, indoor pollution, quality of environment, level of pollution

## INTRODUCTION

Environmental pollution is one of the most vital problems today faced by mankind. The deterioration of the human environment through the population explosion, pollution of air and water, and other disruptions of the ecological balance pose major health hazards and serious challenges. Indoor environment plays a crucial role in determining human exposure to actual pollutant concentration. The environmental conditions of the kitchen includes the physical structure that man uses including all necessary services, facilities, equipment needed for the physical and mental health and well being of the people living or working in that environment. The study was undertaken to assess the quality of environment in the kitchen, knowledge of the respondents regarding the quality of environment and effects of selected variables on the quality of the environment of the kitchen.

## METHODOLOGY

The research design of the study was experimental-cum-descriptive. The experimental design was used to assess the quality of the environment. A descriptive survey method with the help of interview schedule was adopted to elicit data from 150 samples which included knowledge test to determine the level of knowledge of the respondents regarding enthe vironmental quality. To measure the level of air pollution the levels of SPM, $SO_2$ and CO were determined with low volume samples and glass fibre filter and readings were taken with a spectrophotometer. To measure the quality of stored water in the domestic kitchens, water samples were analysed for physical, chemical and bacteriological impurities. The sound levels were measured with a sound level meter. A light meter was used to measure the illumination on the work surface and in the kitchen. A mercury thermometer was used to measure temperature in kitchens. The analysis of data involved categorisation, coding, tabulation, frequencies, percentages, range and mean. Statistical tests like coefficient of correlation, chi-square and t-test were used to test the hypotheses.

## MAJOR FINDINGS

The kitchens were not adequate in size, and in many houses, they were combined with rooms. Environmental quality was found poor to satisfactory in highly populated areas and good in some houses in industrial and railway station areas. Experimental results with regard to air quality, heat stress, lighting, noise and water were not satisfactory. Education and knowledge emerged as important determinants of environment in kitchens. Young homemakers possessed more knowledge. The quality of the environment varied with the locality, i.e., best in residential locality and worst in highly populated and commercial areas. Results of experimental study revealed that spur levels were high in all kitchens; the mean value of CO was found to be the highest when windows were closed, and exceeded permissible limits when flat-bottom utensils were used and when the stove was kept below the counter. Water pollution was more in Shakur Basti than in Sabzi Mandi and Shalimar Bagh. Sound levels were high in all kithchens. Mean temperatures were found to be high; illumination level was poor in Sabzi Mandi but adequate in Shakur Basti and Shalimar Bagh.

***Title: Influence of Selected Factors on Knowledge and Practices of Slum Homemakers with Reference to Environmental Conditions***
*Author:* Hemangini Pawar
*Guide:* Nalini Ogale
*Year:* 1993
*Keywords:* Urban slums, degradation of quality of environment, knowledge and practices on environment

## Introduction

The rapid increase in population has resulted in greater concentration in urban settlements. The urban slum settlements have greater pollution, especially with regard to those of land, air, water and sound. It is important to know about the causes and effects of different types of pollution in order to prevent the disastrous consequences of environmental degradation and unhealthy surroundings. The study was conducted to assess the knowledge and practices of slum homemakers regarding environmental conditions, and to determine the factors influencing the knowledge and practices of the respondents regarding suitable environmental conditions.

## Methodology

The study was descriptive in nature and 90 samples from three slum areas of Baroda city were taken. An interview schedule comprising the knowledge test and practices scale were chosen for data collection. The data were coded, tabulated and analysed in terms of frequencies, percentages and means. The co-efficient of correlation, the analysis of variance and chi-square were computed to test the hypotheses.

## Major Findings

The mean age of the respondents was 34 years. Most of them were housewives with a low level of education. The mean income was

Rs. 1,191 per month. Majority of them were living in pucca and semi-pucca houses with one room combined with the kitchen and no separate bathroom and toilet facilities. More than fifty per cent of the respondents had ventilation in their houses and kitchen, and had a smoke outlet in the kitchen but not sufficient to carry out smoke from it. Most of them used the open gutter facility. Most of the respondents did not know about the meaning of environment, environmental pollution, impact of it and man's role in it, and hence most of them had fair practices of maintaining environmental conditions. A positive correlation was found between the practices and the extent of knowledge. The practices were significantly different due to age and type of family. A significant association was found between the education and knowledge of the respondents.

***Title: A Study of Quality of Drinking Water Available to Households and Water Management Practices of Homemakers from Padra***

*Author:* Sonal Shah

*Guide:* Veena Gandotra

*Year:* 1995

*Keywords:* Quality, Drinking water, Household, Management practices, Homemakers

## Introduction

Water is one of the most important natural resources next to air. Along with ensuring the availability of good quality of drinking water, it is important to see that water is available. Water resources are low and dwindling. This results in non-availability of the water in the taps and, hence, homemakers have to make frequent trips for collecting water from a source which is at a low level. The quality of water deteriorates during transportation and the quality of water available for drinking purpose is an important factor in relation to health. It is also important to know whether water management and sanitation practices have any effect on the quality of water, and keeping this in mind the current study was undertaken.

## Methodology

The descriptive research design supplemented with experimental work was used by employing the interview schedule for collecting data. MPN test was conducted on stored drinking water from 10 households each and five sources of water each from both the areas.

A sample pf 90 homemakers from Jakatnaka and Tankhal lake areas of Padra town were selected by purposive random sampling method. Descriptive statistics used were mean, percentage, frequency, and relational statistics used was canonical correlation.

## Major Findings

A majority of the women were in the age group of 30-40 years and were illiterate. A majority of their husband occupation was service, and the total family income per year was up to Rs. 12,000. Two-thirds of the respondents collected water from a household tap. A majority of them collected water in iron buckets and then stored it in earthen pots; a majority collected water in a container for washing clothes and utensils.

A majority did not cover the water while bringing it back from the source, but covered it with a tight lid at home. A majority of them never washed their hands before taking water out of the container and never cleaned their storage tanks. A majority let the dirty water after washing clothes and utensils collect outside their house. There was prominence of water-related infections, such as malaria and jaundice.

A majority had poor water management practices and fair sanitation practices. The experimental results revealed that the quality of stored water was poor as it was contaminated, but the quality at the source was good.

Testing of hypotheses proved that there is a relationship between age, education, occupation, family income and water management, and sanitation practices followed by them, and as a result it had an effect on their health also.

*Title: Assessment of Micro-environmental Quality of Household Kitchens in Baroda City*

*Author:* Sangita Patel

*Guide:* Veena Gandotra

*Year:* 1996

*Keywords:* Assessment, micro-environmental quality, kitchen

## INTRODUCTION

The environmental quality is being constantly degraded by the activities of man. This is true not only for the macro but also for the micro-environment, that is, the household environment. The quality of micro-environment is degraded to a great extent by smoke and fumes mainly due to combustion of fuels, use of various appliances, sound from various activities, lack of sanitation, lack of ventilation, excess of heat, poor lighting, etc. which affect the health of women as they spend the maximum time in the kitchen. Hence, it was considered essential to study the quality of micro-environment, factors influencing it and its effects on health problems experienced by the homemakers.

## METHODOLOGY

A descriptive-cum-experimental research design was used. An interview schedule was used to collect the data. The study covered household kitchens from three selected localities of Baroda city which included industrial-cum-residential, commercial-cum-residential and residential locality. A multistage purposive-cum-random sampling design was used. Fifty Households were chosen from each locality which comprised total 50 households. Frequencies, percentages mean, standard deviation, correlated coefficient, analysis of variance and 't' tests were used for analysing data.

## MAJOR FINDINGS

The mean age was 36.01 year and the family size was 5.9 members. The mean income was Rs. 1,442.40 per month. The education level of the respondents was very low. Most were not employed, only 37.3 per cent of the respondents had a separate kitchen and the average time spent in kitchen was 4.84 hours per day. The overall quality of micro-environment was average with variations on the basis of the locality in which the respondents lived. Improper orientation of the kitchen, inadequate floor space, inadequate open space in terms of windows and ventilators led to poor ventilation in most of the kitchens. Little more than half of the kitchens were fairly clean and little less than half of the houses had dirty surroundings. The air quality was poor. The quality of drinking water was poor. Most of the respondents lived in very noisy surroundings. The temperature levels were above the recommended comfortable levels, and the illumination levels were below the recommended values in all the kitchens during daytime. Respondents possessed a medium level of knowledge regarding the quality of environment and followed fair practices influencing the quality of micro-environment. Age, educational level and extent of exposure to media affected the knowledge of the respondents significantly. The knowledge of respondents had a direct effect on the practices followed by the respondents which affected the quality of micro environment.

***Title: A Study of Knowledge and Sanitation Practices of Homemakers Regarding Water Pollution and to Assess the Quality of Water***

*Author:* Shalini Agrawal

*Guide:* Veena Gandotra

*Year:* 1997

*Keywords:* Knowledge, sanitation practices, water pollution, quality of water

## INTRODUCTION

Pollution today is very complex in its composition and getting more so all the time. Careless handling, pollution and contamination of our rivers, lakes, streams and underground sources have impaired the quality of the available water resources. The quality of water available for drinking purposes is an important factor in relation to health. It is important to know whether the knowledge of homemakers and sanitation practices followed by them has any effect on the quality of water and how the quality of water affects other household activities.

## Methodology

A descriptive research design was used with the experimental work. A stratified random sampling was used to select the sample. An interview schedule was used to collect data, experiments were conducted to test the quality of water. The water samples were collected from the sources as well as from three different localities selected for collection of data, that is Shishmahal, Amrawati Colony and Kusum Khera. Water samples were collected and physio-chemical and biological tests were carried out. The collected data were analysed in terms of simple frequencies, percentages, mean and standard deviation. Pearson's Product Moment Correlation Coefficient, analysis of variance and t-test were computed to study the relationship between selected variables.

## Major Findings

The respondents had a fair knowledge regarding water pollution and followed fair sanitation practices, while they rarely faced health problems. The quality of water available at the source as well as collected from the households were found polluted, though the quality of water was poor at source. The quality of water deteriorated after rainfall. Moreover it was found that contamination was there during transportation. It was found that education, employment of respondents and total monthly family income were related to the knowledge of the respondents and sanitation practices followed by them. A difference was found in the quality of water collected from sources before rain and after rain.

***Title: Homemakers Environmentally Concerned Awareness, Buying and Consumption Behaviour in Relation to Selected Consumer Goods***

*Author:* Maneesha Shukul

*Guide:* Nalini Ogale

*Year:* 1995

*Keywords:* Homemakers, environment, awareness, buying, consumption, behaviour, consumer goods

## Introduction

Family and individuals in the family take several decisions, while using resources from the environment. Such decisions whether informed and deliberate or uninformed and semi-conscious, affect the environment. Recently, the consumers are becoming increasingly interested in assessing the environmental impact of their decisions. Environmental concern is not only important while buying, but is also equally important while using any product / service and disposing the waste. In India environmental concern in buying of goods remains relatively an uninvestigated area. Hence, a need was felt to find out the extent to which Indian women are concerned about the environment when they buy or consume any product or throw away the waste.

## Methodology

The present investigation was a descriptive survey, conducted on 204 homemakers living in Baroda city, selected through the purposive sampling method. A questionnaire was used to collect data. Frequencies, percentage, mean standard deviation, multivariate analysis techniques, coefficient of correlation, F-test and t-tests were used to analyse the data.

## Major Findings

The mean age was 37.9 years. Thirty-five per cent were graduates, 33.9 per cent postgraduates and 30.9 per cent below graduation. Half of the respondents were employed and half not employed. The mean income was Rs. 12,027. The homemakers had a medium level of awareness regarding problems of environment, and a moderately favourable attitude towards environmental responsibilities as consumers. Most of the homemakers did not know about 'Eco mark'. It was found that though the environment-friendly behaviour in buying, consumption and waste disposal practices was found to be at 'medium' extent very few homemakers had a real environmental concern as reflected in the reasons given for the choices of alternatives provided for each behaviour. The personal and situational variables affected the environmental awareness, attitude towards environmental responsibilities, and environment-friendly buying and consumption behaviour. It was found that the better the environmental awareness, the more favourable was the attitude towards environmental responsibilities as consumers. But the waste disposal behavior was influenced by environmental awareness only.

*Title: Solid Waste Disposal Practices of Homemakers from Selected Housing Societies of Baroda City*
*Author:* Sarjoo Patel
*Guide:* Maneesha Shukul
*Year:* 1999
*Keywords:* Solid waste disposal, practices, opinion, homemakers

## Introduction

Women are the key members of any house, responsible for a majority of the activities at home, especially those related with cooking and cleaning. They are also responsible for the activities, like disposal of garbage, disposal of perishable wastes, solid wastes etc. For this it is essential to know the solid waste disposal practices followed by them, because it is well understood that one of the major sources of the waste generation is the household sector.

## Methodology

A descriptive research design was used for the study. The sample consisted of 120 homemakers: 40 each from three select housing societies of Baroda city: Shreenagar Society where Baroda Citizens Council (NGO) was providing services, Adhyapak Kutir where Beautiful Baroda Council (NGO) was providing such services, and Harkashi Society where the sweeper was appointed by the colony itself, by systematic random sampling method. The interview schedule was used for collecting data.

## Major Findings

The mean age of the homemakers was 36.1 years and the mean income of the family was Rs. 10,428. Nearly 43 per cent were graduates and 35 per cent had education above graduation, nearly 60 per cent were not employed. The homemakers from the colonies where solid waste collection and cleaning facilities were provided by outside agencies had good practices and opinion regarding disposal of solid waste as compared with the society which had its own solid waste collection facilities. The statistical analysis indicated that the solid waste disposal practices of the homemakers varied with their education, family income, housing society and employment status. The opinion of the homemakers varied with the housing colonies in which they resided. The practices and opinion of homemakers were positively correlated with each other.

***Title: A Study of Indoor Air Quality in the Vicinity of Taj Mahal***
*Author:* Priyanka Kulshreshtha
*Guide:* Veena Gandotra
*Year:* 2001
*Keywords:* Indoor air quality, environment, pollution

## Introduction

Environmental pollution and human effects for the betterment of living standards are the two sides of the same coin. The inevitable outcome of this development and human evolution is environmental pollution. Although a lot has been said and done about outdoor pollution, the perception of people towards indoor it has been of disregard and negligence. The focus of this study is on the quality of indoor air due to penetration of outdoor air pollutants inside the house and due to pollution produced within the homes.

## Methodology

A descriptive-cum-experimental design was used for the present study. An interview schedule was used to collect data. Three localities were selected for the present study from Agra city. This is Zalma Leprosy Institute Campus, Taj Ganj and Shaheed Nagar. The total sample comprised 90 households, with 30 households from each locality. Percentage mean, frequencies, t-test, F-test and coefficient of correlation were used in statistical analysis.

### Major Findings

The mean age of the respondents was 30.1 years. The maximum number of respondents belonged to below-graduation group. A majority of the respondents were housewives. The mean income was Rs. 7,020. The mean family size was five members. Majority had kitchens in the north-east direction. An open space was found facing the kitchen. LPG was mainly used as the fuel. All the respondents had an average quality of ventilation in their kitchens. Most of the respondents irrespective of their income and education, had a high level of perception regarding the ill- effects of air pollution. Such knowledge also varied due to educational level, occupation and family size. Health problems perceived by the respondents varied due to the locality in which they lived. The level of concentration of pollutants was found to be much higher than the permissible limits when cooking was carried on in the kitchen.

***Title: An Exploratory Study on Energy Audit in Selected Cases of Residential Units of Baroda City***

*Author:* Vasundhra Gohil

*Guide:* Rachel George

*Year:* 2001

*Keywords:* Energy audit, Residential units

### Introduction

Today, there in increasing awareness of the need for productivity improvements to save energy and conserve scare resources. In this context, energy audit assumes significance. A systematic study of the kind proposed exposed the factors considered, the professional help utilized, if any, and the processes followed in order to create the lighting design, and in purchase of household gadgets that transform energy in various end uses. The study was helpful for the families in understanding the lacunae in their lighting design, and in attaining a higher illuminance level by adopting measures to improve the same. The major objective was to study and build a descriptive case story regarding the illuminance during daytime and night-time in selected residential units, and to study the lighting design and the layout of the sample.

## METHODOLOGY

A diagnostic research design was used for the present study. The method used was the case study approach wherein the main tools to elicit data from the sample included indepth interviews, observation and field measurements, All together, 15 families comprising five from each income group were selected from Baroda City. For data analysis, descriptive statistics employed were frequency, percentage mean, standard deviation and coefficient of variation. The inferential statistics used was t-test, by pooled variance method.

## MAJOR FINDINGS

It was concluded that general lighting, tubular fluorescent lamps and incandescent lamps dominated the lighting design in the cases studies. The lighting design was deficient not only in quantitative aspects but also in qualitative aspects. Most of the respondents from lower income group families were found to be satisfied with the lighting conditions of the home. Very few families were aware of the type of lamps available and they were among the higher income group. The higher income group families were found to possess a varied number of energy-transforming gadgets when compared with the lower income group. The inter-group comparison on expenditure on electricity ranged from Rs. 50 to Rs. 130 among the moderate income group, and Rs 500 to Rs. 1200 among the higher income group. On the cooking fuel, it ranged from Rs. 150 to Rs. 300 in the lower, Rs. 200 to Rs. 300 in the moderate and higher income group. In the case of petrol/diesel, the expenditure ranged from Rs. 300 to Rs. 480 in the lower, Rs. 390 to Rs. 720 in the moderate, and Rs. 1,980 to Rs. 3,000 in the higher income group cases. On the basis of the computed t-test it was concluded that income plays a critical role in a family's average monthly expenditure on all fuel forms, electricity and petrol/diesel.

***Title: Extent Use of Vermitechnology by the Farmers of Bharuch District***

*Author:* Nishi Sharma

*Guide:* Suramya Joshi

*Year:* 2003

*Keywords:* Vermitechnology, Farmers, Extent of use

## Introduction

Organic farming, of which vermicompost is a part, does not cause any harm to the environment. Through this system of farming, the agriculture as a vocation is rendered sustainable. In this, man, animal and plant are positively interrelated. It is easy to practise vermin technology, a way of farming, as for this the resources are locally available. Although a many researches have been undertaken on earthworms and productivity, vermicomposting, green manuring and organic farming, few studies have been done on the problems and satisfaction of the farmers regarding vermin technology. Thus the focus of the present investigation was on problems and the satisfaction experienced by the farmers with the extent of use of vermin technology.

## Methodology

A descriptive research design was used. The interview schedule consisting of the problem scale and the satisfaction scale was used to elicit data. The sample comprised 130 farmers who had adopted vermitechnology since the last two years from Bharuch district, selected through multistage random sampling method. For statistical analysis, frequency, percentage, mean, t-test and chisuqare were computed.

## MAJOR FINDINGS

Respondents of the present study were the farmers who were illiterate. They belonged to the low income group with farming as their main source of income. Nearly half of the respondents prepared the compost more than seven times in a years, and kept vermibed either in their front yard or backyard beneath the *nalias* shade. Thus it showes that the farmers of this region were familiar with vermitechnology. The respondents adopted vermitechnology mainly for soil protection, source of income generation and saving of expenditure on chemical fertilizers, to make the best use of the waste materials and better field of chemical-free flowers, vegetables and fruits. A majority of the respondents used the compost once or twice on the entire land for crop cultivation. They used the compost for rice and tuvar dal, brinjal, tomato, coriander, onion, mango, cluster beans, chikoo, bajra, jowar and maize. Thirteen per cent of the respondents faced to a problems great extent and 56.9 per cent of them had problems to some extent. Nearly one-tenth of the total respondents were somewhat satisfied, very few were dissatisfied and 80.7 per cent of them were satisfied. The extent of the use of vermitechnology problems faced while operating vermitechnology and satisfaction experienced with vermitechnology were not affected by personal and family variables but were affected by situational variables. Also there was an association between the problems faced and the extent of use, and the extent of satisfaction and the extent of use. The extent of satisfaction and the extent of problems faced while operating vermitechnology were inversely related.

***Title: A Study on Energy Auditing of Domestic Units***

*Author:* Srishti Seth

*Guide:* Neena Jaju

*Year:* 2004

*Keywords:* Energy auditing, Domestic units

## Introduction

The energy problems of the world are manifested in large activities, and modern economic systems are greatly dependent on energy supplies. The growing dependence on large quantities of energy has greatly influenced the human life- styles, both in developed and developing countries. Man has become so much accustomed to technology that he is likely to forget that technology is the manifestation of energy transfer and transformation. People, in general, are becoming conscious of the role of energy in human life.

## Methodology

The aim of the present study was to probe the energy usage practices of selected families to gain an insight into the energy expenditure on different energy users possessed by the families. The study was a descriptive research. A sample of 90 homemakers of Vadodara City was selected through convenient sampling technique. The interview schedule developed to collect the data had relevant questions and a scale to find out the energy usage practices which were subjected to the establishment of content validity and reliability through split-half method. The major findings of the study revealed that homemakers of the present study were relatively good in the energy expenditure on the different energy users with regard to energy usage practices. It was found that more than three-fourths of the families followed good practices, while less than one-fourth of them scored moderate on energy usage practices. The analysis of data revealed that there was no statistically significant association between energy expenditure incurred on different energy users and their energy usage practices. However, it was found that the expenditure on electricity and petrol was significantly different with family monthly income and the education of the respondents, and the energy expenditure was significantly different with the age of the house. The ANOVA also revealed that there was a significant variation in the energy usage practices adopted by the families and selected personal, family and situational variables.

# 9

# People with Special Needs

In any society there are groups of people who have their unique problems and need the attention of researchers and policy makers. The research studies conducted in the department have touched few such groups, i.e., disabled or differently able people, aged and retired and females who are heading the households. The studies on disabled or differently able people have considered aspects such as causes and extent of disability, the problems faced by them and their families, the adjustments they make and the coping strategies they adopt to solve these problems. Human life is a continuous process of adjustment and readjustments. Both the disabled and their families need to adjust themselves to this situation. Rehabilitation of these people as productive members of society is the challenge faced by the society. The researchers can contribute by identifying the problem areas and draw attention of policymakers towards it.

Another special group is that of the aged and retired people. Aging is a natural process and the issues arising out of it need to be dealt with immediately. The population of the aged is increasing as the longetivity of people is increasing. Their physical, psychological economic and managerial problems have been studied. Their health financial security, employment, housing and living arrangements are of concern. Few researchers have made an effort to study the problems and practices of the aged of different marital status, problems of their living in old age homes and with families. An assessment of their living conditions is also an area of research. However, a lot more needs to be done as there are marked differences in the stage at which decline sets in. The need to utilise the productive potential of the young aged needs to be looked into and day-care and institutional facilities for aged with chronic limitations of their physical abilities need to be looked into. At the same time housing for them should be given consideration keeping in mind their limitations and utilising their abilities. Retired people also face similar problems and there is a need to channellise their potential for benefit of the society as they are capable but have to retire due to their reaching a particular chronological age.

Similarly, single-parent families also need to be given their due consideration. Not only female but also male members struggling with management issues need to be looked into.

*Title: A Study of Management of Time and Money by Mothers of Orthopaedically Handicapped Children*

*Author:* Aruna Dubey

*Guide:* Veena Gandotra

*Year:* 1984

*Keywords:* Money, management practices, retired people, attitude

## INTRODUCTION

The importance of time and money management by the mother of a disabled child plays a major role in his rehabilitation. The amount of time and effort she spends and the financial resources she diverts in securing medical attention and equipment for the child would affect his rehabilitation. The loss of movement and dependability in daily routine activities constitute the major problems in the rehabilitation of orthopaedically handicapped children. The extent to which a child's potential has developed depends on the help given by the mother in making him self-reliant. If the mother takes it up as a challenge and establishes the child physically and emotionally he would grow into a well adjusted and independent individual.

## METHODOLOGY

A descriptive research study was conducted. The interview schedule was used as a tool for collecting data. The sample for the study comprised 50 respondents selected purposively. For analysis categorisation, coding, tabulation and statistically analysis were used. The data were expressed in frequencies, percentages and mean scores. The coefficient of correlation and t-test were used to find the relationship.

## Major Findings

Delegating work to other family members, adjusting the standard of work, simplifying work methods were other means employed by the mother to adjust the time demand. Mothers made efforts to make children self-reliant by encouraging them to be independent in daily routine activities. Families experienced shortage of funds for meeting some of the needs of the disabled child. The extent of the disability had a direct influence on the expenditure incurred on the disabled child and the time spent in the care of the child. There was an association between the time and money management practices of mothers in general and the problems experienced by them.

***Title: A Study of Money Management Practices of Retired People and Their Attitude towards Money Management and Retirement***

*Author:* Kiran Ghai

*Guide:* Veena Gandotra

*Year:* 1982

*Keywords:* Money management practices, attitude, retired people.

## Introduction

Financial security is of significance at any period; it is of particular importance at the retirement stage of the family. There are various retirement programmes like life insurance, social security benefits, private pensions, annuities or interest on saving and various investment plans that a person must take into consideration before his retirement, so as to provide additional income after retirement. Good management of family finance makes purchasing power available at the right time and in correct amounts for effective use. It is important to highlight the problems of retired people so that concerned agencies like the government may find the result useful and prepare their employees mentally when they are on the verge of retirement about their problems and future plans so that they can have better adjustment in their future life.

## METHODOLOGY

A descriptive research study was conducted. The interview schedule was used as a tool for collecting data. The sample for the study comprised 120 respondents selected randomly from two occupational groups of low and middle income group. The data was categorised, coded, tabulated and were expressed in terms of frequency, range, mean and percentage t-test. The coefficient of correlation and chi-square test were used to test the relationship.

## MAJOR FINDINGS

The average of credit taken by retired people decreased after retirement and they used cash credit rather than instalment credit. A majority of retired persons were able to save before retirement but after retirement only a few were able to save. Different income group respondents reflected difference in their practices of handling money. Income, occupational differences, attitude of persons towards money management and their attitude towards retirement showed decided influence on money management practices followed by the retired people.

***Title: Management Problems and Practices of Homemakers with Disabled Member in the Family***

*Author:* Veena Gandotra

*Guide:* Nalini Ogale

*Year:* 1982

*Keywords:* Management problems, practices, homemakers, disabled

## INTRODUCTION

The fundamental purpose of management is to bring about a change in an orderly manner. The change may be the result of freely chosen goals or of adjustments to the forces beyond the control of the individual or family, such as is in the case of a person born with a disability or affected by it sometime during his life. The adjustments have to be made by the disabled persons themselves but the extent to which they succeed in achieving proper adjustments is very much dependent upon the family in which they live. The disability of a family member is therefore a major crisis in the family which gives rise to a number of psycho-social and managerial problems. The attitude of the homemaker may reduce or aggravate the extent of problems experienced by her. The problem situation thus created may motivate the family to set forth the goals for the rehabilitation of the disabled member or neglect him in despair. The goals set and the resources available form the inputs to the managerial system and give direction to the plans and organisation of the steps to be taken. The plans need to be implemented to bring about output in the form of the extent of rehabilitation of the disabled person and the adjustment made by the family in allocation of resources. Thus the focus of the study was on identification of the managerial behaviour of the homemaker in meeting her problems.

## METHODOLOGY

The population of the study comprised the families of disabled person in the city of Vadodara. A pilot study of 50 families was made to assess the extent of disability of the disabled in order to select the sample and to establish the validity and reliability of instruments prepared for the final study. On the basis of the result of the pilot study, a non-probability purposive, quota sample of 25 families was chosen keeping in mind the age and extent of disability of the disabled family member.

The sample consisted of five families from each group: orthopedically handicapped, blind, deaf-mute, mentally retarded and cerebral palsy groups. Data were collected by personal interview and observations of the selected households and case studies were developed. Descriptive statistics in the form of frequencies, means and percentages were used and relational statistics were used, to study the relationship between selected variables. The test used were t-test, chi-square, Pearson's product-moment correlation and partial correlation.

## MAJOR FINDINGS

The causes of disability were mainly congenital, due to disease and birth injury. Lack of awareness on the part of family regarding preventive measures was also one of the causes in a majority of the cases. The nature and extent of disability had significant effect on problems faced by the homemakers.

The psychological problems experienced by homemakers were: worry, anxiety, fear, frustration, embarrassment, unhappiness and lack of understanding of the disability. The dependence of disabled persons imposed restrictions on social contacts of the respondents and placed heavy demands on time.

The practices followed by the families included setting realistic and specific goals for rehabilitation and joint decisions by parents along with adult disabled were prevalent. Family members, relatives, friends and neighbours extended help when needed. Families tried to educate and train the disabled person to become financially independent. Families resorted to credit to supplement income, and made a cut on their expenditure to meet costs of rehabilitating the disabled. The disabled family member was made to feel as a useful member of the family by allowing him to help in household tasks. Families provided physical aids and facilities to help the disabled family member. The suggestions evolved and the feedback to the homemakers to improve their management were found to be helpful. The result of the follow-up study after a period of six months revealed that the families could tackle the problems of rehabilitation of the disabled person better when they became aware of where to seek advice, ways to reduce work, to seek financial help and improve their resource management in general.

***Title: Problems Faced by Aged and Their Attitude towards Old Age***

*Author:* Deepa Shah

*Guide:* Veena Gandotra

*Year:* 1989

*Keywords:* Problems, aged, attitude

## Introduction

Old age has become a problem in the recent years due to the increase in the life expectancy of an average person. With the breaking away of the joint families and the increasing cost of living it becomes difficult for a family to look after the needs of the aged. The steady increase in elderly population has created problems for the society as well. The society has not been able to meet the situation adequately. Hence, the aged in our country especially are facing a number of problems. In old age the magnitude and extent of the problems is much larger. The social and psychological problems are very much linked with health and financial problems. For achieving the fullest satisfaction from life, management is very important, as lack of it may increase the problems.

## Methodology

The interview schedule was used to collect the data. The sample of the study comprised widowers, widows and couples. From each strata 50 respondents were taken and from couple groups 25 women and 25 men were interviewed. Sampling was done by using stratified purposive sampling method from Bhavnagar city. The data was analysed using frequencies, percentage, mean, standard deviation, chi-square, coefficient and correlation of raw scores for testing the association between the variables.

## Major Findings

A majority of the aged from high and middle income group faced a moderate level of problems. The majority faced more social problems compared to health and managerial problems. Widowers faced more severe problems than widows and couples, and they faced more social problems. Widows faced more health and managerial problems. Couples faced comparatively less problems than widowers and widows. The majority of the respondents were having neutral attitude towards old age. Age, education, income and marital status influenced the problems faced by the aged. Occupation, age and education influenced the attitude of the aged.

***Title: Developing and Testing a Curriculum for Teaching of Home Management to the Visually Handicapped Learners***

*Author:* Sangeeta Khanna

*Guide:* Salma Nadvi

*Year:* 1990

*Keywords:* Curriculum development, teaching of home management, visually handicapped learners

## Introduction

There are around 400 lakh blind in the world out of which 90 lakhs are in India. The dependency rate of the blind and the sighted people are different. To overcome the dependency, the blind should have proper training and education which can be provided through a special curriculum. What we need today is a curriculum for the blind which makes allowance for their lack of sight and makes use of their other senses to the full. After visiting the model school for the visually handicapped of the National Institute for the Visually Handicapped, Dehradun, the investigator found that the existing content of the subjects in home management was inadequate and vague and so far no step had been taken to rectify this. Thus she took up the curriculum development of two home economics subjects, time and money management both very important and useful resources. Thus, the present study was undertaken to evaluate the existing curriculum in the field of home management for the blind children of IX and X standards, to develop an effective teaching package for them and to evaluate the effectiveness of the package prepared.

## Methodology

A case-cum-experimental study was undertaken. An interview schedule was used to gather data and factual observations made on the spot by the investigator. Purposive sampling was done to select 15 students of classes IX and X along with their teachers as respondents. On the basis of the feedback from the interview schedule and observation, the curriculum was developed for the students of IX and X. This package was subjected to content validity. One unit each from both the courses was chosen for implementation. Two written tests were conducted: one prior to the implementation of the teaching package and another after the implementation.

## Major Findings

The curriculum of the school was in accordance with the objectives of the school. The time and money management courses were taught as a part of the home science course, which did not have any specific objective, and the whole matter was taught in maximum two classes of one hour duration each. No teaching aid was used, no learning experiences offered and only one evaluation was taken in home science course in which a question was asked about time and money management. All the students reported that matter taught under time and money management was vague, so they understood only a part of it, though it proved helpful for their self-improvement. After getting the feedback from the students and teachers, the curriculum was developed and implemented.

The evaluation of learning was done by the help of two tests, one prior to the implementation of the package and another after the implementation. The answers given for the test conducted prior to implementation showed very poor results. After conducting the first test, the next step was to make daily and weekly time plans and use the management process in making a time plan in time management and 'budget, its objectives and points to be kept in mind while making it. The students were given two days to go through the matter, doubts were cleared after which learning experiences were provided and a test was taken. A maximum number of students fell within the medium achievement range.

The principal recommended that the following course could be taken up as four to six schools of the blind to note its effectiveness and for standardisation of the package. The teacher suggested the use of audio-tapes to teach in order to save time, but the students did not want the tape alone as a medium of instruction. Audio tape and discussion method along with written material in braille can be combined to teach the class.

*Title: Comparative Study of the Conditions of the Aged Staying in Institutions and with Families*

*Author:* Sneha Kapadia

*Guide:* Veena Gandotra

*Year:* 1990

*Keywords:* Aged, institutions, families

## Introduction

Extension of life has been a recent phenomenon and has been experienced by all countries in the world, developed and developing. A profound change is gradually taking place today in the structure of the Indian population. Improvement in health and arresting of premature death by conquest of killer diseases have raised the expectation of the life of people. This increase in population of older people has come gradually at first, but now very rapidly, and has raised many questions, such as individual financial security, family relationships, maintenance of good health and passing of free time by the aged. Many aged seek help from institutions for the aged, to meet the problems arising due to the changing status of the aged persons in the family. Therefore, it is very important to find out the present conditions of the aged staying in institutions and with families, and to compare the similarities and differences in the nature and type of problems they face, and their satisfaction with regards to their present conditions.

## Methodology

The descriptive research design was used. An interview schedule was used to elicit information. The sample of the study comprised 60 widows staying in institutions and 60 staying with families. It was a comparative study. Data were analysed in terms of simple frequencies, percentage, mean and chi-square and employed for testing the association between independent and dependent variables.

## Major Findings

More respondents staying in families were consulted in family decisions, especially in social and religion areas. A majority of them staying with families bore the personal expenditure themselves. None of the respondents took credit after retirement. Majority of the respondents saved in cashand a majority felt their health poor as compared to those staying with families. Those staying in institutions had a negative attitude towards aging as compared to those staying in families. Among the selected demographic variables the relationship was found significant between the type of family and occupation, decision making and occupation, and the occupation and personal expenditure. The relationship between the time use pattern before and after retirement was found significant in the case of work, leisure and rest time. The relationship between selected demographic variables and the attitude of the respondents towards aging was found significant in the cases of widows staying in institutions and with families.

***Title: A Comparative Study of Conditions of Aged Women in Urban and Rural Areas According to Their Marital Status***

*Author:* Jyotsna Joshi

*Guide:* Veena Gandotra

*Year:* 1991

*Keywords:* Aged women, marital status, rural and urban areas

## Introduction

Aging is a phenomenon that is built into the lifecycle of all organism. In the past the aged were not considered as a problem as the joint family system existed and the aged were automatically taken care of, but with rapid industrialisation and urbanisation the joint family system has become a thing of the past. The increasing cost of living, shortage of space in big cities and changing attitude of younger generation towards the aged has made it difficult for the families to look after the needs of the aged. Women like other human beings face problems since the beginning of the society but the nature of the problems and social status changes when they grow old. While considering the status of the aged women in India one has to make a distinction between rural and urban aged women as a cultural gap seems to exist between our urban way of life and our predominantly rural ethics.

## Methodology

A descriptive research design was used for the study. The interview schedule was used to elicit the data for the present study. The respondents of the study consisted of women above the age of 60 years out of which 30 married and 30 widows were selected randomly from both urban and rural areas. The data was analysed in terms of frequencies, percentage, mean and chi-square, and t-tests were employed to test the relationship between independent and dependent variables.

## Major Findings

More respondents staying in rural areas suffered from health problems as compared to those staying in urban areas. With regard to marital status it was found that an equal number of married aged as well as widows faced problems. Aged women staying in urban areas were satisfied with their financial status when compared to their counterparts in rural areas. A majority of the respondents had a neural attitude, towards old age. Widows had a more neutral attitude towards old age compared to married aged women. Marital status had a significant impact the on overall problem faced by the aged. Family size and place of residence influenced the attitude of the aged. A significant association was found among the family type, marital status, place of residence and the decision making opportunities of the respondents in the family.

***Title: A Study of Problems of Visually Handicapped Adolescent Girls and Their Attitude towards Their Handicap***

*Author:* Noopur Lodha

*Guide:* Asha Dass

*Year:* 1995

*Keywords:* Visually handicapped adolescent girls, attitude, problems

## Introduction

A visual handicap limits the range and variety of experiences, physical mobility and interaction of the individual with his environment. The situation for the visually handicapped adolescent girls is more acute beside her undergoing all the normal changes in the physical, psychological, social, economical and educational development. She has an inability attached to her. The attitudes formed by visually handicapped adolescent girl will be the result of harsh condescending or rejected attitude of the environment. This in terms lead to the formulation of an unfavourable attitude by the usually handicapped adolescent girls. There is a lot of scope for taking up research studies regarding various problems and attitude towards various aspects.

## Methodology

A descriptive research design was used for the study. A questionnaire-cum-interview schedule was used to gather data. The data of 90 visually handicapped adolescent girls was selected by purposive random technique. For data analysis, the descriptive and inferential statistics employed were frequency, percentage, mean, standard deviation, co-efficient of correlation and analysis of variance.

## Major Findings

A majority of the respondents were not aware of the cause of their being visually handicapped, congenital microphthalmas was found to be the major cause, as per the institution's record sheet. Most preferred the leisure activity watching TV and and listening to the radio. A majority of the respondents had a moderate level of problems faced in various aspects of life, such as physiological, psychological, social, marriage, economical, education, management of household. A majority showed a moderately favourable attitude towards their handicap in relation to physiological growth aspect, psychological aspects, social aspects, marital aspects, economical aspects, educational aspect and management of household. The period of stay in the institution emerged as a factor affecting the respondents' attitude towards marital aspects. The attitude of the respondents towards social aspects was found to be influenced by monthly family income.

This affected the economic problems faced by the respondents. The problems faced in various aspects of life were found to be influenced by the attitudes formed by the respondents.

***Title: The Study of Time Use, Activity Pattern and Perception of Retired People towards Their Retirement***

*Author:* Kirti Mehta

*Guide:* Maneesha Shukul

*Year:* 1996

*Keywords:* Time use, activity pattern, perception, retired people

## Introduction

Retirement is a major turning point in adult development since it is the social milestone marking the shift from middle years to old age. In the mind of retiring people, retirement is equated with "old age". Only when the time is employed and utilised in a creative way, it brings satisfaction, happiness and income to them, whereas when people remain idle, the mental physical and social conditions deteriorate. This idleness and loneliness may arise due to a number of reasons such as lack of knowledge, skill, facilities, support and guidance to them. They can be guided in utilising the time from such activities which will give them satisfaction as well as some benefits to themselves or to the family and society.

## Methodology

A descriptive research design was conducted. A questionnaire was selected as a tool to collect data. The sample of the study comprised 80 respondents 40 from non-teaching staff and 40 from teaching staff of the M.S. University of Baroda, selected through systematic random sampling technique. For data analysis descriptive statistics as frequencies, percentage, mean and standard deviation were used, and chi-square, ANAVO and t-test were used to test the hypotheses formulated for the study.

## Major Findings

It was found that teaching and non-teaching respondents spent almost equal time on work, rest and leisure. A majority of them were found to be spending more time on leisure than rest and work. A significant association was found between occupational status and perception, but for other variables such as education, age and personal income association was not found with perception of retired people towards them life.

***Title: Facilitators and Constraints in Utilizing Consumer Rights and Benefits by Disabled.***

*Author:* Ami Majmudar

*Guide:* Veena Gandotra

*Year:* 2001

*Key words:* Consumer Rights, Disabled, Facilitators and constraints

## Introduction

Disabled citizens are also consumers like all able-bodied citizens. They have the same rights and needs as any other consumer. They have some special needs and face different problems such as inaccessibility to shops, public places, and recreational facilities. The government has provided certain special facilities and benefits to them. More utilization of consumer rights and benefits will make them better consumers leading to greater satisfaction and better quality of life. Each consumer exercises his rights in varying extent; the matter requires special attention if the consumer is disabled. A dearth of information led an investigator to assess the knowledge of disabled consumers for consumer rights and benefits provided to them by the state government. It also aimed to find out the extent of utilization and problems faced by the disabled and to identify facilitators and constraints in utilizing them.

## Methodology

The descriptive survey was conducted on 238 disabled consumers selected through proportionate random sampling technique from three institutions working for disabled people in Ahmedabad City. A questionnaire was the tool to collect data. It had various scales as per the objectives of the study, and was subjected to establishment of content validity and split-half reliability.

Descriptive and inferential statistics, ANOVA, t-test, coefficient of correlation, multiple regression analysis were used to test the hypotheses.

## Major Findings

About three-fourths of the respondents were male, the mean age was 26 years; a majority were unemployed; a majority were unmarried. A little less than half were educated up to higher secondary. About two-third respondents lived in joint families and had a mean family income below Rs.5,000 per month. A majority had acquired disability due to disease between one and five years of age. Most of the respondents had good knowledge regarding consumer rights. Sex, age, education, occupation and type of family were the factors which affected the knowledge regarding consumer rights. About half of the respondents utilized the consumer rights to a high extent. A positive significant relationship was observed between the knowledge and the utilization of consumer rights. A little less than half of the respondents had good knowledge regarding benefits and showed low utilization benefits. Age, education, occupation, family income affected the extent of utilization of the benefits as well as knowledge regarding benefits. The study revealed a need for enhancing the knowledge of the disabled regarding their rights and benefits. The researcher gave a talk on All India Radio, Ahmedabad on "Disabled as a Consumer.

# 10

# Gender-based Studies

Female-headed households is an emerging issue and they have their unique lifestyles which are different from the traditional patterns of male-headed households. Their demographic profile is different, their resource base is restricted and their socio-cultural issues are unique. The rise in this group of population is due to an increase in divorce, separation, widowhood and male migration. The women need to assume the role of the protector, the carrier and bearer, and the decisionmaker. But they are not exposed to these situations. Like any other oppressed group women need special consideration in development programmes.

The researchers have focused on the problems faced by this group, the coping strategies they have adopted and the policy issues which need to be addressed. More research work is needed to gain a deeper insight into their problems.

*Title: A Study of Female Child Labour in the Unorganized Sector of Baroda City*

*Author:* Kalpana Dixit

*Guide:* Kamala Srinivasan

*Year:* 1985

*Keywords:* Female child labour, Unorganized sector.

## Introduction

A study of female child labour in the unorganized sector of Baroda City was carried out with a view to find out the extent of exploitation of female working children in terms of their working conditions, wage discrimination, working hours, job satisfaction and the time use pattern of these children.

## Methodology

The research design was exploratory-cum-descriptive. Through an interview the data were gathered from 60 female children below 14 years working in five small scale industries (viz. hosiery, rubber, heeng, ring and soap factories). An attempt was made to study the attitude of the parents of working children towards female child labour. An attitude scale was developed and subjected to establishment of validity and reliability. The sample comprised 30 randomly selected parents.

## Major Findings

The findings revealed that three-fourths of the respondents were from nuclear families, more than half were from migrant families, of which more than one-third migrated due to poverty or for better jobs. Half of the respondents' fathers' income ranged between Rs.100 and 200 per month. The mean monthly contribution of the working girl was Rs.156.98. One-third of the girls were working for eight to 10 months in a year and one-fourth were working for six to eight months. The working girls had to perform dull, monotonous and unskilled work in different industries for long hours. The rest interval period at the workplace ranged from half to one hour. About one-third of the girls got Rs. 5 to Rs. 10 as pocket money every month. The working girls had 2.79 mean hours for leisure, 9.53 hours for work and 8.14 hours for sleep. A little less than half of the girls were dissatisfied with the working conditions of their present job. About half of the parents had an unfavourable attitude towards girls, skill training, their education and 'equality of sex' approach, but had a positive attitude towards female child labour. The study shows migration as a determinant of child labour. The nature of the household and large families has a positive correlation with the female child labour as revealed through the coefficient of correlation. Protection provided at workplace and employer's behaviour were found to be significantly different from industry to industry revealed through the t-test.. The income of the family was found to be a key determinant of job satisfaction of female working children. The study clearly has an implication for making efforts to change the attitude of parents towards girl child labour. It indicates the need to strengthen the law-implementing machinery to give full protection to girl children against exploitation.

*Title: A Study of Female Construction Workers: An Exploratory Analysis*
*Author:* Sudhi Agarwal
*Guide:* Nalini Ogale
*Year:* 1988

## Introduction

Female labour which dominates the labour force in the unorganized sector, contributes critically to the developing economy of India. Also, a woman is the pilot of the family. Her role and status play a very important part in moulding the lifestyle of the family, and the utilization of this woman power resource ultimately affects the growth and development of the country. Females engaged in building construction do hard, physical labour to earn some money as well as manage their family resources for the betterment of their time, energy, money and health. The present survey was carried out to study the lifestyle and status of female construction workers.

## Methodology

The exploratory research design was used for the present study. One hundred females, engaged in building construction, from eight localities were interviewed. Data were collected through the interview and observation techniques. The data were coded, categorized, tabulated and statistically analyzed in terms of frequencies, percentages, mean, median and mode. Chi-square tests were also applied to find out the relationship between various variables.

## Major Findings

In all, 100 respondents were studied from 83 families. A majority of the female workers engaged in building construction were from tribal families. About two-thirds of the respondents had nuclear families. A small family up to four members was found in 60 per cent of the respondents, while one-third had medium sized families (5-7) members). Three-fourths of the families were nuclear in nature. The mean age of the respondents was 24.5 years. All of the respondents were illiterate. Except for two widows and 15 girls, all the female workers were married. Except for one family, all families were engaged in construction labour in Baroda. The women took up this particular job of construction work because of easy selection, minimum requirement for skill and presence of other family members in this area. The living conditions were not proper, and for lighting the workers used kerosene lamps and cooked food on open fire mud or brick chulha. Sanitary and hygienic practices were poor. After taking up the employment their economic condition in terms of income, assets and liabilities had become better. The respondents worked for 8.83 hours a day at the construction site. The social life of the female workers was restricted only to their co-workers near them, because of their frequent change of living place. Common ailments prevalent among these workers were fever and body aches, Seventy-two per cent of the workers had equal status with male workers at their workplace. The status of respondents in the family was much lower as 59 per cent had a low status, 39 had an equal status and only 2 per cent had a high status. An association was also found between the status of the females in their families and their percentage contribution to their family income.

***Title: Female-headed Households of Rural North Bihar: An Indepth Analysis of Status of Women***

*Author:* Manjula Thakur Jha

*Guide:* Veena Gandotra

*Affiliation:* Department of Home Management, Faculty of Home Science, M.S. University of Baroda, Baroda

*Year:* 1998

*Keywords:* Female-headed households, status of women

## Introduction

Bihar state is considered as an underdeveloped state providing very little employment opportunities for the people which leads to migration. The female of these families therefore have to shoulder the entire responsibilities of the family. Further it was of great concern to know how the females of these families managed to discharge their responsibilities, how they took decision at various points of time and how much freedom they had to spend their family income.

## Methodology

The present investigation was a descriptive survey conducted on 200 female heads of households living in the rural area of North Bihar, selected through a multistage random sampling design. An interview schedule was used to collect the data. Descriptive as well as relational statistics were used to analyse the data. The data were scored, categorised, tabulated and presented in frequencies, percentages, mean and standard deviation for analysing various information. Analysis of variance 't' tests and correlation coefficient were employed to study the relationship between selected variables.

## Major Findings

The mean age of the respondents was 34 years; 90.5 per cent of the respondents were illiterate. The mean family size was 5.1. The mean income was Rs. 409.50 per month. About 68 per cent of the respondents were heading the family because of the husband's migration, followed by widows (25%) and wives of physically handicapped males. The respondents had awareness of the developmental programmes but participation was very poor. Among the problems faced, the economic problem was dominating. In the area of personal and social problems feeling of insecurity at night, to entertain male visitors at home due to social criticism, fear of sexual advances from males, were important ones. The support structures of female-headed households were poor. The strategies adopted by female heads were limited due to the lack of awareness or they had no access to the sources of help. Most of the respondents felt that women were being discriminated in the family as well as in the society.

The overall status of the female heads was found to be high. Personal-familial and situational variables were affecting the problems faced by respondents which in turn influenced the status of women. The occupation of the respondents and socio-economic status affected the opinions on discrimination against women.

***Title: A Girl-child Focused Study on Gender Bias in Intra-household Resource Access and Allocation***

*Author:* Rajya Lakshmi

*Guide:* Kamala Srinivasan

*Year:* 1990

*Keywords:* girl-child, gender bias, resource, allocation

## Introduction

Gender discrimination is a drag on development and can lead to macro-problems like population explosion and poverty. The various discriminatory practices carried against girl-children have become a cause for global concern. For this a study was undertaken to study the intra-household practices of resource access and allocation, and, identify the nature and extent of discrimination.

## Methodology

An exploratory-cum-descriptive research design was used. The study also resorted to the case study method to get a deeper insight into the issue. An interview schedule was used for gathering data. The sample consisted of 100 middle income households drawn from six areas purposively. The samples of the study were those households with at least one girl-child and one boy-child, in the city of Rajahumandry, Andhra Pradesh. The units of enquiry were 50 fathers and 50 mothers. The data were analysed using measures of central tendency, measures of dispersion, percentages, and for testing the hypotheses chi-square and t-test coefficient of correlation were used.

### Major Findings

The mean family size was 5.39 members. The mean age of the fathers was 41.28 years and that of mothers was 34.9 years. In both joint and nuclear families, the mean number of daughters was less than the mean number of sons. None of the households were saving money on the named girl-children. In 59 per cent of the households daughters were discriminated in food serving pattern. Parents had negative opinions regarding equality in intra-household food allocation. Parents paid significantly a greater amount of school / college fees for sons' education than for daughters. A clear-cut demarcation of sex-segregated roles in intra-household division of labour was observed. Parents had a negative attitude in the areas of decision making, division of labour, girls' employment and food-serving pattern. Mothers-work status and educational level emerged as a significant determinant of both attitude and actual practice of discrimination. Fathers shared a more progressive attitude than mothers towards girl. A positive correlation was found between actual practices of discrimination and parents attitudes.

***Title: A Study of Factors Associated with Discrimination of Girl-child***

*Author:* Anita Patel

*Guide:* Veena Gandotra

*Year:* 1991

*Keywords:* Discrimination, girl-child, gender bias

### Introduction

Women constitute nearly half of a country's human resources. An effective management of a country's human and non-human resources leading to their optimum utilisation, is vital for its growth and the development. No society can progress if awareness and developmental urge are absent among the women. As compared to boys, girls have always been a neglected part of the family. The birth of a girl-child does not arouse as much ado and excitement as the birth of a boy. Scientific tests such as aminocentesis, is being abused to conveniently get rid of female feotuses and like a forest fire, it is spreading fast among the various segments of our society. A daughter is never regarded as a full member of her family, and she is kept under much more discipline and restriction as compared to the sons. The preference for sons, thus, is an increasing day by day and hence there is increase in the discrimination of girl-child. Thus, it has become a matter of concern for the social scientists to examine the status of girl-children in the present socio-economic conditions. These girls can act as catalysts in the development process. Thus, the study was undertaken in this area to focus the discrimination towards a girl-child and the factors which directly or indirectly affects her growth and development.

## Methodology

An interview schedule was used to elicit the data for the present study. The investigator approached each home personally, having at least one girl-child and one boy-child, and the homemakers who were non-employed from the three different income groups. The data were tabulated and analysed in terms of simple frequencies, percentage and chi-square tests to test the relationship between the independent and dependent variables.

## Major Findings

Overall the study showed that the extent of discrimination in the treatment towards a girl-child observed in LIG was greater than that in MIG and HIG. In the case of attitudes of mothers towards a girl-child, it was found that a majority of the respondents in LIG had a negative attitude towards a girl-child and a majority of the respondents in MIG and HIG had a neutral attitude towards a girl-child. A striking difference in the treatment of mothers towards a girl-child was also found between low-educated mothers and highly-educated mothers. A low discrimination was observed in highly-educated mothers. The discrimination in the treatment of mothers towards the girl-child was also observed as high in joint families than in nuclear families. A low discrimination was observed in a majority of small families and a high discrimination was observed in large families. A majority of the respondents have a welcoming attitude towards the birth of the girl-child. It was found that there was a positive relationship between the income and the attitude of the mother towards the girl-child. Therefore, it can be said that as the income increased the attitude of the mothers became favourable towards the girl-child.

***Title: Women of HO Tribe of Bihar: An Analytical Study of Their Role in Managerial Decisions, Status in the Family Participation in Developmental Programmes***

*Author:* Mary Martha Thomas

*Guide:* Nalini Ogale

*Year:* 1994

*Keywords:* Tribal women, Managerial decisions, Family participation, Developmental programmes

## Introduction

The social and economic status of Indian women has changed to a considerable extent; their condition is not yet satisfactory, especially that of rural and tribal women. Their participation in family decision making is very limited. Effective decision making is an important factor in their development. There are many developmental programmes implemented by the government for the welfare of tribal women. But their participation is always a question. The situation varies from one tribe to another. The condition of "HO" tribe of Bihar was neglected by social scientists for empirical researches. Hence, an investigation was done to explore "HO" tribal women's role in managerial decision, their status in the family, participation in developmental programmes and impediments preventing them from participation.

## Methodology

The investigation was the descriptive survey conducted in two blocks of Singbhum district of Bihar. The sample of 200 tribals, 100 men and 100 women, were selected purposively. Half of them were literate and the other half illiterate. The interview schedule consisted of questions to elicit information as per the objectives.

It contained a scale to find out the opinions of the sample about tribal women's status in the family and society. It was subjected to the establishment of validity and reliability.

### MAJOR FINDINGS

The mean age of the women respondents was about 37 years; half of the sample was illiterate; and a majority of the respondents were employed as wage labourers during the lean period. The decision-making pattern for most of the households and agricultural tasks were of democratic type. Decisions related to household assets were influenced by the educational level of the respondents. Women's manifold responsibilities allowed them to exercise more freedom in spending money. Women of 'HO' tribe did not face restriction of participation in social, religious and cultural activities; however the extent of their participation was low mainly because of their involvement in household and field work. Many women expressed that developmental programmes were not to their interest. Exposure to mass media and urban environment was limited to a few women. The study revealed that the women of 'HO' tribe enjoyed a medium level of status in their society. If the literacy level of these women could be raised, their status would become still higher.

***Title: An Exploratory Study on Empowerment of Women Beneficiaries through Government-Sponsored Economic Upliftmen Programmes (GSEUPs)***

*Author:* Razia Begum

*Guide:* Rachel George

*Year:* 1998

*Keywords:* Empowerment of women, Economic upliftment programme

### INTRODUCTION

Empowerment is an international ongoing process which involves change. The change may be in attitudes, customs, behaviour, etc. Access to and control over resources is viewed as imperative for empowerment of women. Poor women whose families are below the poverty line are given access to monetary resources for self-employment and income generation so as to bring them into the mainstream of economic development and social accounting system. A number of Government Supported Economic Upliftment Programmes (GSEUPs) are introduced from time to time to draw the economically poor into the mainstream of national economic development. Some of these programmes have women as a special target so that the income-generation capacity is enhanced which would result in higher self- esteem and empowerment. A study was undertaken to measure the extent of empowerment of selected women beneficiaries through Government Supported Economic Upliftment Programmes and compare it with non-beneficiaries.

## Methodology

The study was exploratory in nature. The data were gathered through an interview of 196 women beneficiaries of IRDP and DWCRA programmes of the government. These women were selected through multistage purposive sampling from 18 villages of Rudrapur and Bajpur blocks of Nainital District (UP). A sample of comparable non-beneficiaries was also selected which was about 50 per cent of that of the beneficiaries. The interview schedule comprised three scales developed by the investigator, viz., attitude scale, practice scale and self-esteem scale. The scores obtained by the respondents measured the extent of empowerment.

## Major Findings

A majority of the women beneficiaries were middle aged, had little education, belonged to landless or marginal farm households, to lower middle and lower socio- economic status category. Women beneficiaries in large numbers belonged to families above the poverty line. They were engaged in varied income-generating activities, the most popular being dairy, with financial support under Government Supported Economic Upliftment Programmes. About half of the sample women, their husbands and family members jointly took decisions on the use of income from income-generating activities. The extent of involvement of women beneficiaries of DWCRA was higher in income-generating activities than those of IRDP scheme. Family commitment towards income generating activities under GSEUPs was the same for both the schemes. The high empowerment scores amongst all beneficiaries in contrast to low scores were characterized by older family heads with more education, who had larger landholding, higher investment and involvement in income-generating activities, and their families had higher commitment to their income-generating activities. This led to higher income. The education level of beneficiaries was directly associated with the extent of empowerment. The beneficiaries were empowered to a greater extent than their non- beneficiary counterparts.

***Title: Intra Household Resource Allocation and Division of Labour amongst Children in the Households of Bihar***

*Author:* Anupama Sinha

*Guide:* Maneesha Shukul

*Year:* 2005

*Keywords:* Households resource allocation, Division of labour, Children

## INTRODUCTION

Women in India constitute nearly half of the population. Hence they cannot be left out of any endeavour for the building up of nation. Man and women have an equally important role to play in the development of their nation but they are discriminated in the very early age of their life. The girl child is socialized right from her childhood to take female roles. From her childhood her play materials are dolls and kitchen materials. In school, girls are encouraged to take up needlework and cookery, and thus in their socialization process in a family, sex stereotypes play their part. Since the investigator belongs to Bihar and discrimination was observed between the boy and girl child in families, she thought it important to draw empirical evidence through research so that the findings can enlighten the government and non-government organizations for taking various programmes. This would reduce the discriminating behaviour of the families, since, literature reveals there is a lot of gender discrimination present in our society.

## Methodology

The descriptive research design was adopted for the present study. A survey was carried out on the sample at 120 parents, both mothers and fathers, and those having at least one girl child and one boy child within the age group of 13-19 years, belonging to middle income group of one rural and one urban area in the state of Bihar. The snowball technique was adopted to select the sample. An interview schedule was used as the instrument of gathering data. The data were coded, categorized, tabulated and statistically analyzed in terms of frequencies, percentages, mean, median and mode. ANNOVA, t-test and coefficient of correlation were also applied to find out the relationship between various variables.

## Major Findings

More of the family belonged to either other caste or were Rajput, in both urban and rural areas. A majority of people spoke Maithili in the rural areas and Hindi in the urban areas. About three-fourths of the families were nuclear in both areas, with four-five members in each family. The mean age of mothers was 40.50 and fathers 45.30 in the urban area; in the rural area, the mean was 37.55 for mothers and 41.83 for fathers. Most of the fathers from the urban and more than one-fourth from the rural area were graduates; among mothers, a little more than half from the urban area and most of the mothers from the rural area had education till secondary school. A majority of the fathers were employed and mothers were not employed. The mean family income was Rs.15,598.47 in the urban area and Rs. 10,864.41 in the rural area. The mean age of daughters was 16.4 and sons was 15.14 in the urban area; in rural area, it was 17.89 for daughters and 1683 for sons. Most of the mothers in the urban as well as the rural areas and fathers of the rural area had an unfavourable attitude towards a girl child. One-third mothers in both areas and a little more than a third of the fathers had a neutral attitude towards a girl child.

In both areas most of the respondents had poor practices regarding intra-household resource allocation amongst children. There was discrimination of their children on the basis of gender. Girls were given less money on every aspect of their life as compared to boys. On testing the hypothesis, using the ANOVA, 't' test and coefficient of correlation, it was found that the attitude of parents towards the girl child, division of labour amongst children, practices regarding intra-households resource allocation and expenditure incurred on children varied with age, education, occupation, number of children, caste of the respondents. So, it can be concluded that there is discrimination of children on the basis of gender.

# 11

# Energy Management

Energy has always been the key to man's greatest goals, and to his dreams of a better world. The caveman started on the path to civilisation when he discovered the energy in fire and light, and utilised the energy in his body to hunt for food and survival. Today, man has come a long, long way, and discovered innumerable ways to make various forms of energy work for him. But the saddest thing is that a lot of people carelessly waste energy. In kitchens, gas and kerosene stoves sometimes burn unnecessarily.

The black soot you see coming out of automobiles means a big waste of petrol. In factories and farms, tons of precious oil is wasted through bad working methods. As long as we continue to waste our precious energy, all the efforts are of little use. That is why conservation or using something without waste is being popularised everywhere.

The researches are carried out almost all over the world to find out the consumption pattern of the families so that methods of conservation can be suggested. In the Department of Home Management also researches on the estimate of cooking time with different fuels, fuel management practices of homemakers, consumption pattern, fuel conservation practices, performance of improved chulhas, etc. have been carried out.

But this is not enough. A lot more researches can be undertaken on the related issues, and based on the findings booklets can be prepared to make people aware of the energy conservation and the need for it.

*Title: Time and Money Cost of Cooking Rice with Different Fuels*

*Author:* Mariamma Mathew

*Guide:* Elizabeth Beveridge

*Year:* 1964

*Keywords:* Fuels, cooking, cost, time cost, money cost

## Introduction

Fuel is an essential material resource for man in his day to day living. Every home consumes some fuel for cooking, the selection of which is primarily a question of availability and price. To enable the homemaker make a wise decision related to preferring such amongst various options of tests, information based on practical experience of others or research findings is required. There is a dearth of such database which when used can yield the greatest satisfaction from choices made. Hence the present investigation was undertaken to build a database in comparative time and money costs of cooking a constant quantity of rice with charcoal, gas, kerosene and wood under controlled conditions in the laboratory.

## Methodology

Based on a preliminary survey of 20 homemakers selected at random from four localities of Baroda, the fuels, namely, charcoal, gas, kerosene and wood, and the heating appliances, namely sigdi, gas burner, pressure and wick type kerosene stoves and a portable wood burning chulha were identified for the laboratory test. The time and monetory cost of cooking rice on each of the stove with its respective fuel were estimated. In all the tests the same utensil (brass vessel) was used throughout the experiment. The time of the test was recorded with the initial lighting of the chulha till the cleaning up of the utensil used in the experiment with data on lighting the stove, cooking time and cleaning-up time being recorded separately. In all the cases of fuels, the monetary cost was calculated by multiplying the mass of fuel consumed in each test by the unit price of the fuel. The data generated were analysed in terms of comparative time and money cost of cooking the given quantity of rice with charcoal, gas, kerosene and wood.

## Major Findings

Gas was the least time-consuming while charcoal was the most time-consuming. The wick-type kerosene stove, wood and pressure-type kerosene stove ranked in this order in time consumption.

Lighting time and clean-up time varied from one fuel to another. It required the longest time to light the charcoal and the least to light the gas. The utensil used on wood fire took the longest time to be cleaned. The difference between the fuels in their time cost was highly significant.

Charcoal proved to be the most expensive and kerosene the cheapest. Wood and gas ranked in between coal and kerosene. The cost varied for cooking the same amount of rice between the two kerosene stoves though the same fuel was used. The pressure-type stove proved to be cheaper than the wick-type kerosene stove by 37.25 per cent.

Statistical analysis showed highly significant results which confirmed the difference between the fuels in their money cost. The study covers comparative time and money costs of each fuel for cooking the same amount of food.

The process of getting ready included collecting all the needed equipments from the respective places and placing of equipments and fuel, measuring the rice and water, weighing the fuel, putting all equipments in place, bringing the required amount of water up to the starting temperature of 85°F and all the other steps until the time to start lighting the fuel.

The time required for lighting included the time between the lighting of the match until the ignition of the fuel. Cooking time referred to the time between the placement of the vessel on the fire until the food was cooked. Clean-up time was counted from the moment when the worker started cleaning, until it was considered clean according to the standard set by the investigator.

*Title: A Study of the Use of Solar Cooker by the Beneficiaries of the Subsidised Solar Cooker Scheme, Baroda*
*Author:* Gada Ranjan
*Guide:* Rachel George
*Year:* 1982
*Keywords:* Solar cooker, energy

## Introduction

Of all the alternatives available to the human being one with the promise of cheap, reliable and clean supply of energy in the shortest span is that of solar energy. Solar energy could be utilised for domestic and industrial purposes. Solar cookers were invented in the latter part of the eighteenth century. The Gujarat Energy Development Agency (GEDA) ventured to popularise solar cookers for domestic cooking. As a result solar cookers were supplied to enthusiastic consumers on a subsidised scheme. A feedback in relation to the extent of use made of solar cookers by the beneficiaries of the scheme would throw light on the responses of the users, and their merits and demerits as a cooking unit as well as on the revision needed in its promotional strategy. Hence this study was undertaken to ascertain practices, problems and extent of satisfaction of beneficiary housewives regarding solar cookers. It also aimed at assessing the extent of acceptability of solar cookers in day-to-day cooking. The investigator proposed to recommend promotional strategies based on the findings.

## Methodology

A descriptive research design was employed for this study, with an interview technique to gather information. Using a split-half technique or Spearman Brown Prophecy Formula the reliability of the attitude scale was established at 0.72. The coefficient sample comprised 80 beneficiaries of the subsidised solar cooker scheme. The data generated were coded, tabulated and analysed. The statistics applied included frequencies, percentages, mean and chi-square test. The Pearson product moment formula was used to estimate the correlation coefficients between selected dependent and independent variables of this study.

## MAJOR FINDINGS

The prime motivating factors for the respondents to purchase a solar cooker was the concessional rate at which it was available and its novelty. The solar cooker was mainly handled by the homemaker. Most of the homemekers used it on the terrace, mostly once a day. The users in general were aware of the fact that they had to adjust the solar cooker to the sun's position and they did so. A few home makers were not satisfied with the base material of the pans and therefore used ordinary stainless steel pans or aluminium pans. Very rarely was the solar cooker preheated. Mainly boiling, baking, and roasting were the cooking methods followed to cook food in the solar cooker. The most prominent problems faced by homemakers were the heaviness of the cooker, difficulty in solar cooking in the early morning or late afternoon hours. On an average they were quite satisfied with the solar cooker distributed by GEDA. The high income group showed a more favourable attitude than the lower income groups. Income and the education level of the homemakers did not exert any significant influence or relationship on the satisfaction, acceptability or attitude of homemakers towards the solar cooker. However, there was a definite positive relationship between the attitude of the homemakers and the satisfaction in relation to the solar cooker, and the attitude of the homemakers and acceptability of the solar cooker as a device for domestic use. The strategies for promotion and enhanced acceptability are highlighted in the recommendation of the solar cooker along with other research needs in the dissertation.

*Title: **Fuel Management Practices of the Homemakers of Baroda.***
*Author:* Seema Chaturvedi
*Guide:* Nalini Ogale
*Year:* 1984
*Keywords:* Energy, fuel, management practices

## Introduction

At present, families in our country are facing the problem of fuel shortage coupled with the sharp rise in prices of fuel. They face a difficult challenge in maintaining a well-fed family within their limited income and fuel constraints. In order to overcome the problems of ignorance of the urban homemaker in relation to the economical use of fuel, there is a great need to educate them about good fuel consumption practices. The present study was undertaken with a view to find out the types of fuels used, fuel conservation practices followed, knowledge of the homemakers about the effect of fuels on the health and environmental pollution, and about the time of energy-saving equipment.

## Methodology

A descriptive type of research design classified as a survey method was used. A questionnaire was adopted as a tool to gather data. Through purposive sampling technique a sample of 150 homemakers of Baroda city was selected for this study. Mean, standard deviation, frequency and percentage were the descriptive statistics, while the Pearson product moment correlation and analysis of variance were the inferential statistics employed for data analysis.

## Major Findings

Many respondents used more than one cooking unit and fuel to cook their food. Gas was the most commonly used fuel. The quality of food management practices of a majority of the homemakers was just average. Fuel management practices followed by a majority of the homemakers with respect to fuel conservation, effect of fuels on health and environmental pollution, increasing the equipment's efficiency and the use of time- and energy-saving equipment were also only average. As the income increased the percentage of total monthly family income spent on fuels decreased. Most of the respondents considered the gas range and the cooking gas itself to be the most efficient cooking unit and fuel. The knowledge of a majority of the respondents about all the aspects of fuel management was just average, except with regard to the efficiency and cost of the cooking units and fuels about which the homemakers possessed commendable knowledge. Most of the homemakers had just about average knowledge regarding time- and energy-saving equipment, fuel conservation practices and effect of fuels on the health and environmental pollution. All the homemakers possessed knowledge with respect to the need for proper ventilation in the kitchen. Homemakers with higher knowledge about fuel management also revealed better fuel management practices. People from different income ranges and educational levels varied greatly in their fuel management practices. Age did not have any influence on the fuel management practices and knowledge related to it. There was a negative correlation between the education of homemakers and the knowledge about fuel management practices.

***Title: Rural Domestic Energy Survey and Fuel Efficiency of Selected Models of Chulhas***

*Author:* Kirti Chauhan

*Guide:* Rachel George

*Year:* 1985

*Keywords:* Energy, rural, domestic, fuels, efficiency, chulha

## Introduction

Rural households have been dependent on fuel wood as the main source of energy to power most of the household activities. Presently it is facing an energy crisis and unless some drastic measures are taken soon, the households would find themselves in a miserable condition brought forth by non-availability of fuel wood in sufficient quantities. Since chulhas will continue to be the basic cooking appliance for many years to come, these assume paramount importance in national programmes and research. Moreover, there is a need to provide an available solution to homemakers who are the principal participants in the cooking fuel cycle. Hence the present study was undertaken to ascertain the kitchen layout, identify the fuels and fuel use technology for cooking, determine the type of utensils used, food habits of rural households, and to assess the efficiency of selected models of chulhas in the laboratory for identifying the most fuel-efficient ones.

## Methodology

Survey research design was chosen. Interview schedule was the principal tool used to gather information. Purposive random sampling technique was used to select a sample of 60 households from Jaspur village. For the data analysis, descriptive statistics, namely, frequencies, percentages and means were computed. An experimental design was formulated to test the efficiency of seven models of chulhas, namely, open fire, rural chulhas, KVIC, Improved Junagadh, PRAI, Jal Nigam and Priyagni. Water boiling tests were carried out to ascertain the fuel efficiency. A standard data record sheet was used for recording the information. Aluminium pans with flat and round bottoms were used. Mean and standard deviations were the statistics employed in data analysis.

## Major Findings

For cooking devices and cooking fuels, mud floor and brick wall with tinned roof were the most common. Round and flat-bottomed aluminium pans were found to be common among all the households. 'U'-shaped single-pot-hole chulha was found in almost all the households. The orientation of the chulha was mainly either east or west. Food was cooked outside in the yard during certain seasons of the year. Wood and agricultural wastes were found to be most common fuels used for cooking. Homemakers did not vary much in regard to their satisfaction derived regarding fuel forms and type of stove unit used. Procuring fuel was reported to be a matter of concern to them as it affected their daily routine due to longer hours spent in collecting the same. Almost all the families were vegetarians, having two meals – one in the morning and the other in the evening. The awareness of homemakers with regard to new technology was found to be very low. The performance of Improved Junagadh was the most efficient than all the other chulhas tested, open fire was the least efficient with more fuelwood consumption. Round-bottomed pans proved to be more efficient than flat bottomed pans. Shielded stoves like Pryagni and closed stoves like Improved KVIC, Improved PRAI and Improved Junagadh revealed significant potential for conserving dwindling sources of energy.

***Title: Use of Solar Cooker by Rural Households and Fuel Conservation Potential of Selected Models of Chulhas and Solar Cooker***

*Author:* Bela Goyal

*Guide:* Rachel George

*Year:* 1985

*Keywords:* Solar cooker, chulhas, fuels, conservation, energy, cooking

## INTRODUCTION

A large amount of heat loss in cooking occurs in the domestic sector. More than half the world's kitchens use wood burning stoves for cooking. The efficiency of these stoves in extremely low and hence requires larger amounts of fuel-wood in cooking. Considerable research and development have taken place in providing alternate devices for cooking, viz., solar cooker and improved chulha.

Solar cookers were promoted by Vadodara Urban Development Authority (VUDA) during 1983-84 Empirical information on energy resource conservation through solar cooking would be of immense value to make comparison with other fuel-based chulhas and also for its promotional activity.

The present study was undertaken to ascertain practices in relation to the use of solar cooker under VUDA promotional programme problems faced and extent of satisfaction realised by them in using solar cookers. Moreover it was also directed to ascertain the survey that could be effected in fuel wood consumption through the adoption of solar cooker and selected models of chulhas in preparing the standard meal.

## Methodology

A survey research design along with an experimental design was adopted. An interview schedule was used to gather data for survey research. All the households that were provided with solar cookers in Talsat and Jaspur villages formed the sample of the study. Frequencies, percentages and mean were the statistics applied for the data collected through a survey research. For experimental design, seven models of chulhas, namely, open chulha, rural chulha, Priyagni, Improved KVIC, Improved PRAI, Jalnigam and Improved Junagadh were tested and efficiency of each chulhas was ascertained through standard meal test. Time, money and fuel cost in preparing the meal was computed for the selected chulhas and solar cooker. Fuel efficiency of all the selected models of chulhas was compared from the experimental data. Mean and standard deviations were the statistics employed.

## Major Findings

The solar cooker was mainly handled by the homemaker and mostly used in the yard. Most of the households kept the solar cooker in the proper direction while it was being used. They stored the solar cookers in the room adjacent to the place of its use. The solar cooker was not used to full capacity by a majority. Three-fourths of the sample were seen to open the solar cooker in between and used it to prepare one to two items at a time.

The most prominent problems faced by households were the special care of the mirror and the inability to do cooking as and when desired. Almost all the households were satisfied with almost all different aspects of the design, quality of food, and ease of handling except its weight. Most of the respondents felt that the solar cooker could not be used as the main cooking device, and it took too much time to get the food cooked.

Different fuels consumed by rural households were wood, agricultural waste, dry sticks and kerosene, out of which only kerosene was bought and the others were gathered. The solar cooker failed to create any impact on the rural household.

Improved models of stoves tested possessed varying degrees of efficiency. Fuel wood consumption for preparing the standard meal was maximum in the case of open fire, minimum in the case of the Improved Junagadh stove. In relation to chulha with deeper fire bones, round bottomed vessels gave higher efficiencies. The fuel- and money-saving potential of different models of improved chulhas against open fire was very remarkable. Solar cookers showed cent per cent potential in saving the fuel wood in selected items where no conventional cooking was required to partially process the food.

*Title: Urban Household Energy Resource Consumption*
*Author:* Preeti Talati
*Guide:* Rachel George
*Year:* 1986
*Keywords:* Energy, resource, consumption, households

## Introduction

In India the household sector is the largest consumer of energy accounting for about 50 per cent of the total energy consumption. The area of domestic energy consumption has drawn the attention of a few researchers in recent years. Though a few studies have been undertaken in the past regarding fuel consumed by urban households and mean monthly outlay on fuel forms, very little effort has been made to identify factors that affect expenditure on fuel forms. The present study was undertaken to ascertain the structural attributes of housing, the lifestyle of households, the energy consumption behaviour the factors that affect their monthly outlay on fuels, and the attitude of housewives towards energy conservation.

## Methodology

A descriptive research design was thought to be the best. An interview method was employed to collect data for the study. The attitude scale exhibited a reliability coefficient of 0.726. A total sample of 120 housewives were chosen from Baroda city by purposive random sampling technique. For data analysis descriptive statistics employed were frequency, percentage, mean and standard deviation, and inferential statistics used were analysis of variance and coefficient of correlation.

## Major Findings

A variety of commercial fuels were consumed by households of which a majority were non-renewable ones. The largest mean monthly outlay was on petrol, followed by electricity and then cooking fuel. Households had a variety of energy-intensive goods in their possession. The most popular ones were TV, radio, refrigeration, blender and iron. Among new vehicles, two-wheelers were the most popular. Entertaining at home was a part of socialisation. Most of the households cooked moderately complex meals. Most of the foods consumed were cooked at home rather than purchased. Stainless steel and aluminium were popular base materials for cooking utensils. Factors such as need, reputation of manufacturer, durability, size of household, purpose and number of burners were given priority in the selection of equipment and cook stoves. The attitude of most of the housewives was favourable towards energy conservation. Factors like monthly income, household type, goods possessed and the number of rooms emerged out as significant variables affecting the monthly outlay and energy consumption behaviour of households.

*Title: Thermal Efficiency of Select Models of Wood Electric Burning Cook Stoves*

*Author:* Marilyn Patel

*Guide:* Rachel George

*Year:* 1986

*Keywords:* Efficiency, energy, chulhas, wood burning, cook stoves, cooking, firewood

## Introduction

Firewood is a primary source of energy. In the rural Indian households with the increasing scarcity of fuel wood and the problem of deforestation, the concept of Improved Chulhas (IC) offers an attractive option to conserve conventional biomass energy forms. As a result of near complete combustion, cooking on IC is expected to lead to a cleaner and healthier environment within the kitchen. A number of ICs are designed, developed and promoted by various agencies. The present study was undertaken to ascertain the thermal efficiency of selected wood-burning stoves, using pans of different base materials, to ascertain open fire and rural chulha. Further it was also intended to project fuel and monetary savings possible through the adoption of improved stoves.

## Methodology

An experimental research design was required for the present study. Ten models of chulhas, namely, open fire, rural chulha, Priyagni, Damru, Jalnigam chulhas, Improved PRAI chulhas, Improved KVIC chulhas, Improved Junagadh chulha, Thapoli chulha and Magan stove were tested. Water-boiling test was conducted to ascertain the thermal efficiency. The test procedure was standardised on both one and two-pot-hole chulhas. A standard data record sheet was used for recording the information. Aluminium and stainless steel pans with round bottoms were used in all the tests. Two test procedures were used to test the stoves. Mean, standard deviation and 't' tests were the statistics employed in data analysis.

## Major Findings

The improved stoves revealed better net efficiency figures than the open fire for the different phases (high and low powers) of the experiment models of chulha revealing varying efficiency figures. The potential to conserve fuel wood was thus seen to vary from stove to stove. Single-pot-shielded stove – Priyagni stove – which is a metal lightweight portable stove was seen to perform with higher thermal efficiency than some models of closed two-pot stoves. The improved Junagadh stove, Priyagni stove and Thopoli stove revealed the highest potential for conserving fuel wood. Stoves with low thermal mass gave higher efficiency than those with higher thermal mass by IVE procedure and vice versa by VITA procedure. Closed stoves performed better than shielded stoves and open fire with regard to smoke and soot formation. Better combustion took place in stoves with a grating. Aluminium pans gave better thermal efficiency than stainless steel pans.

***Title: Response of Rural Women towards Improved Chulhas and Field Testing of Improved Chulhas***

*Author:* Vandana Vingle

*Guide:* Rachel George

*Year:* 1987

*Keywords:* Rural women, improved chulha, field testing, energy, traditional chulha, cooking

## INTRODUCTION

India is one of the developing countries of the world where nearly 70 per cent of energy requirements in villages are met by firewood and other agricultural wastes, most of which are burnt in traditional chulhas every year for cooking purposes, with increasing fuel wood crisis. Various fuel / energy conservation programmes are undertaken by the central government of India. The National Project on Demonstration of Improved chulhas (NPDCC) is one such programme which aims at promoting improved, well-designed, fuel-efficient, low-cost and appropriate cook stoves. The present study was undertaken to ascertain the practices related to use of improved chulhas by the beneficiaries of NPDIC during 1984, and also to assess the performance of improved chulha in laboratory and in the field through water boiling tests.

## METHODOLOGY

A combination of descriptive research design and experimental research design was adopted for the present study. A survey method was used for the descriptive research design and an interview schedule was employed to collect the data. The sample comprised 32 households in Jaspur and Dholikua villages who had improved chulhas under NPDIC. Data analysis were planned in terms of categorisation, coding, tabulation and statistical analysis. Means, frequencies, percentages and 't' test were computed. An experimental research design comprising water boiling tests were carried out on improved chulhas in the laboratory as well as in the field. VITA test procedure was used to test the stoves efficiency. Flat-bottomed aluminium pans were used. Mean, standard deviations, co-efficient of variation and 't' test were the statistics employed in data analysis.

### Major Findings

The beneficiaries had opted voluntarily for the improved chulha. Nearly half of the respondents used the kitchen for cooking-cum-dining purposes. The sudy revealed poor fuel management practices. All cooking activities were done on the chulha and thus the chulha was the primary cooking device. Heavy dependence (81.8 per cent respondents) was seen on fuel wood gathered from farms and forests. Gathering was done mainly during summer season, basically by husbands and sons of respondents. Improved chulha was used for either making all or few items. Dry wood and twigs were used most commonly to light the chulha. 'Too much smoke', 'blackening of walls', 'soot on pots and pans', 'irritation in the eyes' and 'respiratory problems' were the common problems faced on traditional chulha. The problem faced on improved chulhas was 'difficulty in feeding fuel wood through the small mouth of the stove'. Most did not use both pot-holes together although they did cover the second pot-hole when not used.The chimney was cleaned by a very few respondents. Landholding size household and income influenced the extent of the use of the chulha significantly. The extent of the use of chulha was assessed by assigning scores to the responses on the frequency of the use. There was a slight difference in the mean score earned by users belonging to upper income group and households in the larger landholding.

***Title: Comparative Study on the Performance of a Selected model of Improved Chulha and Shielded Conventional Chulha***

*Author:* Jaya Tewari

*Guide:* Rachel George

*Year:* 1988

*Keywords:* Improved chulha, shielded conventional chulha, chulha, thermal efficiency, feedback, acceptability of improved chulha

## Introduction

The energy crisis in India is primarily due to the scarcity of fuelwood and the escalating prices of liquid fuels. To combat the fuel wood scarcity and to achieve conservation of fuel wood in the domestic sector, a key programme initiated by the government of India is promotion of the improved chulha. The present study focuses on studying the performance of a selected model of the improved chulha and comparing its efficiency with the conventional chulha. The specific objectives of the study were to assess the performance of the improved and traditional chulha by controlled cooking test, to ascertain the fuel consumption, and to study the responses of housewives towards the selected model of the improved chulhas in terms of their acceptability, problems, benefits and suggestions for improvements of the improved cook stove.

## Methodology

Experimental and case study approaches were chosen for the present study. Water Boiling Test (WBT), Controlled Cooking Test (CCT) and Kitchen Performance Test (KPT) were adopted to assess the performance. Data record sheets and interior schedules were utilised to gather data in relation to the experimental method and case studies. Data collected were subjected to tabulation and analysis. Five households were selected purposively for case study. Experimental work was carried out both in the field and the laboratory. The performance of the chulha was analysed in terms of mean thermal efficiency, mean standard specific consumption, mean specific fuel consumption, mean power rating, using WBT in terms of mean net of overall efficiency and mean specific consumption using CCP. On the other hand, mean specific daily consumption, mean fuel consumption per day, mean weight of processed food mean time to reach boiling point were computed based on the data generated through KPT.

## Major Findings

All the households had 'horse-shoe'-shaped traditional / conventional chulha. In most of the households fuels were stored in the verandah. Fuel consumption was reported to be the most during the winter season. In a majority of the households, daughters attended to cooking and tending fire in the chulha in the absence of their mother. The least quantity of processed food was found to be associated with the lowest mean fuel consumption. The maximum net efficiency attained at TC was low.

The Improved Junagadh chulha (IJC) showed a commendable potential to save fuel in comparison to the traditional chulha. The mean net and overall efficiencies of the traditional chulhas were relatively smaller in relation to those of IJC. The turndown ratio of traditional chulhas was very low. The chulha needed to be tended carefully, otherwise the fire died out. Cooking on IJC required less cooking medium since it was a slower cooking process. The turndown ratio of IJC was higher than that in TC and this facilitated maintenance of contents in pots at simmering at low burning rates. IJC, if effectively and efficiently managed, has a remarkable potential to conserve fuel wood. Though the respondents had been using TC for years, they became interested in IJC once they came to know about it. They volunteered to use it. The feedback showed that a majority of them used it occasionally. At large proportion of users complained about the small pot size. Most had not made any changes in the chulha. A shielded chulha was preferred by the households, but a slight modification to accommodate larger vessels was needed in the chulha. IJC was found to perform significantly better than TC. The performance of IJC was seen to be influenced by fuel management practices.

***Title: A Comparative Study on Energy Consumption Behaviour of Students Enrolled in Maharaja Sayajirao University of Baroda***

*Author:* Vandana Puri

*Guide:* Rachel George

*Year:* 1995

*Keywords:* Energy, petrol/diesel, fuel consumption behaviour

## INTRODUCTION

The greater the scientific and technological developments, the greater the desire for the acquisition of power-based consumer-durable goods and the higher the demand and consumption for energy to run these. This is evidenced through the use on two-wheelers automobiles and consumer-durable goods, like refrigerator, recreational equipment, and lighting and fan use by nearly every segment of the society. The youth, especially students, are energy intensive. A need exists to create an awareness amongst the youth about the ill-effects of over-consumption of fossil fuels, scarcity of natural resources effects of fuel shortage on their lifestyle in future. To achieve this goal, it is necessary to build a database on their energy consumption behaviour with special reference to two wheelers, and aid uses like lighting, fans, TV VCR, music systems and refrigerators. The buying habits of students related to petrol, and their attitude towards energy conservation and social responsibility were other aspects on which the information base was to be built.

## METHODOLOGY

A descriptive research design with a survey method was used. A questionnaire method was employed to collect data. Reliability coefficients of energy conservation behaviour scale and attitude scale were 0.849 and 0.873 respectively. A purposive random sampling technique was chosen for selecting the sample which comprised 70 boys from the Faculty of Technology and 35 girls each from the Faculty of Home Science and the Faculty of Technology respectively, thereby totalling 140 students. Data were descriptive statistical analysis, like estimation of frequencies, percentages, mean and standard deviation, and inferential statistical analysis, like analysis of variance, 't' test and correlation coefficients.

## MAJOR FINDINGS

A majority of the male students belonged to fourth year graduation , while most of the female respondents to the third year. Most of their families did not receive reimbursement for petrol and electricity. In most of the families, the monthly expenditure of petrol on all vehicles owned was between

Rs. 500 and Rs.1,000. In most of the cases, pocket allowance of respondents did not include allowance for their personal petrol expenditure. Mostly, their source of financing was parents who doled money as and when required. Most of the male respondents checked their petrol consumption on a regular basis while most of the females checked at times to keep a control on its use. Most of them refilled their vehicles once in a week and their vehicles always went into reserve before refilling. Most of the respondents checked their petrol consumption pattern. They considered energy crisis very serious and felt that the cost of petrol and electricity would increase in the future. 'Increasing energy consumption' and 'increasing population' were the reasons for the present energy problem as reported by male and female respondents. They felt that energy conservation was necessary to avoid wastage of energy.

According to the sample "use of non-conventional energy sources" and "educating the public about energy conservation techniques" were the most important methods to tackle energy problems. Most of the respondents revealed a moderate energy conservation behaviour. Most of the respondents had a neutral attitude towards energy conservation and social responsibility. Educational background, ordinal position and family income emerged as factors affecting the energy consumption behaviour of the students while ordinal position and energy consumption behaviour emerged as factors related closely with the attitude of students towards energy conservation and social responsibility. Those with a favourable attitude towards energy conservation and social responsibility, were more energy conserving in their behaviour.

# 12

# Gainful Employment of Women

India with its ancient culture and civilisation has held the position of women in high esteem around the inner circle of hearth and home. Together with the new technical developments and social changes, the standard of living has urged the homemakers to seek outside gainful employment.

'Women and work' has been a topic of study with emphasis on different aspects from time to time. People have different views regarding employment of married women outside home. Some of them may be favourable while others are unfavourable towards it. Thus, efforts should be made to minimise the inconveniences of female labour which will increase the productivity of the place of job, as well as result in better utilisation of female potentials who form half of the population of a country.

A number of researches have been undertaken on this aspect, like the reasons of gainful employment, attitudes of married and unmarried women about gainful employment, opinions of Indian men and women about the same, economic and psychic cost-cum-benefit analysis of gainful employment of married educated women, motivating factors, socio-economic and business profile of the entrepreneurs, etc. Though many researches have been undertaken on the employment of the women, some aspects are lacking, like whether the employed women really have a decision-making authority regarding financial matters. Sometimes it is seen that though women are employed they do not have the right to their money. So a need to investigate the extent to which the employed women have power over their money is felt. In the real sense, the women will be empowered if and only if they are involved in the decision-making tasks.

*Title: A Study of the Reasons why Married Homemakers Accept Gainful Employment Outside the Home in the City of Ernakulam, Kerala State*

*Author:* Sister Mary Irminia

*Guide:* Jyoti Dangoria

*Year:* 1965

*Keywords:* Gainful employment, reasons, married home makers, attitude

## Introduction

India with its ancient culture and civilisation, has held women in high esteem. This study is concerned with an attempt to find out the reasons why married homemakers accept gainful employment outside the home is Ernakulam city. The objectives of the study were to find out the economic position of families of working homemakers, the reasons for accepting outside employment, to assess the attitude of the gainfully employed homemakers towards their job, and the attitude of the other members of the family on the whole towards the working women. The economic factor and the desire to serve society have influenced them in the choice of their career.

## Methodology

A survey was conducted using a questionnaire schedule which was pretested among 20 working homemakers. From a list of married women in gainful employment, through a stratified random sampling, based on the total family income per month, the sample was selected. Out of 100 questionnaires administered personally 98 were returned. The data were analysed in averages and percentages.

## Major Findings

The time spent by the homemakers outside the home ranged from 4 to 9 hours daily. More than 55 per cent of the total sample maintained personal bank accounts. Most of the homemakers spent their earnings on food, clothes, equipment, furniture, education of children, rent and luxuries. Economic factor was the predominant reason for accepting outside employment by the homemakers of the lower income groups while the homemakers of the highest income groups were influenced by making use of their education and training in serving society. As to the attitude of the working mothers towards the family, most of them were fatigued when they returned and found their time schedule tight and exacting. They were satisfied with the financial returns of their job though they had to spend more on items like clothes and food due to the homemaker's absence at home. Nearly 71 per cent of the homemakers found the job quite pleasant and were enthusiastic about it. Mostly teachers found their job unpleasant, troublesome and difficult at times.

Most of the homemakers sent all or some of their clothes to the laundry and in some families children of pre-school age were looked after by other female family members. Most of the homemakers were satisfied with the available holidays to do certain responsible duties at home and many had somebody to share their domestic responsibilities. The other members of the family were of favourable, cooperative, pleasant and sympathetic attitude towards the working homemakers in the case of a majority of these women. Thus, outside employment provided the means for a better living and future financial security, and also secured economic independence in the case of majority of the gainfully employed homemakers.

***Title: A Comparative Study of Attitudes of Employed and Non-employed Married Women towards Gainful Employment of Married Women***

*Author:* Veena Kalia

*Guide:* Jyoti Dangoria

*Year:* 1965

*Keywords:* Attitudes, employed women, non-employed women, married women, gainful employment

## Introduction

Combining home and career is one of the major issues concerning women since the past few years. Inadequacy of the income of the bread-winner, exigency conditions, increased education, industrial revolution, urbanisation and technological advances have integrated and resulted in the steady increase of the number of women engaged in gainful employment outside home. The present study made an attempt to throw light on the attitudes of married women towards gainful employment of married women. It meant to measure whether the attitudes of society are favourable or whether people still attach importance to the traditional role of women. It also tried to study the attitude towards the presence or absence of children and their age, if present, reason for employment, approval or disapproval of employment by husband, and preference for employment status. The study was limited to only employed and unemployed urban married women having at least one child.

## Methodology

A checklist was used as a tool for recording the observations of the interview to collect data. A stratified sampling technique was used to select the total sample of 60 employed and non-employed homemakers. The sample of employed women comprised 10 teachers, five clerks, five nurses, five industrial workers and five women working counsellors, doctors and administrative officers. The data were analysed by systematic comparison and mathematical calculation.

## Major Findings

The attitudes of employed and non-employed respondents differed with the reasons given for gainful employment of married women. Economic reason was accepted by all the respondents for employment of married women. There was no significant difference in the attitudes of the two groups on the economic reasons. Employment of women having no children was totally accepted by both the groups of respondents. Out of 60 respondents 59 felt that approval of husband was essential for a married woman who seeks outside employment. The employment of a divorcee or a widow was readily accepted than that of a married woman with the husband as the main provider. Only 29 women favoured full-time employment of a married woman and it was favoured more by the employed than non-employed. There was no significant difference in the attitudes of employed and non-employed groups of women on good effects and bad effects of employment of a married woman. The preference for the jobs suitable for a married man was teaching, medicine, social work, nursing and as a librarian. The employed women preferred the job of a social worker while the non-employed preferred that of a nurse. The five least approved jobs were those as a worker in the labour force, sales woman, personal secretary, modelling and interior decoration. These findings could be used as a guide when the conditions, advantages and disadvantages of gainful employment of married women are considered.

*Title: Opinions of Indian Men and Women about Employment of Married Indian Women*

*Author:* Leela Iqbal Gulati

*Guide:* Margaret D. Liston

*Year:* 1965

*Keywords:* Opinions employment, married Indian women

## Introduction

The present study was concerned with measuring attitudes of Indian men and women regarding employment of educated married women in India outside of their homes. A need for such a study was felt with the progress of education, cultural influences from the West, universal franchise, and recognition of equality. The structure of the society is changing. In order to understand the significance of this change and its application on future policies, a need was felt to conduct the present study. One general purpose of the study was to develop an instrument which would measure, with some degree of efficiency, the attitudes held by Indian men and women.

## METHODOLOGY

A survey method in which respondents fill out a series of questionnaires was selected to gather the data. An attitude-belief inventory (Likert technique), paired comparisons, polar adjective checklist, attitude belief inventory (Wolen's degree of certainty type) techniques were used to obtain required information. The population to be interviewed was based upon lists made available by the India Students' Association and the foreign student adviser. Fifty-eight of the respondents consisting of 35 men and 23 women were willing to take the test. After being edited, coded and tabulated on flow sheets, the data were punched onto IBM cards to facilitate descriptive and analytical interpretation. Frequency distributions, mean scores and scale analysis by paired comparisons were the statistical techniques used.

## MAJOR FINDINGS

One-half of the respondents were students, one-fifth were wives and about one-seventh were staff members. Through the Likert type attitude belief inventory it was found that the reasons most frequently approved for married women to take employment seemed to be essentially financial in nature. However, women respondents favoured personal considerations more frequently than the men. In the attitude belief inventory, productive use of education was found as the most frequently approved reason for the wife's employment.

The most possible undesirable effects on the traditional roles of Indian women, as viewed by the respondents, were that the family would find it more difficult to have all its meals together, maintain control over the servants, make the home attractive, and entertain relatives. More men than women felt that she would find it difficult to build wholesome relations. The detrimental effects that was felt by the respondents, and particularly by the male respondents, were that the working wife would become more independent.

Men, on the whole, seemed more conservative than women regarding paid employment for married women. The degree of certainty type inventory of attitudes and beliefs dealt mostly with various roles of the wife and her functions in the family.

The respondents approved with a high degree of certainty that women should be as well educated as men and that they should receive equal pay as men. A polar trait adjectives technique was used to obtain the opinions. Four out of five respondents viewed an employed homemaker as sociable, time conscious, forward looking, practical, well-groomed, organised and active. The method of paired comparisons was employed to order seven selected reasons on a continuum with respect to their degree of motivating Indian women towards paid employment. The responses along the continuum or descending order were use of education, increase money income, feeling useful, occupying time, feeling respected, enjoying outside contacts and avoiding household routine. There were significant differences in the scale positions of the values. The reasons given for taking employment by one-third of the group were use of education, personal development, and service to the community. It was noticed that men seemed to be more willing to allow their own wives to combine their family responsibilities with participation in public life but more women felt they would rather work for money and gain economic independence than do voluntary services to the community.

***Title: Attitudes of College Teachers and Students towards the Employment of Educated Married Women***

*Author:* Sucheta Carrol

*Guide:* Mariamma Mathew

*Year:* 1969

*Keywords:* Attitudes, employment, educated married women, views

## Introduction

'Women and work' has been a topic of study with emphasis on different aspects from time to time. People have different views regarding employment of married women outside home. Some of them may be favourable while others are unfavourable towards it. Whatever the attitude may be, it can have a direct leaning on an individual's and a family's decisionmaking, particularly in deciding whether the wife should be employed outside the home or not. The present study was therefore undertaken to construct a reliable and valid instrument for measuring the attitude, and then use the same for identifying and measuring the attitudes of people towards employment of married women. The other objectives of the study were to ascertain the attitudes of college teachers and students towards the employment of educated married women, to find out the differences in the attitudes of teacher and student respondents, male and female respondents and married and married teacher respondents, and to ascertain the reasons for favourable or unfavourable attitude, and identify the hierarchy of importance of the reasons.

## Methodology

Thurstone's Equal Appearing Interval Method was used for studying the attitude of people towards the employment of married women. Content validity and reliability were established for the scale. The correlation coefficient was 0.73. A questionnaire was used to collect the data. The sample was selected randomly with the help of the table of random numbers for the three groups: male teachers, male students and female students from M. S. University of Baroda. The sample comprised 240 respondents, 120 each for the teachers and students, 60 males and an equal number of females in each case. The data were coded and analysed by frequencies, percentages, means, factorial design of analysis of variance and chi-square tests.

## Major Findings

In general, the attitudes of the respondents were scattered and diversed. The proportion of females who had a favourable attitude was more than the males. The results of ANOVA showed that the male and female respondents varied significantly in their attitude towards the employment of married women. The teachers and students did not vary significantly in their attitude towards the employment of married women. Marital status, income and designation of the teachers had no association with their attitude scores obtained. Financial reasons like 'to add to the family income', 'to raise the standard of living' and 'to relieve family of financial debts if any' were mostly accepted by the respondents as reasons in favour of the employment of married women.

More female than the male respondents accepted the reasons pertaining to the personal development and interest of wives. The differences in ranking by the male and female respondents were found significant for the reasons 'to feel useful', and 'to support in educating the family members'. 'Children are neglected', was the reason that was accepted as being the most justifiable reason not in favour of married women's employment.

*Title: Economic and Psychic Cost-cum-benefit Analysis of Gainful Employment of Married Educated Women*

*Author:* Kavita Choudhary

*Guide:* Kamala Srinivasan

*Year:* 1981

*Keywords:* Economic cost, psychic cost, cost-cum-benefit analysis, gainful employment, married educated women

### Introduction

Women have been entering into remunerative occupations and professions in increasing number. The activities she performs and the responsibilities she shares at home have a direct or indirect bearing on the country's economic and social progress. Thus, efforts should be made to minimise the inconveniences of female labour which will not only increase the productivity at the place of the job, but also result in better utilisation of female potentials who form half of the population in our country.

Therefore, the present study was undertaken to determine the role-related expenditure which reflects the economic cost-benefit of gainful employment of married educated women, to assess the psychic cost and benefit of gainful employment of married educated women, and to measure the job satisfaction and attitudes of the respondents.

## METHODOLOGY

A descriptive survey was adopted as a research design for the present study. A structured questionnaire was tested and reliability was established for both descriptive rating scale and attitude scale by using the Spearman Brown Prophesy formula. The reliability coefficient was 0.92 for the descriptive rating scale and 0.98 for the attitude scale. A stratified random sampling was used to select the sample from three occupations, viz., teachers, clerks and lecturers. By using the table of random numbers, the total sample of 100 employed wives was selected randomly for the above three groups. The data were coded, tabulated and analysed by frequency, percentage, mean, median, mode and standard deviation. 't' test of pooled variance was used for testing the hypotheses. The Karl Pearson formula of coefficient of correlation was also computed to find out the association between the job satisfaction and attitudes of the respondents.

## MAJOR FINDINGS

A majority of respondents had permanent jobs. The reasons, for feelings of objections by husbands towards wives in jobs were: inadequate care of child and neglect of household responsibilities. In case of teachers and clerks categories, joint decisions were made which shows a syncretic cooperation, whereas in the case of lecturers category, the women were taking autocratic decisions. The lecturers category was less economically oriented for job as compared to other two categories. The husband's help was more in teachers and clerks categories, whereas paid help was more in lecturers category which is an account of their higher occupational status associated with higher income. Lecturers had more of a single bank account in their own name compared to the other two categories. Expenditure on personal clothing and hiring services was positively associated with a higher occupational status associated with income. But with regard to expenditure on eating outside and transportation, occupational status partially accounted for significant differences between the three categories. Purchase of household durables, outlay on house construction and on savings was dependent on the occupational status. The study revealed that economic benefit increases with higher occupational status at an increasing rate while economic cost tends to increase with higher occupational status at a diminishing rate. The psychic benefit increased with higher occupational status as reflected by mean scores of three occupational categories. The job satisfaction followed an increasing tendency with a higher occupational status. With the increasing status, the achievement level of children was significantly high. There was a tendency to have more of positive attitudes towards the job with a higher occupational status. Thus, the clerks categories had a relatively higher cost, both economically and psychologically, followed by teachers category, whereas in the case of lecturers category, psychic-cum-economic benefit were relatively more.

***Title: A Comparative Study of the Attitude of Husbands whose Wives were Employed and Those whose Wives were not Employed Regarding Gainful Employment of Married Educated Women***

*Author:* Bina Bhatt

*Guide:* Asha Dass

*Year:* 1983

*Keywords:* Attitude, gainful employment of wives, married educated women

## Introduction

In our country, a husband is the head of the family; he is the dominating power. His attitude towards the employment of married educated women, therefore, plays an important role. It may be acceptable for unmarried women to work but according to the attitude of husbands some may have to discontinue their employment after marriage while others continue their job. Therefore the study was designed with the main objective to study the attitude of husbands whose who wives were employed and of those whose wives were not employed, and regarding the employment of married educated women. It also aimed to study the relationship of some demographic factors with attitudes towards gainful employment of married educated women, to construct a scale to measure the attitude and views of husbands towards the employment of educated married women and to determine the differences between the attitude of husbands whose wives are employed and whose wives are not employed. The study was limited to lecturers, readers and professors of M.S. University, Baroda, having nuclear families.

## Methodology

A structured questionnaire was used as a tool for collecting data. An attitude scale was developed which was given to the experts for content validity. Reliability was determined through test-retest method. A sample of 120 male teaching staff of the M. S. University was selected. After the collection of data, it was coded, tabulated and analysed. Simple frequencies, mean, percentage and chi-square tests were used for analysing the data.

## Major Findings

Out of the total sample of 120 respondents, half of the respondents had employed wives while the other half had non-employed wives. Nearly half of the employed wives were post-graduates and nearly 80 per cent of the non-employed wives were graduates. A majority of the sample had four to six members in their families. The mean income of the employed group was Rs. 3,211 per month and of the non-employed group was Rs. 2126 per month.

Regarding 'marital relationship', 'household work', 'personal traits' and job, a majority of the husbands whose wives were employed were having a positive attitude while a major proportion of the non-employed group was having a neutral attitude. Referring to the specific contents, like 'child care', 'marital relationship', 'household work', 'personal traits', and 'job', there was a significant difference in the attitude of both the groups. The income of the family and the age of the husband had some effect on the attitude of the subjects whereas the size of the family and the wife's occupation had no effect on the attitude of the subjects.

*Title: A Study of Female Labour Force Participation in Development: Its Extent and Impact of Family Living in Rural Bangladesh*
*Author:* Feroza Sultana
*Guide:* Kamala Srinivasan
*Year:* 1984
*Keywords:* Female labour force, development, family living

## Introduction

The utilisation of women power for national goals must be planned in a development framework that protects women's rights and needs by including them in the development as both participants and contributors. It is widely known that women's inequality has tended to be related to the importance of their economic participation. Women are definitely a disadvantaged group in the matter of their labour force participation. The present study was undertaken in Bangladesh to determine the extent of female labour force participation and its characteristics, to analyse the occupational pattern of both employed and unemployed women, and to study the consumption expenditure pattern and the family behaviour pattern of households in selected areas indicating the status of women in the home and the community.

## Methodology

The research design of the present study was mainly a descriptive survey. The survey covered 200 rural married women, both employed and unemployed, and their households. A three-stage sampling procedure was adopted. It was a purposive selection with the union and villages at the first and second stages, respectively, and in the third stage, households were selected by a stratified and proportionate random sampling method. Data were collected through personal interview and observation. Elementary statistics used in the analyses were percentage, measures of central tendency and measures of dispersion. Analysis of variance, t-test and chi-square test, linear and stepwise multiple repression were used to see the significant difference and relationship between different variables.

## Major Findings

The mean age at the marriage of the wives was less than 15 years. The sex ratio in the present sample was 1:0.9 (male to female) indicating the lower position of women. The mean number of children born (5.66) along with the mean birth spacing of children (2.38) years showed lack of control over fertility by the housewives. Both the literacy level of wives and the socio-economic status of households had a direct relationship with fertility. The female labour participation had a clear negative relationship with the fertility behaviour. Religion had a significant relationship with fertility. A small family size was positively related to female labour participation. Hindu women were found to be employed more significantly than the Muslim wives and employment rate decreased with the increasing literacy level. A majority of the women belonging to the extreme poor households were engaged in very low wage-paid activities the Bidi making, rope making, vegetable, like vending or as maidservants. The extent of dissatisfaction was more among the women employed in low paid jobs. Most of the respondents expressed their willingness to learn skills provided there was an opportunity. Literacy, socio-economic status, religion, family size, only literacy and religion were found to be significant in influencing the status of women, on the basis of t-test and F-test. Through stepwise multiple regression, male labour participation and literacy were found to be significantly affecting the status. There was no significant difference between the expenditure pattern of employed and unemployed women's households as per the poor and extreme poor status of households.

***Title: A Study of Job Satisfaction/stress and Coping Styles of Educated Mothers Gainfully Employed Outside the Home***

*Author:* Vandana Kapoor

*Guide:* Kamala Srinivasan

*Year:* 1984

*Keywords:* Job satisfaction, Stress, Coping styles, Educated mothers, Gainfully employed

## Introduction

There is a need for an indepth research, especially with respect to organizational role, stress, and physical and psychological health of the working women. Therefore, a study was undertaken with the broad objective of identifying the determinants of job satisfaction, the stress of working mothers, the impact of job satisfaction/stress on their health aspect and the varying coping styles adopted by them. This will help the management experts to formulate appropriate guidelines for them working mothers, provide a basis for future researches and open opportunities for employment in a variety of fields concerning women welfare.

## Methodology

The descriptive research design was used. An interview-cum-questionnaire schedule was used to collect data. The study was done on 100 homemakers belonging to four occupational categories: doctors, nurses, teachers and lecturers, selected on the basis of purposive-cum-quota random sampling techniques. The descriptive as well as relational statistics were used for data analysis.

## Major Findings

The mean number of years of job held was 9.08 years. Only 11 per cent reported of the workplace to be far off. It was encouraging to note that the respondents perceived that their husbands were satisfied to have a working wife. Dissatisfaction was found mostly by children. Major reasons for objection were neglect of household, less care of children and burden of household responsibilities. The nurses category showed a higher job satisfaction and doctors the least; overall the sample reported average health. It was found that there were more psychological problems than physical health problems. The nurses' category reported maximum job satisfaction. Overall the coping styles did not reveal any unhealthy practice. The socioeconomic status shared significant variations in I status class and II status class respondents. Job satisfaction was more among nurses, followed by teachers, doctors and lecturers. The psychological problems were found more among all the four occupational groups. The nurses' category had the maximum job satisfaction and the minimum stress.

***Title: An Inquiry of Nature and Causes of Non- participation in Gainful Employment of Educated Married Housewives, Their Stress, Coping Styles and Attitude towards Gainful Employment***
*Author:* Geeta Malik
*Guide:* Kamala Srinivasan
*Year:* 1985
*Keywords:* Gainful employment, educated wives, married housewives, stress, coping styles, attitude

## INTRODUCTION

Education becomes an important input in the productive process to determine the quality of the human factor. The level of development, in fact, between countries is often directly compared in terms of the proportion of the educated in a given population. A woman's intelligence and capacity to work is as valuable as a man's and her right to work is as valid as his. Today, women are entering into a number of professions and these women, being educated, join careers due to a number of reasons. Many researches have focused on the employed women but to the investigator's knowledge no study has been done on educated women not participating in gainful employment and their reasons for non-participation in it. Hence the present study was conducted to find out the causes of educated married women for non-participation in gainful employment, stress at home and coping styles, and their attitude towards gainful employment outside the home. The study was limited to a 100 married educated women with minimum high school certificate pass.

## METHODOLOGY

The study was based on a descriptive research design. A survey method was used and interview-cum-questionnaire schedule was framed to collect the data. A sample of 100 educated married women was selected on the basis of random sampling technique. For attitude scale the content validity was tested and reliability (0.98) was established by using the Spearman Brown Prophesy formula. Data were analysed and presented in terms of frequency, percentage and the measures of control tendency. 't'-test of pooled variance was used for testing the hypotheses postulated for the present study.

## Major Findings

The mean family size was five members. The male to female sex ratio was 1:0.91 and the mean age of respondents was 32.05 years. The mean per capita income was Rs. 551.72 which is lower than the national per capita income. The time spending pattern showed that maximum time went to rest and sleep (approximately nine hours). Most of the sample reported satisfaction with the existing standard of living as a reason for non-participation. Other reasons quoted by respondents for non-participation were 'household chores', 'objection by husband and in-laws', 'children-oriented reasons' and 'job conditions'. Few reported of taking pills, shouting at husband and children, crying out silently which are not desirable ways of overcoming stress. The tendency of a positive attitude was there though it was maximum in the high income and minimum in the low income category. Family type, size and family income as determinants of non-participation were partially accepted. There was a significant difference of coping styles between low and high, middle and high-income categories. Family income as a significant variable of attitude scores was partially accepted. Family type was found to influence attitude scores whereas educational category was found to be non-significant.

***Title: Women's Work Pattern and Economic Contribution to Family Resource Development in Rural Households of Haryana***

*Author:* Savita Singal

*Guide:* Kamala Srinivasan

*Year:* 1989

*Keywords:* Work pattern, economic contribution, family resource development, rural households

## Introduction

Rural women's work pattern revolves around a variety of jobs in home, farm and livestock management. Domestic work is made up of many purposeful activities, resulting in the production of goods and services which enable the family to function as a unit. In most developing economies, women are exclusively responsible for the domestic work; in other words, this unpaid domestic work is everywhere seen as women's work, women's responsibility. However women's contribution to this income through their tremendous labour input is largely ignored because it is separate from the market economy. Factors as diverse as stereotyping men as breadwinners, excluding women's economic contribution from official statistics and assuming that women will benefit from the trickle-down effect of a family-oriented development programmes kept women's real and potential contribution to family resource development largely invisible.

## Methodology

A descriptive study was conducted and an interview schedule was used as a tool for gathering data. The sample of the study comprised 120 respondents through a multistage sampling technique. Data were statistically analysed using appropriate tests like measures of central tendency, dispersion, chi-square, correlation, t-test, F-test multiple regression analysis.

## Major Findings

Housework (child care, household chores) and economically extended work (fetching fuel, water and making cowdung cakes) crucial for families' survival are still exclusively women's responsibility. Agricultural tasks, especially during the peak season, involved the use of body in squatting and bending positions. Time-use analyses of rural women reflect that besides house work, their contribution in terms of real income through agricultural production and livestock management is enormous. More that 50 per cent of the rural women contributed to the family through money income by involving themselves in various types of paid activities.

*Title: Women at Work – A Comparative Study of Doctors and Bank Officers*

*Author:* Kalpana Srivastava

*Guide:* Asha Dass

*Year:* 1990

*Keywords:* Women, work, employment

## Introduction

Women of today are trying to combine two things together satisfactorily – management of home and outside employment. Management of home as such is a full-time job, so those women who take outside employment with it have to make several adjustments in order to make a satisfactory combination of management of home and outside employment. Mostly, it had been found that doctors have very irregular hours of work and for lady doctors with small children it is a great problem. Whereas bank officers have fixed hours of work yet they have to stay out of home for long hours and when there are young children then it becomes a problem to combine home and job responsibilities. Therefore, the study was designed to know the reasons of employment and opinions from lady doctors and bank officers regarding employment, child care, household responsibilities and leisure time, its causes and measures of solving.

## Methodology

The descriptive survey method was used for the present study. The interview schedule was adopted for collecting data. Hospitals and nationalised banks were selected by a purposive sampling technique. The two occupational groups, viz., lady doctors and lady bank officers, formed the two strata for the present study. A quota of 30 respondents from each strata, who were mothers of children between the age group of 0 and six years, was selected. The data were coded, tabulated and analysed. Statistical analysis used were frequency, percentage, mean, association of attributes and correlation coefficient.

## Major Findings

Half of the respondents belonged to the age group of 31-35 years and lived in joint families. The mean income of the respondents was Rs. 4,200 and the mean income of the family was Rs. 7,333. Almost every respondent their income and contributed to the family expenditure. Most of the respondents had the problem of a heavy workload because of overwork due to lack of staff. Little more than half of the respondents felt satisfied with their job and did not have any job-related problems. Most of the respondents had problems that satisfactory care of the child was not taken by the servant as the servant was too lenient and respondents were not able to spend much time with their child due to lack of time.

Families who lived in joint families had less problems as compared to nuclear families, who got help mostly from family members. Physical care of the child was positively associated with the joint family, income and number of children, whereas attributes, such as two professionals, bank officers and lady doctors, and the hours of service of the working homemaker were not associated positively. All the attributes, such as joint family, two professionals, income and the hours of service of working homemaker, were negatively associated with the domestic chores. Leisure time was positively associated with the attributes, such as two professionals, number of children and age of the children, whereas attributes, such as joint family and hours of service of working homemaker, was negatively associated.

***Title: A study of Awareness and Post-effectiveness of the Self-employment Programme for Rural Women in Three Selected Villages of Najafgarh Block, Delhi.***

*Author:* Vandana Dogra

*Guide:* Salma Saifullah

*Year:* 1990

*Keywords:* Awareness, Self-employment programme, Rural women, Post effectiveness

## Introduction

Women are the most important human resources in the development of countries' economic. If this human power is not properly utilized, no economic and social transformation of society is possible. After reviewing the literature it was found that various studies were conducted but they all mainly deal with the administrative aspect, like training methodology, problem of finance problem, selecting the beneficiaries, etc, but the emphasis is on the awareness of women beneficiaries, their problem during and after training, the impact of the programme, the problem of the beneficiaries, etc. So, in the present study, the investigator tried to make this study more beneficiary-oriented as the findings of this study may be helpful for planners, administrators and future researchers to know the bottlenecks which act as a major hindrance for the successful implementation of any programme.

## Methodology

For the study, the survey method was used. The research design was descriptive in nature. The purposive sampling technique was used. The interview schedule was used for data collection. The study was limited to 150 women respondents of Najafgarh block, Delhi. The descriptive as well as relational statistics were used for data analysis.

## Major Findings

Most of the trainers had a medium level of awareness. Most of the trainers learned this skill in meeting the household needs, thus saved money and also by taking orders from others to earn-money. Different opinions were also given by the trainers, like stipend as a motivation for learning the skill, work arrangement done by the government, timings of training, etc. A majority had problems of raw materials, lack of marketing outlet, size of classroom, lack of confidence in returning the loan, etc. To overcome these problems all the trainers suggested that the size of the classroom and equipments in the centre should be increased. There was found to exist a great association between the level of awareness and self-employment, income, general criteria and facility provided. The association was also found between the training and increase in income of the trainers after training.

***Title: Socio-economic and Business Profile, Motivating Factors and Problem Solving Strategies of Male and Female Entrepreneurs: A Gender Focused Analysis***

*Author:* Mitali Bali

*Guide:* Kamala Srinivasan

*Year:* 1992

*Keywords:* Business profile, socio-economic profile, women, entrepreneurs, motivating factors

## Introduction

Among the factors of production, it is the "entrepreneur", i.e., the human resource component who co-ordinates the other factors. Studies have indicated that entrepreneurship development in a society depends on the prevailing economic, social, religious, cultural and psychological factors. Therefore, the traditional picture of a woman being docile, dependent, obedient, led to blatant neglect of woman power from the development scene. But with industrialisation, urbanisation, democratisation and other factors, like higher education of women and breakage of joint family system, women have stepped into the economic scene and has left their indelible mark on it. In order to bring women in the main stream of development of business world, it is very important to study the gender dimension in the area of entrepreneurial development. Hence, the present study was undertaken to study the socio-economic and business profile, motivating factors and problem solving strategies of male and female entrepreneurs.

## Methodology

The research design of the study was exploratory-cum-descriptive. A survey method was used and the tool for collection of data was questionnaire-cum-interview. A purposive sample of 30 female and 30 male entrepreneurs of Baroda was taken. Their initial investment is above Rs. 50,000 with a minimum of three years' experience. The statistics applied were frequency, percentage distribution, measures of central tendency. Chi-square test, Spearman's rank correlation and Karl Pearson's co-efficient of correlation were used to test the hypothesis.

## MAJOR FINDINGS

Both the samples were from affluent families of liberal views giving ample opportunities, especially to females, to take decisions on their own, take the initiative and risks. There was cent per cent awareness about financial assistance from banks and other institutes, and a very few utilised the infrastructure facilities available in terms of incentives like training inputs and technical knowhow. A higher percentage of females and males were in marketing and manufacturing respectively. Most of both the samples were sole proprietors. The reasons for the choice of products showed no significant variation among the gender. However there was a significant variation among the gender on variables of "sources of help in project proposal", females being more dependent on "relatives" and males on friends". No significant variation was found among the gender on variables of 'financial', 'social', 'personal' and 'family-centered reasons' for entering into the entrepreneurial world. Females scored significantly higher than the males in the business competency test, showing a higher level of entrepreneurial traits than males. High correlations were found between the genders on variables of production and management problems, and infrastructural problems. There was no significant variation among the strategies adopted by both the sexes when faced with a difficult problem.

***Title: Training Programme for Self-employment, Trainees' Perception Its Impact – A participatory-cum-Action-oriented Research***

*Author:* Razia Begum

*Guide:* K. Srinivasan

*Year:* 1993

*Keywords:* Training programme, Self-employment, Perception

## Introduction

Despite the fact that multi-pronged training programmes in women's entrepreneurial development have been undertaken at different levels, government centre and states, it is very disappointing to note that the self-employed women constitute a mere 1 per cent (Vinzem 1987). This strongly reveals the need for the involvement of other institutions such as the educational institutions in general and higher educational institutions in particular, through their extension research and development activities. Based on this a study was undertaken to organize and conduct a knowledge-cum-skill development training programme to selected batches of females through participatory-cum-action oriented research that would help them to become self-employed.

## Methodology

The experimental component with appraisal before and after training was built within the research design. The interview schedule was used for data collection. The training programme for self-employment was started in two voluntary institutions which was helping poor students: Methodist Technical Institute and Friends Society. The income- generation skills training, i.e. food processing and preservation, was for one year and handicraft work was of four-five months' duration.

## Major Findings

The overall data analysis and findings showed a significant improvement in the entrepreneurial traits of the trainees. Trainees also revealed a significant progress in the skill performances. The knowledge input given by a bank on credit use and by DIC on how to start and run an enterprise resulted in trainees seriously inquiring for eligibility for grant of loan amount for starting their own enterprise. The exposure to the different types of trades which can be started by women entrepreneurs at Diamond Jubilee Cottage Industries and lectures on motivation and managerial competencies given by CED had a positive effect on their entrepreneurial skills.

***Title: Attitude of Female Students about Multiple Roles of Career Women of Dual Career Families of 21st Century***

*Author:* Aradhana Bhuyan

*Guide:* Rachel George

*Year:* 1994

*Keywords:* Attitude, multiple roles, career women, dual career

## Introduction

The role of women in the developmental process in the Third World countries has received attention and close examination only over the last two decades. The economic contribution of married women had far reaching effects on their perceptions and performance of their familial roles and expectations from others. The attitude of different members of the society towards the employment of women can affect the actual employment of married women. So it is important to investigate the views of society regarding this issue. Hence the present study was framed to determine the attitude and beliefs of female students towards the multiple role of career women of dual career families of the twenty-first century, to determine the perception of female students about the problems of career women, and to ascertain the operations of female students and ranking of career goal in relation to other goals identified by them.

## Methodology

A questionnaire schedule was used to gather data. Descriptive rating scales were prepared to measure attitude towards multiple roles of career woman, beliefs about the image of career women of dual career families of twenty-first century. Reliability of these rating scales was established by a split-half technique. The sample comprised 165 female students of M.S. University selected at random. The collected data were coded, categorised and analysed. The descriptive statistics employed were frequency, percentage, mean and standard deviation while inferential statistics employed were analysis of variance and correlation coefficient.

## MAJOR FINDINGS

A majority of the respondents were very young and first-born, and belonged to the nuclear family and the high income group in the urban area. Most of the respondents had given first preference to career than the other roles, and teaching profession emerged as the most popular career choice. Most of them thought that they would be able to achieve their goals beyond AD 2000. Familial problem was the main hurdle for a majority of the respondents in goal achievement. Most of the respondents had a favorable attitude towards multiple roles and positive beliefs towards the different roles in future that career women would be playing, the income of the respondent's mother, the age of father, the beliefs and perceptions of respondent's towards problems of future. Career women emerged as factors affecting respondents' attitude towards multiple roles of future career women. The age of the father, the attitude related to familial responsibility, gender equity, political and religious roles and the perception of respondents towards problems emerged as factors affecting respondents' belief towards different roles of future career women. The income of the mother, the total attitude score, attitude and beliefs towards familial responsibility, and images emerged as factors affecting respondents' perception towards problems would be faced by future career women.

***Title: A Study of Job Satisfaction among Career Women in Managerial Position***

*Author:* Rakhee Sheth

*Guide:* Rachel George

*Year:* 1994

*Keywords:* Job satisfaction, career women

## INTRODUCTION

There has been remarkable changes in the status or position of women in India, especially after independence. More and more women have been entering educational institutions, professions and public life. In spite of the added role as a working woman and the additional status as an economically independent person, she is expected to carry out the role of a traditional housewife and to do household chores all by herself with / without paid or unpaid help. Job satisfaction gives happiness, efficiency and success in the work. It gives harmony to the individual and progress to the society. The present study was planned to study the job satisfaction of married career women in managerial positions, to assess the role strain experienced and the coping strategies adopted.

## Methodology

A questionnaire schedule was used to gather data pertaining to the present study. A descriptive rating scale was prepared to measure job satisfaction of career women, their role strain and the coping strategies adopted that they adopted. Ninety-five married career women residing in Baroda were selected by purposive random sampling technique. The data were coded and categorised. For data analysis the descriptive statistics employed were frequency, percentage, mean and standard deviation while the inferential statistics employed were analysis of variance and correlation coefficient.

## Major Findings

The mean age of respondents was 43.56 years and of their spouses the 43.33 years. A majority of the respondents and spouses belong to the high level of education group, i.e., postgraduation or above postgraduation. The mean size of the family was 4.19. More than 50 per cent of the respondents were involved in dealing with managerial or administrative work. Most of them perceived a cooperative climate in their organisation. Most of the respondents' spouses helped them in household chores, marketing and payment of bills and banking work while their children helped in household chores and marketing work. Most of them had part-time paid help to accomplish routine household tasks. Most of the respondents were moderately satisfied with their job and experienced a moderate role strain. Most of them adopted moderate coping strategies to cope up with their dual role. Age and the number of years of work in the present organisation influenced the job satisfaction. There was a negative correlation between the relationship with their superior and the number of years of married life. A positive correlation was found between (i) job clarity/security, (ii) relation with colleagues and the hours of work done at job. There was a negative correlation between authority/power, relation with superior and colleagues, physical surroundings and working conditions, total score of job satisfaction and role strain. A positive correlation existed between physical and mental exertion and total annual income of family. Coping style and overall job satisfaction as well as satisfaction regarding remuneration, job clarity and security were positively correlated. There was a negative correlation between coping with life regarding organisation and the number of years of married life, between role strain and job satisfaction, between stalling and number of years of work in the present organisation. There was a positive correlation between compartmentalisation and hours of work, the number of family members, and the total score of coping style with role strain. Role strain was influenced by the number of family members.

***Title: Impact of Economic Role Performance on Household Development and Women's Status in "Gaddi" Tribes of Himachal Pradesh***

*Author:* Jatinder Kishtwaria

*Guide:* Nalini Ogale

*Year:* 1995

*Keywords:* Economic role, impact, household development, women's status

## Introduction

Involved in an unbelievable variety and multiplicity of activities, millions of poor Indian women live below the poverty line, and work for the purpose of providing for the survival needs of their families. Their multiple roles as workers, child rearers, and family maintainers through a variety of overlapping activities account for much debated invisibility of their unpaid labour. There is a tendency to view women's unpaid work in household agriculture and allied spheres as having less or no value resulting in an underestimation of their economic role. Attention needs to be paid to identify and input the value of women's unpaid work because the support derived from this work generally provides the very basis for the family's survival the particularly amongst the extremely poor. The policy makers are largely unaware of the dimensions and extent of rural women's work or they choose not to notice it. The result of that ignorance or disregard of the problem causes omission of relevant policies. There is need to gather enough data to sensitise planners and policy makers to the massive contribution of women who play a pivotal role in subsistence activities of their families, especially in rural and tribal areas.

## Methodology

A descriptive type of survey design was considered to be appropriate for the study and a multistage purposive-cum-random sampling method was followed to select the area, villages, households and respondents. The sample of the study comprised 200 women (100 employed and 100 non-employed) An interview scheduled was used to collect the data, and the analysis was done by using both descriptive (frequency, percentage, mean and standard deviation) and relational statistics (chi-square, z-test, pearson correlation coefficient, t-test, multivariate test of significance, univarate, f-test scheffe's procedure and multiple regression analysis).

## Major Findings

Tribal women were invariably responsible for the performance of dual tasks. Employed women spent less time than non-employed women on non-market work. Economic contribution through non-market work to family income was higher in the case of non-employed women than employed women. Employed women enjoyed more authority in delegation and supervision of work at home and observed less of customs and traditions as they had less time. More leisure time was available to non employed women that employed women. In spite of active participation of tribal women in decision making they still gave importance to the men's opinion as male superiority was a way of life. Visible economic contribution due to women's employment accorded them a higher status than non-employed women. Higher economic role and contribution of women led to significantly higher developed households.

*Title:* ***Occupational Health Problems: Impact on Output and Household Development of Women Workers of Rural and Urban Handloom Industries of Panipat***
*Author:* Santosh Kumari Sharma
*Guide:* Nalini Ogale
*Year:* 1995
*Keywords:* Occupational health, Handloom Industries, Impact on household women worker

## Introduction

Occupational health comprises measures for protecting the workers against any health hazards arising out of their work or conditions under which it is carried on. Proper promotion of occupational health by the industries results in labour turnover, reduction in absenteeism, reduction in incidence of disease, lengthened span of working hours and increased productivity.

Paradoxically many Indian workers work in deplorable conditions and are exposed to extremely severe occupational hazards. Women workers are no exception to this. Their earnings are essential for the survival of poor households. If they suffer health problems, then the reduction in their working capacity would affect the wages they earned and would hinder the development of their households.

Realizing a need for reliable and factual information regarding occupational health problems a study was undertaken to assess the extent of suitability of occupational environment to women workers of handloom industries in terms of work, workplace and organizational factors, to assess the impact of occupational environment on their occupational health problems, and its impact on output as perceived by them. The study also aimed to find out employers' view about facilities provided to workers and the improvement they want to make.

## METHODOLOGY

The research design was descriptive. A multistage purposive sampling design was adopted through which 252 women workers from 18 industries (9 from urban and 9 from rural industries) were selected. From each of the six processes of production of carpet 42 workers (half from the urban and half from the rural areas) were selected. The data were gathered personally through an interview schedule which comprised various sections to elicit necessary information as per the objectives. It also comprised a scale to assess the awareness of women workers about the source of occupational health problems which were subjected to establishment of validity and reliability. Chi-square, t-test, linear stepwise multi-regression, co-efficient of correlation were applied to test the hypotheses.

## MAJOR FINDINGS

The mean age of the women was 44 years, and many were illiterate. A majority lived in nuclear families and had a mean monthly family income of Rs. 2,820. A majority of the women had temporary jobs, were semi-skilled workers and all worked nine hours every day, having only one break for an hour. Their mean monthly wages were Rs. 863. More percentage of workers felt the streneous work posture and repetitious work great extent. A significant difference was found between rural and urban occupational environment. A wide majority had an average level of awareness about sources of occupational health problems. Most of the women workers always felt the strain on their shoulders, pain in the hips, neck and back, headache, pain in arms and fingers, and overall physical fatigue. Half of them suffered from frequent cold, irritation in nose and throat, redness of skin and abrasion on hands. A majority of the problems resulting from work and workplace factors affected the physical health of women workers. Many women in wool-sorting process suffered from too many problems. Frequency of occurrence of occupational health problems was significantly more in rural than in urban areas. The mean actual output of women workers was more in urban than rural workers. A negative significant relationship was found between the frequency of occurrence of occupational health problems and the output of women workers. Occupational health problems due to particulate matter emerged as the most important determinant causing variation in output. A negative significant relationship was found between the frequency of occurrence of occupational health problems and household development. Most of the employers did not want to employ more women as they were considered to be physically weak and had higher absenteeism.

***Title: A Study of the Improvement in Economic Status of Families of Women Trained in Income Generating Activities by the Voluntary Organisations***

*Author*: Mona Shah

*Guide:* Asha Dass

*Year:* 1996

*Keywords*: Economic status, income generating activities, women, voluntary organisations

## INTRODUCTION

Women employed in the labour force perform a great variety of tasks during the working day, and their output is accorded with little economic value. They are also expected to continue to undertake domestic responsibilities in addition to their job. Voluntary organisations play a useful role in social development, people's participation and institutionalisation of women's programme, and integrating them with the ongoing economic development programme.

The present investigation, thus attempted to study the improvement in the economic status of families of women who have been trained and thereafter being employed in selected income-generating activities, like stitching, embroidery, papad making, masala making and pickle making, by the voluntary organisations. The study also attempted to study about awareness, motivation and various reasons for undergoing the training, opinions regarding expectations from the training and various problems faced by the respondents due to their employment.

## Methodology

A descriptive research design with an interview method was adopted for the present study. The data were collected with the help of a questionnaire. A simple random sampling without replacement was chosen to select the sample which comprised 120 respondents from three organisations. The data collected were coded, tabulated and analysed. Descriptive statistics of mean and percentage were used. Canonical correlations and multiple regression analysis were applied to test the hypotheses.

## Major Findings

A majority of the respondents belonged to the age group of 31-35 years and nuclear families. The mean income of the family was Rs. 4,020.63 per month. The mean saving of the respondents was Rs. 536.36. The most important reason for saving money was to "get children/relatives married". Family members were the sources of awareness and motivation to join income-generating activities. 'Supplementing family income' (93%) was the main reason for undergoing the training by a majority of the respondents. Most of the respondents were satisfied by the way training was given to them and helped them to acquire certain personal attributes, such as "better ability to socialise", "better confidence", and "better knowledge" from the training. In the case of improvement in the economic status, possession of consumer durable items like TV, radio, vehicle showed a tremendous increase. In the case of non-durable items, clothing and more of nutritive food along with an increase in buying of fruits and vegetables had increased. "Leg pain" due to stitching and embroidery, respiratory problems of "coughing" and "asthama problem", due to papad making, masala making and pickle making, were the problems faced by the respondents. Most did not face any interpersonal problems due to their jobs. There existed an excellent relationship between the reasons for undergoing the training with improvement in the economic status and the various kinds of job with the job-related problems whereas no significant relationship was found between selected family variables and improvement in the economic status.

*Title: Determinants of Entrepreneurial Growth Process Among Women Entrepreneurs*
*Author:* Neerja Jaiswal
*Guide:* Nalini Ogale
*Year:* 1996
*Keywords:* Entrepreneurs, growth process, entrepreneurship

## INTRODUCTION

Entrepreneurs are seen as major determinants of growth of a nation. Women form one half of the nation's potential for growth. Women entrepreneurship has gained momentum in developed countries but has also been noticeable in small measures in the developing countries. In India the women entrepreneurship is still at the level of small and medium scale industry. To uplift the status of women, to make them self-reliant and to achieve a faster growth rate, women entrepreneurship is very important.

The present study was undertaken to identify the determinants among women entrepreneurs which have helped them in the growth process of their enterprise. The purpose of the study is to identify factors responsible for the initiation of the enterprise, resources and constraints faced in establishing the enterprise, the extent of participation in decision making, their managerial abilities and determinants of entrepreneurial growth process based on the performance of their enterprise.

## METHODOLOGY

A sample of 245 women entrepreneurs were approached out of which 113 fulfilled the criteria decided for the study. An interview schedule was constructed for the study. Content validity, clarity and feasibility of the schedule were tested. Data were gathered by interviewing the respondents personally. The data was analysed by frequency, mean and percentage. Relational statistics of Hoteling's $T^2$ test and 'F' test, canonical 'r' linear model and factor analysis were used.

## MAJOR FINDINGS

The personal data revealed that respondents were opportunistic/ chanced entrepreneurs with the mean age of 39.3 years and belonging to Gujarati community. A larger percentage was untrained and learned business skills on their own. Personality traits, such as self-confidence, and taking initiative were dominant among two-thirds of the respondents. Risk taking and use of influence strategies were the least dominant traits and were found to be absent among the majority (92.0%) of the respondents. The enterprise profile revealed that nearly half of them were sole proprietors and more than one-third were engaged in the manufacturing enterprise. The line of trade were beauty clinics, crèche, garment industry, and other, i.e., chemicals and pharmaceuticals, industrial, commercial and domestic goods. Involvement of women was more in the operation of their enterprise than in its establishment; 61 per cent invested 1 lakh in their unit. The net worth ranged from Rs. 25,000 to Rs. 22,20,61000. Nearly half of the respondents were satisfied with the performance of their units. Economic independence ranked first as the motivational factor followed by utilisation of skill and opportunity to exercise creativity. Support and constraint profile revealed that husbands provided the major support, i.e., moral, technical, marketing, liasoning legal and personal. Banks provided the institutional support. Constraints reported were limited working capital, delays in sales / cash realisation. Difficulty in repair and maintenance and lack of specialised skill were technical problems. Non-availability of skilled labour and absentism were labour-related problems. Marketing problems were related to stiff competition, corruption, multiplicity of legal compliance red-tapism, etc. Respondents' decision making status was low in financial aspects. Overall decisions were taken by others in all enterprise functions. One half of the respondents had a high decision-making status. However their independent contribution was high in the operation (51.60%). The relationship among variables revealed that the performance of trained entrepreneurs did not differ significantly from those who were forced or chanced into being entrepreneurs. Personal, familial and situational variables were significantly related to performance. Decision-making ability, decision implementation, ability and managerial ability were not significant determinants of growth process.

*Title:* ***Stress Experienced and Role fulfilment by Career Women in Dual Career Families***

*Author:* Neerja Telaprolu

*Guide:* Rachel George

*Year:* 1998

*Keywords:* Stress, Role fulfilment, Career women, Dual career families

## INTRODUCTION

Dual career families are fast increasing in India. The pursuit of higher education by women and increase in equal employment opportunities have contributed to increased prevalence of dual career families. The women who aspire for both marriage and career may face incompatibility of demands between career and familial roles. When the demands put up by various roles exceed their capacities, these women experience stress, which in turn influences their role fulfilment in employment as well as in family, and vice versa. There is a need to understand the stressors, the extent of stress experienced and how it is expressed in the behaviour of people and how to cope with it. A study was undertaken with the objectives of measuring the extent of stress experienced by carrier women in dual career families, and to develop and measure stressors from family and employment, the stress- coping strategies adopted and the social support that would be extended by employment and family organizations.

## METHODOLOGY

The research design was descriptive. A sample of 541 career women in dual career families were selected through multistage sampling from various organizations/institutes of Hyderabad. The questionnaire comprised scales to assess the perception of sample on stressors pertaining to employment and family organization. Higher scores indicated the higher score of stressors. Other scales were to measure the extent of social support from family and employment. All instruments were subjected to establishment of validity and reliability.

## MAJOR FINDINGS

The mean age of the respondents was about 40 years. Nearly half of the respondents were postgraduates, career women in dual career families, who spent a major portion of their time daily on their paid work and the least on personal care. They worked for 17 hours daily and for a mean of 17 years. Most of them had a higher perception of employment organization work stressors' perception. More than half of them had higher scores on family organization overall stressor perception. Regarding the mode of coping with stressful situations, three-fourths of the women said that they would neither follow escape nor control the mode of coping predominantly. A majority of the respondents revealed that they would get social considerably high level of support as revealed through the scales. The PGI health questionnaire revealed that a majority of the career women were able to cope with multiple responsibilities without undue stress. Many women experienced backache, headache, poor digestion, etc. Listening to music, seeking company of family, watching TV taking a nap, going to temple were some of the most commonly used practices to overcome stress manifestations. The extent of stress experienced was higher for older women, having a relatively higher personal income with more number of years of service as revealed through co-efficient of correlation and stepwise regression analysis.

***Title: A Comparative Study on Self-Assessment of Managerial Skills of Male and Female Entrepreneurs.***

*Author:* Aditi Majumdar

*Guide:* Neena Jaju

*Year:* 2002

*Keywords:* Self assessment, Managerial skills, Male, Female, Entrepreneur

## Introduction

An entrepreneur is a person who displays courage to take risk of putting his own money into an idea, have the courage to take on competition, leap into an unknown future and create a new enterprise that shows growth and propels the nation forward. Management excel concentrates on building managerial skills. The managerial skills will decay unless a person keeps on utilising them. Assessments play a major role in fighting against the decay of managerial skills. Assessment may also be used to evaluate mastery of skills by managers as it is very essential for a manager to know which skill he possesses. The prime objective of the study was to gain an insight into the self-assessment of managerial skills (SAMS) of male and female entrepreneurs, and study the interrelationship between self-assessment of managerial skills of male and female entrepreneurs and selected personal, family and situational variables.

## Methodology

The descriptive research design was thought appropriate to carry out the present investigation on self-assessment of managerial skills of male and female entrepreneurs. A sample of 120 entrepreneurs (60 males and 60 females) was selected through the simple random sampling technique. A questionnaire schedule was resorted to build up the data for the present study, which constituted the personal and project profile of the respondents, Maudsley's Personality Inventory and a scale on self-assessment of managerial skills which was developed and standardized by the investigator. The scale was tested for its content validity and reliability. Descriptive statistics like analysis of variance and t-test by difference were computed for analyzing the data of the present research.

## Major Findings

Major findings revealed that three-fourths of male and female respondents were in the age range of 35 to 44 years and 30 to 39 years. It was further found that 35 to 40 per cent male and female respondents were grouped into the category of low neuroticism-high extraversion. One-third of the male respondents and one-half of the female respondents were professional degree holders. Data revealed that the SAMS of female respondents differed significantly at 0.01 levels with regard to their age, personality type, number of years of experience and the family type. However, in the male respondents the SAMS differed significantly at 0.01 level with regard to their years of experience only. The analysis of data revealed a significant 0.05 level in the SAMS of male and female entrepreneurs, wherein male respondents assessed themselves higher as compared to females. On observing the score range and the mean scores it was found that they overestimated themselves with regard to their SAMS.

***Title: Problems and Problem-solving Strategies of Entrepreneurs during Procurement and Repayment of Finance***

*Author:* Nidhi Jain

*Guide:* Neena Jaju

*Year:* 2003

*Keywords:* Problems, Problem solving, Strategies, Entrepreneurs, Procurement, Finance

## Introduction

Entrepreneurship is a purposeful activity indulged in initiating, promoting and maintaining economics for the production and distribution of wealth. An entrepreneur is a critical factor in economic development and transformation. Entrepreneurship cannot have its effectiveness, if an urge to take risk, uncertainties and leadership, i.e., capacity of showing things in a way, which afterwards proves to be true, is not there. While going through the journey of enterprise development, an entrepreneur faces many types of problems, and to solve the problems he develops or adopts some strategies so that he can overcome the problems and run his enterprise smoothly. The prime objectives of the study was to gain an insight into the problems and problem-solving strategies of the entrepreneurs during procurement and repayment of finance, and to study their interrelationship with selected personal, family and situational variables.

## Methodology

The descriptive research design was used to carry out the present investigation. A sample of 120 entrepreneurs of Kota city of Rajasthan was selected through the purposive sampling technique. A questionnaire schedule was resorted to build up the data for the present study, which constituted the personal profile of the respondents, their business profile, problems faced by the entrepreneurs and problem-solving strategy adopted by them during procurement and repayment of finance. For the latter part, a scale was developed by the investigator. The scale was tested for its content validity and reliability. Besides, descriptive statistics, inferential statistics like analysis of variance and co-efficient of correlation was used to analyze the data of the present research.

## Major Findings

Major findings of the study revealed that entrepreneurs of the present study encountered a relatively higher number of problems related to their managerial competence and those related to the financial institution during procurement and repayment of finance as compared to rapport building and technical competence. It was found that a little less than one-half of the entrepreneurs of the study adopted a moderate type of strategies to solve their problems related to procurement and repayment of finance. More than one-third of the entrepreneurs adopted a high number of strategies and about one-fifth of entrepreneurs adopted low number of strategies. Analysis of data revealed that there was no statistically significant association between problems and problem-solving strategies of the entrepreneurs and age, gender, professional qualification, number of years of experience, personal income, type of family, income of family, business inheritance and annual turnover. Also, there existed no relationship between the problems encountered by entrepreneurs during procurement and repayment of finance, namely, rapport building, managerial competence, technical competence and problems related to financial institution with their respective problem-solving strategies. However, it was found that there existed a positive relationship between the problems related to the financial institution and the technical competence strategies. Thus it can be said that the higher the number of problems an entrepreneur encountered related to the financial institution, the greater would be the extent of technical competence strategies adopted by the entrepreneur with regard to procurement and repayment of finance.

***Title: Employed Muslim Women : A Study of Problems, Management Practices and Coping Strategies***
*Author:* Ashiyabanu Shaikh
*Guide:* Maneesha Shukul
*Year:* 2003
*Keywords:* Employed Muslim women, management practices, coping strategies

## Introduction

Today women are playing the dual role of a homemaker as well as an income earner. Technological advancements have offered women various types of labour-saving devices and equipments, so that the homemakers finds it easy to cope with the two responsibilities of homemakers as well as income earners. Liberation for a woman does not mean being like a man; she cannot take up the male task; she has a separate role to perform, which is allotted to her. Men and women thus are performing different roles in their field and limitation. It has been observed that Muslim women have been increasingly taking up gainful employment outside the home. But due to social, religious, family and health reasons, they find it difficult to manage their resources, especially time and energy to meet the heavy demands and expectations of the family.

## Methodology

The study with a descriptive research survey was carried out on a sample of 120 respondents of Baroda city. There were Muslim women who were gainfully employed or self-employed at the time of data collection. The snowball technique was used to select the samples. An interview schedule was used as an instrument for gathering data. Descriptive statistics of frequency, percentage and mean were applied. An analysis of variance, t-test and coefficient of correlation were computed to test the relationship between selected variables.

## Major Findings

It was found that personal reasons were more prominent due to which women were gainfully employed or self-employed. Problems regarding time, energy and work were experienced with higher intensity by the gainfully employed respondents. A majority of the respondents had a moderate quality of management practice regarding time, energy household work management as well as money management. The self-employed women faced more problems and hence followed the coping strategies to a high extent. The extent of problems faced by Muslim employed women varied only with the occupation of the respondents. It was found that there was a relationship between problems faced by Muslim employed women and the coping strategy by them.

***Title: A Study of Organizational and Familial Climate as Perceived by the Managers of the Selected Corporate.***

*Author:* Mukti Upadhyay

*Guide:* Neena Jaju

*Year:* 2004

*Keywords:* Organizational and familial climate managers, Corporate firms

## Introduction

The prime objective of the study was to gain an insight into the organizational climate and familial climate as perceived by the managers, and to study the interrelationships between the organizational climate and familial climate as perceived by the managers with respect to selected personal, family and situational variables.

## Methodology

The descriptive research design was thought appropriate to carry out the present investigation on organizational climate and familial climate as perceived by the managers. A sample of 120 managers was selected through the purposive sampling technique. A questionnaire schedule was resorted to build up the data for the preset study which constituted the personal and organizational structure profile of the respondents. Maudsley's personality inventory was developed to study the personalities of the managers in respect to neuroticism and extraversion. The scale on leadership style developed by Marshall Shaskin (1998) was utilized to access the leadership styles of the managers. The scales on organizational climate and familial climate as perceived by the managers were developed by the investigator. The scales were tested for their content validity and reliability. Besides, descriptive statistics, inferential statistics like analysis of variance and t-test were computed for analyzing the data of the present research.

## Major Findings

Major findings revealed that the mean age of the respondents was 47.4 years. It was further found that 34.2 per cent of the respondents were ordinary graduates. The mean monthly income of the respondents was Rs.22,663. Further, it was found that the mean scores on neuroticism and extraversion nature of the respondents were more or less similar, i.e., 1.98 and 1.97. Regarding the leadership styles, about 64.2 per cent of the managers were practising the participative leadership styles (high task-high relationship) reflecting that they were concerned both with their employees personal welfare and work performance. However, testing of hypothesis revealed a significant difference in the perceived organizational climate and educational qualification, and management level of the managers. No significant differences were found with regard to other selected variables. Correlation values indicated that there was no association between the organizational climate and familial climate as perceived by the managers. The computed ANOVA revealed that no significant differences existed in the organizational climate and familial climate as perceived by the managers amongst the three selected corporate firms.